LAKE HOUSE

A culinary journey in country Australia

ALLA WOLF-TASKER

PRINCIPAL PHOTOGRAPHY BY SIMON GRIFFITHS
PAINTINGS BY ALLAN WOLF-TASKER

Hardie Grant Books

I do hope you enjoy reading our story
Alla W-T

CONTENTS

- vii   Author's Note
- 1   Foreword: A Very Special Family
- 7   CHAPTER ONE Beginnings
- 19   CHAPTER TWO Our Place
- 35   CHAPTER THREE Our Food
- 61   CHAPTER FOUR Local Food
- 67   CHAPTER FIVE A Day in the Life of the House on the Lake
- 101   CHAPTER SIX The Apple Never Falls Far from the Tree
- 125   CHAPTER SEVEN From the Soil
- 145   CHAPTER EIGHT Watery Creatures
- 179   CHAPTER NINE Plucky Birds and Game Friends
- 219   CHAPTER TEN From the Paddocks
- 253   CHAPTER ELEVEN Sweetness and Fruitful Anticipation
- 279   CHAPTER TWELVE Basics and Embellishments
- 299   CHAPTER THIRTEEN Decades of Change
- 304   Index
- 310   Acknowledgements

AUTHOR'S NOTE

The recipes in this book range from fairly basic to considerably challenging. Before embarking on one, please ensure that you read it thoroughly and are aware of what you are in for in terms of equipment, ingredients and timing. The professional cook's *mise en place* – that essential ingredient for averting disasters and ensuring efficient delivery – is equally important in laying the groundwork for any enjoyable and successful cooking session.

Other than perhaps in patisserie, recipes can often only offer guidance in matters such as timing, temperature and quantities of liquids, sugar and seasoning. Much depends on the produce and equipment you are using. The shape and size of your pots and pans will determine how quickly something sears, cooks, reduces, and how much liquid will be needed. A healthy dose of commonsense is always required. Pay attention to visual clues. If something looks like it is about to boil dry it will require more liquid – regardless of what the recipe may say. Similarly variations in produce can alter the outcome of recipes. Tasting frequently is essential.

At Lake House and for these recipes we always use unsalted butter. Unless otherwise specified we use large free-range (60 g/2 oz) eggs. When organic free-range eggs from a reliable local supplier are available, we grade these ourselves and the smaller ones are relegated to the breakfast buffet. The sheet or leaf gelatine utilised in our kitchen is gold-grade, and each leaf weighs 2 g (1/10 oz). The oils we use are discussed on page 283, as is salt on page 290. We use pink Murray River salt flakes on our restaurant tables. Other general instructions on the recipes and equipment can be found in Chapter 3, Our Food (from page 35).

For my parents, Anatoli and Katya, and the thousands of others whose homeland was far away.

Foreword
A VERY SPECIAL FAMILY

A very special family has contributed to the fibre of our place. My artist husband, Allan, always the wind beneath my wings, has been my lifelong support and partner in our house on the lake. Retreating from his own personal ambitions for his art, he devoted considerable time in the early years to working the floor. In due course he was also sensitive enough to let go much of the decision-making. In part, it is to his understanding of how many chiefs a business can tolerate and the need for clear divisions of labour, that I attribute the longevity of our relationship.

Most couples who commenced in hospitality about the time that we did, have not survived the tumult that involvement in the industry produces in one's personal life. There were plate-throwing episodes of course, driven by crazy working hours, economic difficulties, my own interminably manic aspirations for the place and simply the continued stress of making absolutely each service the best in this, the most intensively scrutinised of industries.

Allan's easy grace and the ability to chat with guests remains a trademark of the place whenever he is around. 'Al's bar with a little jazz' for residential guests has become something of an institution. But he also now pursues his painting full time. Many of his pieces adorn the walls at Lake House as well as those of private and public collections around the world.

Our daughter, Larissa, grew up in the business and spoke hospitality before much else. She rode in the baby seat as I delivered function food and sat in the stroller as I shopped at the markets. I still recall her asking at age four what sort of menu the day's large function was having: 'Is it á la carte today, mama?' 'Horror days' (hollandaise), 'a mute' (a minute) and 'weesheff' (Oui, Chef) are words she mumbled to herself as she set her dolls up at a miniature table to eat, having heard this terminology – and much else – day in and day out. 'Terrassamolata' (taramasalata) was her favourite childhood spread and fried crumbed brains with browned butter and capers were what she knew as hamburgers.

Originally in the playpen in the corner of the kitchen or with my mother upstairs, Larissa grew up surrounded by many very busy adults who afforded her much love but little time. Her friends were gardeners and dishwashers, cooks who offered her tastes of extraordinary things and provedores who stopped at the kitchen door for a yarn. Like Robert Jones from Tuki Springs, who had his kids in tow, some are now an important part of their own flourishing and expanding concerns. Because of the nature of the property there was always some place for Larissa, unlike many city-restaurant kids often relegated to being minded elsewhere. She had her own small strawberry patch and tree house. Yabbying and riding the rickety billycart down the hills were favourite pastimes as was picking fruit with my mother. Later, she earned pocket money by filling sugar bowls, cutting butters, arranging petits fours and eventually was trained for floor service on weekends and holidays.

While at university she cut her teeth at various city restaurants, including working as a bussy with Paul Wilson at Georges and also with the Grossi family. After graduating, she was at somewhat of a loss. She loved the house on the lake and deeply wanted to be involved, but was not particularly keen on settling into just the food and beverage area. Gradually she proceeded to carve out a niche in the marketing and sales area and now deals with all our international and domestic tourism partners as well as handling public relations and brand management and development. She spends some part of the year travelling around the world on many gruelling trade missions, as an ambassador of sorts, speaking to various travel houses. She is also on hand to welcome new guests and catch up with many regulars. Expansion of our brand now includes the retailing of Lake House produce as far afield as Harvey Nichols in London, the availability of our Salus mineral water to Australia's restaurant tables, and the supply of our Lake House Swiss–Italian sausages, based on recipes from the original settlers of the region, to various gourmet specialty shops.

My mother, Katherine (Katya), was of enormous help through the early years at Lake House. She looked after Larissa, gardened, polished glasses and cutlery, fretted about the hours I worked and tutted about the language of the cooks in the kitchen, while at the same time swearing, in several languages, at the birds attacking the fruit trees. Larissa called her 'baba', short for *babushka*, or grandmother, in Russian. The name stuck and many of the Lake House staff over the years have known her only as that.

My father, Anatoli, did not live beyond the first few years of Lake House. Orphaned at fourteen, and displaced by the war, his difficult life took its toll. I owe him my love of literature, music and hospitality, and my fluency in Russian and much more.

My extended Lake House family is very much the heart and soul of the place. Shelley Ryan, our general manager, arrived on the scene some years ago for what she thought to be a little bit of waiting work while she sorted out whether she wanted to continue with her criminology degree. She has moved through the ranks taking on increasingly senior roles and now runs a smoothly efficient ship. I know my baby is in exceptionally fine hands.

Martin Fairhurst, our restaurant manager, also arrived at Lake House as a waiter and is now a very well-known face among our clientele. With a natural gift for hospitality and attention to detail, Martin has an uncanny ability to remember people's favourite drinks and wines, often years after the event. He relishes ownership of our dining room, together with his immensely talented team.

Mathew Macartney, my head chef, commenced working at Lake House eight years ago, while an apprentice. Since then I have watched his growth and development with considerable pride. He has worked 'stages' in Sydney and at Daniel Boulud in New York and has represented Lake House as far afield as Fiji and Dubai. He and his wife Carla are now the proud parents of two wonderful children, whom Martin already has pegged for front-of-house duties – as soon as they can say 'confit duck'.

Denise Robinson walked into our lives some thirteen years ago with a basket of tussy-mussy posies to be offered to guests on Mother's Day. She has been with us ever since, filling the place with an abundance of beautiful flowers and her good-humoured nothing-is-a-problem attitude. A committed crew of local growers now supply her with magnificent peonies, old-fashioned scented roses, camellias, rhododendrons and exquisite foliage for our large decorative floral displays, room flowers and a remarkable variety of wedding and special occasion floristry.

The other members of our larger team, including some who have passed through and left their mark, are too many to mention. Over burst pipes in hotel rooms, failures in the local electricity grid, state-wide cessation of gas supply, impossible building and painting deadlines with every new project, it has always been a team with its shoulder to the wheel. Some days are infernally difficult and others are exhilarating. Relationships bloom, babies are born. People travel and return. No matter what, each person contributes to the daily workings of a place that is dedicated to the enjoyment of our guests. From the expertly dusted and polished surfaces, the floral arrangements and immaculate gardens, to the welcoming smiles at the front desk or the spa, all speak of the complete involvement of these very special people.

Chapter One
BEGINNINGS

It was sheer madness really ... the late 1970s was not a time when people journeyed into the Australian countryside for any sort of special culinary experience. Devonshire tea or a good counter lunch – perhaps. But fixed-price menus with an *amuse bouche* to start and waiters in long white aprons in a small village that did not even boast a coffee machine – what could I have been thinking?

my father, a dreamer and stirrer of pots

Fresh from kitchen and restaurant experiences in French rural establishments and after some time as a caterer and cookery school proprietor in Melbourne, I was convinced that a country restaurant was what I wanted. Daylesford, a forest-rimmed village a mere 100 kilometres from Melbourne seemed a reasonable bet. I had spent many childhood summers here. It had been a pretty, down-at-heel, impoverished little town then, in the sixties. But for many postwar migrants the place, with its undulating hills, church spires, distinct seasons and European trees, reminded them of home. And then there were the waters, known for centuries in Europe for their healing properties. The region had the largest number of naturally occurring mineral springs in Australia. Drinking and bathing in mineral waters were activities relished by the dispossessed Europeans.

Property was cheap. Many Europeans purchased small cottages for a few hundred pounds and set about turning them into summerhouses and weekenders. And so it was with my parents. Our little country house, or *dacha*, was set beautifully high on Wombat Hill with enchanting views over the valley and its lake. Very Australian from the outside with its double-gabled miner's cottage roof, requisite 'thunder box' and resident tiger snake out the back, inside it bore portraits of Pushkin and Chekhov, family religious icons and reproductions of famous Russian paintings. On the back stoop there were always crocks of pickled cabbage and dill cucumbers and tomatoes. The orchard supplied an abundance of fruit. The garden was planted out with herbs and vegetables and interspersed with roses.

Both my parents were great cooks. My mother was of the more disciplined kind, great with pastry and preserves. My father,

We stumbled upon the site one day when we noticed an old 'for sale' sign nailed to a rotting gum tree in a paddock overlooking an overgrown arm of Lake Daylesford.

a dreamer and stirrer of pots, sang along in three languages to his 78 recordings, while stews and soups of thrown-together ingredients bubbled away on the stove for hours. The war, rationing and loss of family and homeland were still recent memories. Love and caring were expressed through the sharing of food. Every weekend the Russkies came bearing pickled herrings, smoked eels, marinated mushrooms. When people visited they were fed, regardless of the time of day.

And so it was at our Daylesford summerhouse. A pot of borscht or stew simmered on the wood stove. The large kitchen table was set with embroidered cloths. People came, shared food, made way for newcomers, moved on to play cards under the Morton Bay fig or wandered down to the lake for a swim. Talk of politics and the war went late into the night. And, as with all Russian gatherings, there were recitations and songs about the motherland. Much vodka was drunk and often laughter was interspersed with tears. My fondest childhood memories are of those celebrations of abundance and the hospitality of the table. I am sure they have much to do with my becoming a chef and restaurateur.

BUILDING THE DREAM

It was a big leap, however, from the pleasures of the table with family and friends to building a country restaurant in Australia in the late 1970s. We stumbled upon the site one day when we noticed an old 'for sale' sign nailed to a rotting gum tree in a paddock overlooking an overgrown arm of Lake Daylesford. It had been for sale for many years. The word around town was that it was a useless patch of dirt. The back of it sloped down to 'the swamp', as that part of the lake was then known. Indeed, the immediate area was in a terrible state. So much so that the few houses that existed on the other shore all faced the road rather than the water. And an adjacent fire-access track was used by locals to drive to the water's edge to dump rubbish.

But the paddock was cheap, even by our standards, and so in 1979 we became the proud owners of this badly eroded, gorse-covered and blackberry-infested piece of land on the swampy end of Lake Daylesford. My mother wept when she saw it.

'You're building a restaurant where?' was the reaction of friends and colleagues in the industry. There was little or no tourism in the place. One could shoot a bullet down the main street on a Saturday and not hit anyone. The traditional local industries – timber and wool – had slowed considerably. Unemployment was rife. The local council granted us a permit only after cautioning us that we were likely to lose our money. Daylesford was not a place for a restaurant. No one much visited and there were already several take-away food shops in the town.

We would not be swayed. While waiting to commence construction my immediate instinct was to attempt to revegetate the area as quickly as possible. The south-west-facing slope was exposed to winds that would slow the development of garden beds until a good protective canopy could be established. After clearing the site of half a dozen car wrecks, my earliest gardening efforts were thwarted by a winter of 27 consecutive black frosts, during one of the worst droughts on record. Local century-old peppercorn trees perished so what hope had my paltry little

There was the momentous and bitterly cold day when Allan nailed on the last piece of roofing iron and we took a picnic to a paddock on the other side of the lake to view what was now a fully formed building.

twigs? Hugely pregnant with Larissa, I hand-bucketed tiny saplings while my mother, eyes rolled to heaven, exhorted all the Russian saints to bring me to my senses.

Allan, Renaissance man that he is, turned his hand to drafting and eventually building. We designed a large timber restaurant and residence over two levels, with a roofline that echoed some of the large local establishments of the long-gone guesthouse era. Having eaten our way around the few restaurants that existed then in various provincial cities, where once inside you may as well have been back in Melbourne, we were determined to create a sense of place. Large windows were to provide a view of the surrounding countryside and a huge skylight ensured that the room would be light-filled even in the depths of a Daylesford winter.

Much to the bemusement of many locals, who watched us from the road, we plunged into an arduous three-and-a-half-year period of landscaping and construction of the restaurant building. Some thought we were building a nursery, such was the amount of planting and hand-watering that was done. We kept our jobs in Melbourne and camped in a caravan on-site at weekends while we built. A screened-off old tin bath served as a bathroom and an electric urn supplied hot water. As far as the building was concerned only plumbing, painting and electrical work were contracted out.

By this time Larissa had been born and, after managing to get her to sleep in the afternoons, my role was one of builder's labourer with nail bag strapped on. We stopped for respite as we

ran out of energy or money and then recommenced. Everyone thought we were mad. We scoured the classifieds for cheaper building materials, sometimes carting them down from the other side of Melbourne on a tandem trailer hooked onto our trusty jeep. Occasional visits from friends buoyed our spirits.

The building grew and took shape. There was the momentous and bitterly cold day when Allan nailed on the last piece of roofing iron and we took a picnic to a paddock on the other side of the lake to view what was now a fully formed building. The little orchard looked bleak indeed with each tiny tree surrounded by a galvanised tin collar to keep the rabbits at bay. We celebrated being able to sleep inside at last, albeit in a structure with unlined walls and no ceiling.

In some mad Chekhovian flight of fancy I had always wanted an extensive cherry orchard and proceeded to plant two dozen trees. Of those only two remain, their fruit never setting beyond the onset of the black slug that inhabits the hawthorns of the region. My earliest effort to eradicate this menace consisted of climbing the young trees and dumping the branches with talcum powder – a strategy that worked only while the trees were small enough to coat. The sight of me with the talcum powder and later my nocturnal habit of stomping on snails in my vegetable garden – still in chef's coat after an adrenalin-charged service, with flashlight in hand – are probably what in those days earned me the title among townsfolk of 'the strange foreign woman by the lake'.

I still recall an exchange with a local woman who came down our drive one day for a chat.

'Planting lots of trees?' she enquired.

'Yes,' I said, pleased that someone had noted my labours.

'Why are you doing that?' she asked. 'Someone's paid a lot of money to clear this land.'

OPENING THE RESTAURANT

In very early 1984, after stitching tablecloths, cushions and the covering for the banquettes, and finding the money to put the last knives and forks on the table, we opened as a 45-seater restaurant.

The country proved to be a tough turf. I had not considered that as well as there being no culture of journeying to the country for good food, there were really no good local suppliers. There was no little fromagier down the road, no specialty-vegetable grower or someone who raised pheasant or quail for the table. When I placed an advertisement locally asking for supplies of baby vegetables, I was offered only potatoes. Thus began my regular treks to the wholesale markets in Melbourne.

There were no deliveries – no one else needed the sort of ingredients I required. Nor was there a pool of trained local staff and city professionals did not wish to relocate and live in what was a sorry little town in those days.

We commenced with my husband Allan on the floor with one waiter, both in long white monogrammed aprons, and me in the kitchen with an assistant. We initially opened only on Friday, Saturday and Sunday. Allan kept on with full-time employment in Melbourne for a further four years and I persisted with my Melbourne cooking school for two years. There really was no

choice but to supplement the restaurant income, especially if we were to continue to improve and grow.

They were manic times. No local linen service being available, we bundled the lot into the car on Sunday nights to take back to the city. Larissa was in the baby seat in the back. Monday was a day of paper work and preparation for cooking classes, which I ran from the extended kitchen of our house in Melbourne on Tuesday, Wednesday and Thursday nights. Each night there were 30 students, ranging from doctors, lawyers, journalists and housewives to plumbers and trainee chefs. Each class was followed by a sit-down sampling of food with matched wines. There was a lot of laughter and relationships were forged that have lasted over two decades.

It was a time of a huge and growing fascination with cooking and techniques that sometimes took professional chefs years to master. Bread was baked, pasta and pastry were made by hand, sauces were reduced for days and ice cream was churned by people holding full-time jobs and living exceedingly busy lives. Full-on French culinary techniques were used to deliver beautiful time-consuming food, often resulting in an exhausted host. Our French counterparts of the time, and the inspiration for our labours, meanwhile picked up a fabulous terrine, apple tart and a terrific cheese on the way home from work and perhaps put on a splendid Bresse chicken to roast for main course. The equivalent of those sorts of resources really only became available to Australians a decade or so later.

On Fridays I returned to the restaurant just after dawn, via the markets, to prepare for the weekend services. At 5pm, after a day of prepping, I would collect Allan with Larissa in tow from the nearby Ballan railway station, just in time for him to change and welcome the first dinner guests. Many of our earliest visitors to the restaurant, travelling salesmen en route to Ballarat or Bendigo, were not sure what they had struck. Devonshire teas, toasted sandwiches and roasts with three vegetables were frequent requests. 'Beef and Burgundy' clubs and other gastronomic societies from local provincial cities had more heightened culinary aspirations. Membership of these, however, was often confined to 'gentlemen', with wives being invited to Christmas functions only.

My first kitchen at the restaurant was fitted out on a shoestring. In it stood a mighty 18-year-old reconditioned eight-burner Waldorf. Purchased for a song then, she remains the centre of our cooking hub today, despite being some 44 years old. She is fondly referred to as the old dragon as she burns along at only the most ferocious of temperatures. She is surrounded now, of course, with many much more sophisticated ovens and burners. Strangely over the years many kitchen appliances developed female names. The new Garland stove was of course Judy, the smooth white curvaceous mixer was Marilyn. I was also the proud possessor of a brand new Italian electric ice cream churn. The hand-cranked salt and ice model disappeared forever. Nowadays we cook with sophisticated combination steam and dry-heat ovens, use vacuum sealing both for cooking and storage, and lust after a Pacojet. My how things have changed.

We opened with a fixed price of $24 and an *amuse bouche* to start. My first handwritten menus included squab with a garnish of poached grapes in shiraz glaze, jellied rabbit rillettes, and quenelle of yabby and trout in a freshwater fish consommé.

Clearly the demand for sandwiches and scones had not deterred me. We were rewarded with a gratifying review in the

We were rewarded with a gratifying review in the Melbourne Age from Rita Erlich headed 'Enchanting Lake House'.

Melbourne *Age* from Rita Erlich some months after opening, headed 'Enchanting Lake House'. The trickle of visitors grew, most ringing to ask for directions to Daylesford. Allan and I eventually gave up our other jobs and plunged headlong into the all-consuming activity of running a breakfast, lunch and dinner business, 365 days a year.

In time we developed accommodation and all manner of other facilities for our guests. Supply of good produce over the years became easier as local growers and producers emerged. The Australian palate has become more sophisticated and there is no longer any bemusement about encountering a restaurant like Lake House in the country.

Chapter Two

OUR PLACE

Initially inspired by the restaurants of provincial France, Lake House continues to evolve and be enriched by experience, my own culinary journey and the enthusiasm and ideas of the special people who work here.

BENCHMARKS AND INSPIRATIONS

The memory of my first experience of Roger Vergé's Moulin de Mougins in France in the late 1970s inspires me to this day. I had already spent countless hours with my nose pressed to the windows of France's boulangeries, pâtisseries and charcuteries. With money earned washing dishes I had dined at the wonderful belle époque brasseries and the famous literary bistrots of Paris. On the roads of provincial France, eating *plats du jour* with truckies at Relais Routiers, I came to understand that at all levels of the population this was a nation with a dedicated gastronomic culture.

It was not until some considerable time later that I raised the funds to experience the rarefied atmosphere of some Michelin-starred gastronomic temples. Interestingly it was the country restaurants that instantly struck a chord with me. Somehow the city Michelin restaurants of the day seemed overblown and stuffy but the gems of regional France were much more approachable. Often situated in tiny villages, they were referred to with enormous pride by local residents. Georges Blanc at Vonnas, L'Auberge du Père Bise in Annecy and Raymond Thuilier's Oustau de Baumanière in the Baux-de-Provence were memorable. But walking into Roger Vergé's Moulin de Mougins was an especially revelatory moment of understanding and confirmation. This is where I belonged and what I wanted to do.

It was about the effortlessness of seamless delivery of knowledgeable service: a room filled with an abundance of flowers; a verdant garden shaded with enormous white market umbrellas (this was the 1970s!) and edged with perfect hedges; crisply double-clothed tables, impeccable china and glassware; a sommelier and a cellar of note; food flavours based on local produce that still stir my palate memory; the bubble of conversation and laughter and the clink of glasses. Elegant and sexy, it was a restaurant where once your coat was taken, you wanted for nothing. All was anticipated and delivered. You were in the hands of true professionals and you were lavished with love. Regardless of the trends that have come and gone in the past three decades, this was a benchmark that has never altered for me.

In regional Australia of the early 1980s, emulating even a sliver of my Mougins experience was akin to climbing Kilimanjaro. Lack of local suppliers and trained staff seemed an insurmountable hurdle. And we had done everything on a shoestring budget. The surrounding area was still considerably constrained economically and although our diners were growing in number through word of mouth, there was little more than a steady trickle of visitors to the region.

I devoted myself to various local economic development and marketing committees. It was clear that if the region developed and grew, we stood a good chance of prospering along with it. Struggling with establishing the outdoor spaces in any spare moment, working ridiculous hours, I dreamed of verdant gardens, of battalions of crisply attired waiters and of discerning clientele.

REALISING THE DREAM

Daylesford is now a thriving village of some 3000 residents whose numbers regularly swell with travellers looking to escape, recharge and indulge. Our site takes up just over six acres of land, with terraces tumbling down towards the lake's edge.

We eventually won the battle with the blackberry and gorse. In the overgrown gully we discovered an old spring-fed watercourse that is now a place of fern-filled enchantment, with a series of small waterfalls and a timber and rope bridge that guests negotiate on the way to their rooms. In spring this place is filled with thousands of bluebells and in summer a myriad of hydrangeas enjoy the willow-dappled shade. Parts of my early orchard of apples, nashi pears, plums and quince still remain, alongside the more recent garden pavilion that overlooks the tennis court. A kitchen herb garden supplies just-picked freshness. Wisteria, honeysuckle, lilac and climbing and standard roses occupy many secluded spaces throughout the property. As I write in early summer, the air is headily perfumed with nearby cascading boughs of *Philadelphus*. The abundance of white birches, many planted with my mother, are of course just a little of our Russian essence, relocated. There are many bits and pieces that I come across occasionally that I know originated from her garden. Old nameless roses, ivy that she encouraged me to plant to achieve some quick groundcover to stop the never-ending weeds, and sorrel which I pick to this day – splendid in a soup or a sauce for fish – and which seems to thrive regardless of occasional neglect.

The abundance of white birches, many planted with my mother, are of course just a little of our Russian essence, relocated.

For some years now the garden has been in the hands of John Beetham, who set about rectifying much of my original mania to fill every space as rapidly as possible. We now plant with an eye for water tolerance as well as posterity. Recent plantings include *Santolina*, English and French lavender and olive trees as well as a garden of fleshy red sedums, tall ornamental grasses and *Kniphofia*. Escalonia, lumas and box form hedges here and there. The cherry orchard never eventuated but many of the tiny tubers bought at school fetes and markets and planted 27 years ago, while I was pregnant with Larissa, are now 20-metre tall trees. Cockatoos, kurrajongs, magpies, rosellas and many kinds of finches inhabit the overhead canopy.

Today Lake House is a small boutique hotel of 33 rooms and suites, with various resort facilities and a current staff team of 80, including many long-term employees who are more like family and friends. The restaurant, together with outdoor terraces overlooking the lake, seats well over a hundred. It has gone through many transformations and refurbishments. Revitalising and refitting at least once every five years is always on the agenda. Initially a 45-seater on one level, with our residence upstairs, the considerably expanded dining space now occupies two levels. A spacious foyer greets the guest and an abundance of daylight shows off the canvas-hung walls. Aubergine-coloured chairs and banquettes are softened by pale silvery sage walls and extensive views taking in trees, gardens and lake.

Staircases, which lead from one level to the other, and the bar are adorned with iron worked in a local forge. Further stairs lead to our extensive cellar, which for many years has been noted by New York's *Wine Spectator* magazine as offering one of the world's most notable restaurant wine lists. The short-term cellar area includes a private dining facility with a magnificent locally hand-adzed American-oak table. A door from the cellar leads to another terrace that looks directly onto the small lagoon at the bottom of the garden.

One of the original features of our dining room, the swing doors to the kitchen, deliberately provides a small, framed glimpse of the action within. From my vantage point in the kitchen the doors originally offered me much-needed connectivity with the goings-on out front. Nowadays, with more time on the pass, I get a sense of where the dining room is at by standing behind the barman at the adjacent bar and looking out at the diners. No, we have no cameras trained on the guests. Despite having encountered these in many restaurants, I feel it is an intrusive practice.

In contrast to most kitchens I have worked in, the Lake House kitchen windows offer essential daylight, fresh air and the pleasure of a view of trees and the lake. Beyond the kitchen is a staff terrace overlooking the lagoon. Capturing plenty of afternoon sun it provides much-needed respite during busy times.

Our Terrace room is a very large function and event centre where corporate meetings give way to glamorous parties and weddings. We hosted our wonderful Two Decades Dinner there with a raft of friends and colleagues from the media and the industry. Each year in February there is a Regional Producer's

Day, when the Terrace room converts to a huge market area to showcase local wines and produce. We host charity balls here, with the space transformed by silk ceiling sails and glowing candelabra. The facility also includes its own kitchen, where Penny and others toil over an endless array of preserves. One wall folds back to reveal the demonstration kitchen where we offer classes and seminars run by visiting guest chefs and myself and the team. Outdoors is our grill, barbecue and wood-fired oven kitchen. Used extensively for various functions and groups it also serves to provide particularly delicious flat breads, pizzas and slow roasts for staff dinners in the summer months.

Our state-of-the-art day spa, Salus, features private hot mineral water spas in enchanting cedar tree houses and eight treatment areas with the latest in spa products and technology.

TRAINING AND DEVELOPMENT

Having a sole visionary in an enterprise such as ours would have had a limiting affect on our sustainability and success. The toil of running the business, together with the sheer physical demand of maintaining its momentum, would eventually take its toll. When Allan decided it was time to return to his paints it was clear that I needed to build a strong team around me.

Developing young people has been one of my most rewarding achievements at Lake House. Management team members, some of whom have been with me for many years, act as role models for new staff. 'That is someone you could be in three or four years' time,' is frequently heard at induction time.

Some aspects of training have become problematic nowadays. Getting raw recruits to understand front-of-house procedures is hindered by the rarity of family dining in contemporary Australia. The family dinner table seems to have all but disappeared. Dinners in front of the television, computer, or on the run on the way to sports practice or other activities have yielded a generation with few good dining habits. We frequently find that a basic understanding of table setting cannot be assumed with new young staff.

Front-of-house and kitchen teams regularly meet for food-tasting and wine-pairing sessions. The information is available for all staff across the property from housekeepers and maintenance crew to those in the front office. One of the maintenance crew leaning on a shovel in the sunshine, caught in an exchange with a guest about their favourite Heathcote shiraz, is an encounter worth observing. Cooks gathering herbs in the kitchen garden will often stop for a chat about current produce with customers.

It was clear that I needed to build a strong team around me.

SERVICE AND STYLE

Lake House is about fine dining with its top button undone. Our food is served on crisp double-clothed tables by young people whom we train to be knowledgeable, accommodating and discreet. For most the job is a profession. We maintain a cellar that is internationally renowned and we have at least two sommeliers on the team at any time.

Regular refurbishments and updates notwithstanding, the place has been around for long enough to have an appealing patina and systems in place that afford consistency. An abundance of fresh flowers, preferably from the local area, is an ever-essential part of our décor.

We have many longstanding guests but are delighted to have also captured many of the younger generation as regulars. Just recently, in one week, we hosted members of two well-known pop groups, one famous in the 1970s and the other making a big impact today. Showing my age I noticed the presence of the former, but had no idea about the latter until I saw the front-office team in an excited huddle. Many celebrity folk pass through our doors, relishing the serenity, service and discretion that the property provides.

Over the years we have avoided fads but remaining current is an important part of our philosophy. We are aeons away from the concrete bunker, noisy shared table and very casual approach now often a part of everyday modern eating out. A happy celebratory ambience should not mean one has difficulty in talking or being heard. How on earth does one manage to whisper the sweet nothings so integral to romance? And romance has always been on our agenda.

As well as degustation dinners with matched wines and gloriously formal banquets, we also offer lighter and very inexpensive lunches, alfresco dining on the outdoor terraces overlooking the lake and happy celebratory family parties. I relish the rooms filled with flowers, lamp light, laughter and conversation, the clink of glasses and the effortless gliding service of the floor staff. Watching service from a specially set up table upstairs is now one of my favourite very indulgent activities.

I am often asked whether all this was the plan when we first began. In fact there was no plan but rather the boundless optimism and energy of youth. Had we sought professional advice or done some market research, I have no doubt that we would have been told not to bother. In the back of my mind there was always the frivolous hope of leaving a tiny toe print in Australia's culinary landscape. Of perhaps creating a restaurant, which in the words of the Michelin guides, was worthy of a detour or even a journey.

For me Lake House is truly the fulfilment of what I would have seen as an impossible dream. Through many national and international awards we have been afforded gratifying recognition from the media, the public and our peers. The baton is now firmly in the hands of a passionate team of young professionals – culinary and service wizards who pursue the dream with a zeal all their own.

Chapter Three

OUR FOOD

It was always important to me that the restaurant and its food offer a sense of place in terms of location and climate. The building was constructed to include extensive views of the lake and surroundings. Guests walked from their cars through the newly planted orchard.

REFLECTING THE SEASONS

Seasonal appropriateness has always made perfect culinary sense to me. Located as we are on the hip of the Great Dividing Range and at an altitude of close to 700 metres, the seasons are keenly felt. Often it is the weather outside that dictates how successful a dish will be and how well it will be received. From my very first menu, the food on the plate reflected the seasons that were so apparent through the large dining room windows.

Autumn at Lake House heralds a succession of colours in the leaves of our giant deciduous trees, ranging from the gold of the poplars to the reds, russets and scarlets of fruit trees, pin oaks and Japanese maples. I forage for mushrooms in the local forests, using the skills taught me by my parents and their friends to distinguish the edible ones. Russians have always been mad about mushrooming and their literature is full of stories of mushrooming parties. My young cooks are now equally enthusiastic. Larissa has picked mushrooms since she was two.

Local hare is frequently seen on our autumn menus as are the farmed game birds that come into season at that time of year. Quinces arrive in huge quantities, reflecting the size of the trees in the region. Placed in large bowls, they perfume the air throughout the property. We roast them ruby red for the breakfast table or convert them to quince jelly and paste. Figs are stuffed and baked or pickled. Chestnuts begin to arrive.

Winter days are framed with the bright red tips of willows and lichen-covered branches of maples. There are frosts, mists and the occasional snowfall. Guests go for long rambles along leaf-strewn woodland paths that run beside rushing creeks and waterfalls, returning to the warmth of log fires, a glass of good wine and the company of friends. Dishes become more robust and we offer our version of classic cassoulets and choucroutes. There is a preponderance of the delicious vegetables of the season – leeks, parsnips, celeriac and brussels sprouts – done as a purée or sautéed and served with chestnuts and lardons of local bacon.

Spring brings with it much welcome rain and a dramatic incandescent iridescence in the garden. Everything is bright green with new shoots. There is a vitality and energy that is reflected in the produce. The 'primeurs', the first baby vegetables, are eagerly anticipated and are paired with spring lamb – already available for several weeks. There are also white and green asparagus, peeled broad beans, baby peas, artichokes shaved and served raw in a salad, and aromatic locally picked morel mushrooms, which we string up and dry for later if it is a good season, and much, much more.

Summer follows swiftly, bringing splendid local berries, currants and cherries, which we bottle and brandy. Later there are stone fruit and of course heavenly, just-picked tomatoes and basil. There are masses of elder bushes in the area – you can stick a twig from one of the bushes in the ground and it will grow. Elderflowers are delicious as fritters served with tea. We use the berries in our elderberry glaze.

We use local morello cherries, which are too sour to eat raw but offer great flavour in cooking and preserving. Sweet cherries are just so beautiful fresh that I feel loathe to cook them. In season they sit glistening in a large bowl in the middle of our breakfast buffet. When I was very young there were few morello cherries around, yet they are the stuff of many European recipes. A blackforest gateau simply is not the same without them. The arrival at our household of sour cherries (*vishni*) from a friend's tree was greeted with great excitement. My father would set about poaching some in order to produce the sweet syrup that he mixed with alcohol to produce *vishnievka*, a cherry liqueur. My mother made beautiful sour cherry dumplings, which we ate dusted with sugar and slathered with sour cream.

Before making brandied cherries you need to decide whether you are more interested in the fruit or the resulting syrup. Cherries are ready to eat after bottling in brandy for a month – more than three months and their flavour will be mostly overwhelmed. The fruit can still be used but generally as a garnish only. We allow the cherries to steep for six months. It is the liquor we are after, which is eventually turned into our house cherry brandy. We serve this with our sour cherry trifle or Sour Cherry and Almond Pithivier (see page 269). Try it also with a classic Limousin clafoutis. The remaining alcohol-soused cherries are used to garnish the cherry brandy or the ice cream that accompanies the dessert.

BRANDIED CHERRIES

a quantity of firm, ripe cherries, with no bruises
2–3 cups sugar per 1 kg (2 lb 3 oz) fruit
brandy

Rinse the fruit, whole, and allow it to drain on a towel. Clip the stems to about half the normal length. Prick the fruit all over with a new wooden skewer then pack it tightly, in layers, into sterilised jars, just covering each layer with a layer of sugar as you proceed. If you have them from using cherries elsewhere, place a small handful of cracked cherry pits wrapped in muslin in each jar. These add a nuance of almond flavour. When a jar is two-thirds full, cover the fruit and sugar with the brandy. Put the lids on tightly and shake the jars daily until the sugar is dissolved. We simply up-end our very large jars every couple of days. Store in a cool dark place. Refrigeration tends to slow the flavour exchange.

❧ Cherry brandy ☙

After six months and up to a year, we convert the brandy in which the cherries have been bottled to Cherry Brandy with the addition of a cherry syrup. Over the years I have attempted to come up with precise guidelines for the syrup to brandy ratio, with little success. The variety of fruit used, its ripeness and sweetness and whether it comes from an irrigated orchard all play havoc with exact formulas. It is simply a matter of adding sufficient cherry syrup to the bottling liquor to provide the sort of drink you enjoy. The tasting and adjusting makes for a pleasant afternoon with the opera playing. Any remaining cooked syrup and fruit are a delicious topping for ice cream.

CHERRY SYRUP

750 g (1 lb 10 oz) cherries, stemmed and pitted
1 handful cherry pits, cracked with a hammer and tied in small muslin bundle
juice of 2 lemons
4 cloves
2 cups sugar

brandy liquor, strained from Brandied Cherries (see page opposite)

To make the cherry syrup, place the cherries, cherry pit bundle, lemon juice and cloves in a pan and dredge with the sugar. Mix well, bring to a simmer and cook gently. Give the occasional stir to ensure the sugar is dissolving in the emerging cherry syrup. Continue to cook for about 10 minutes or until it is clear that the cherries are not dropping any more juice. Strain off the juice, reserving the cherries for another use. Boil the juice to reduce it to a syrup then allow it to cool. To finish the brandy, combine the syrup, to taste, with the strained brandy from the bottled cherries. You will need to experiment with a little of the brandy and the cherry syrup to start. The result should be syrupy, smooth and pleasantly rather than overwhelmingly alcoholic.

❧ ELDERBERRY GLAZE ❧

Makes about 2.2 litres (75 fl oz)

My mother cooked de-stalked elderberries, dredged with sugar, until they dropped their juice and then, on a little further cooking, eventually thickened into a dense syrup. I remember the result being too pungent for my taste. The following is a recipe for a more savoury version, particularly good for deglazing the pan after roasting rich meats and for tossing through hot baby beetroot.

900 ml (30 fl oz) red wine
750 g (1 lb 10 oz) sugar
6 strips orange peel, with no pith
3 dried bay leaves
6 cloves
750 g (1 lb 10 oz) de-stalked elderberries

Place all the ingredients, except the elderberries, in a large saucepan. Bring to the boil and simmer for about 20 minutes or until the alcohol is cooked off and the remaining liquid is syrupy. Add the de-stalked elderberries, boil for 30 seconds then allow them to cool. Leave the berries in the liquid to steep, preferably overnight. Strain the glaze through a muslin-lined sieve and pour it into sterilised bottles. Store in a cool place.

❧ PICKLED FIGS ❧

Pickled figs are lovely with pork or served with a lamb tagine in the depths of winter. Like all preserves they offer a delectable taste of seasons past.

2 cups brown sugar
3 cups red wine vinegar
1 cinnamon stick
3 cloves
2 pieces star anise
5 cardamom pods
1 kg (2 lb 3 oz) firm but ripe purple figs

Place all the ingredients, except the figs, in a pan and bring to the boil then simmer for 15 minutes. Add the figs for about 5 minutes, ensuring the syrup never cooks beyond a bare simmer. Using a slotted spoon, remove the figs and pack them into warm sterilised jars. Taste the syrup. If it is overly sharp, boil it for a few more minutes then pour over the figs and seal. If you are using very sweet purple figs, the addition of 1 teaspoon of black peppercorns to the pickling liquid adds a nice touch of spice.

Menus at Lake House generally change twice a season but I am ever cautious about being constrained by a printed page. Mother nature marches entirely to her own drum and the much-anticipated seasonal produce can be early or late depending on her climatic whims. Many a time I have salivated in anticipation over pre-planned dishes – luscious fat white asparagus spears with sautéed morels perhaps – only to be thwarted by a dry spring or late frosts. When you dine at Lake House you may find the waiter explaining last-minute menu changes if perhaps the summer beans delivered are not up to scratch, figs are still a little green or a late summer downpour has spoiled the local berries.

Rousseau's Sleeping Chef, *the painting used on our menu covers (also shown on page ix) is an adaptation of* The Sleeping Gypsy *by Henry Rousseau. The image features Alla, her passion for food and art so intense it invades her dreams. Her dog, representing all other distractions, competes for her attention against the almost blank landscape that awaits her creativity. The 14 culinary implements represent our 14 years at Lake House in 1997, the year in which I completed the painting.*

ALLAN WOLF-TASKER

OTHER INFLUENCES

In the early years of my career I worked in some torturous Australian restaurants where fine dining menus then ran to a formula of seafood cocktail, pepper steak, chocolate mousse and after-dinner mints (in little brown envelopes) with coffee. Chefs were predominantly alumni of Swiss and German hotel schools. It was rare to come across an Australian head chef. One particular place was an old schooner that made forays into the bay regardless of weather. Below decks we jammed in 80 à la carte covers. Upstairs held an even greater number for birthdays and other celebrations.

We sweated over duck *à l'orange* and pan-fried freshwater trout – both bizarre choices for an at-sea menu – in a tiny galley, as the boat pitched and yawed late at night in often very rough seas. The band played on regardless, with a frequently inebriated singer at the helm. It was not an unusual dining experience for the times.

Travelling in France exposed me to all manner of culinary possibilities and *Mastering the Art of French Cooking*, volumes one and two, were bibles I fell asleep with. Later it was Jane Grigson, Simone Beck, M. F. K. Fisher and Richard Olney who provided late-night reading. The revolutionary Fernand Point, Fredy Giradet, Roger Vergé and the brothers Troisgros were my heroes. Nowadays the likes of Marc Veyrat, Pierre Gagnaire and Thomas Keller provide stimulation. Although I am much more likely to be surfing the web at 2am for current New York menus or chatting to a chef in Manhattan about Hudson Valley foie gras than reading about it in a book. What a gift global interconnectivity is.

When I look over the menus at Lake House for the past two decades there are reflections of all these influences. Grounded in solid French culinary techniques of stock-, sauce- and pastry-making, our contemporary food has evolved along with the Australian culinary sensibility. Like much of contemporary Australian cooking, our cuisine is a complex fusion, each dish an evolution of traceable influences of tradition, culture and contemporary culinary thought. Our extensive repertoire of Lake House charcuterie is a nod to lessons learned in rural France as is our take on many French classical dishes. Our composed salads are wayward descendents of Point's Salade Delice and the Troisgros' Salade Riche. These were absolutely *le dernier cri* in the eighties among many of us cooks.

The childhood memories of fabulous Russian banquets have also clearly left their mark. Their influence can be seen in the smoking, pickling and seasonal preserving that we do – a sense of putting things down for a leaner season. The notion of Russian *zakúska*, or small bites, inspires our various tasting plates. Ingredients such as eel, beetroot, tongue, jellied pork, horseradish, pickled cabbage and sour cherries are a part of my earliest palate memories.

I also think that the Jungian notion of a collective unconscious possibly applies particularly to cooks. Often ideas, combinations and presentations come into my head, and just work. Many times when I have sought and found a solution for working with a particular ingredient, I later find a photograph in a magazine or an image on the web indicating that some cook halfway around the world has recently come to the same conclusion. And of course

OUR FOOD ✱ 43

as you cook you continue to learn. There is something new all the time.

Nowadays the Lake House repertoire continues to evolve, shaped by life experience and the talent of ideas that pass through our kitchens. Visiting guest chefs also leave a little bit of themselves in an exchange and sharing of ideas that we truly relish.

Many dishes have traceable derivations: a recollection of flavours, something that has been read somewhere, something someone else has made, something I have been taught or a dish spurred on by the availability of a special ingredient or by the person who has grown or produced it. Many dishes, if they could speak, would tell anecdotes about people or stories of places and ideas.

Some years ago a most elaborate idea for a salmon coulibiac layered with blini instead of pastry and baked in a tall tin came from my visit to the kitchens of the Grand Hotel in St Petersburg in Russia. It was not long after perestroika and the first Russian hotels owned jointly with foreign corporations were bustling with foreign businessmen, eager to capitalise on this very large, new free-market economy. It was an extraordinary time. Metal detectors were at every hotel entrance as pinstripe-suited locals, looking like gangsters, checked their guns in at the door. Meanwhile in the kitchen huge blocks of frozen meat arrived. The individual components of these were only identifiable on thawing. But blini, caviar and sour cream were at every service, with an innovative and interesting take on the classic coulibiac on the dinner menu. With a few minor changes it was also on ours.

Photographer and friend Earl Carter and his partner, Wanda, once sent me a beautiful, tiny wooden box from Vienna containing a delicious miniature Sacher torte. This became the inspiration for the apricot version of our Chocolate Fondant Sacher (see page 276).

On visits to Australia, Graham Pushee, noted Australian countertenor, was a frequent weeklong guest at Lake House during the years he lived in Switzerland. At a critical time in his life he had toyed with the notion of starting 'just a little hotel and restaurant' in the south of France and asked to work in my kitchen for experience. Just a week of generously spaced rosters put paid to any future in hospitality. It was the peeling, coring and chopping of five boxes of quinces that proved the undoing of the dream. The requirement to answer 'Oui, Chef!' rather than 'Okay, okay it's coming' when being hurried along, was just the final straw. Our next quince dessert was dedicated to him and named the Pushee Quince. Graham orders it whenever it is available, to remind him of his close call.

As I developed my culinary skills and the repertoire of our kitchen, things also changed in Australia. The various European migrant influxes altered the food culture forever and laid the groundwork for the later waves of Asian cuisines. Nowadays we salute the availability of a global supermarket of flavours. We utilise ingredients from the cuisines of many nations and coax them into dishes where they unmistakably speak Australian. Increasingly they are also speaking the particular food language of our region.

COOKING FROM THE GROUND UP

The kitchen brigade is currently ten strong with cooks and an additional four kitchen hands. Its size is considerable for today's culinary economic climate in Australia and especially for a regional restaurant. From the outset we have worked from the ground up producing our own bread, pastries, charcuterie, jellies, jams and relishes. The output of work is breathtaking. To the untrained eye, the transformation each couple of days of boxes and boxes of incoming produce into pots of simmering, bubbling and reducing concoctions, a myriad of julienne and dice of vegetables cut just so, meat, fish and birds broken down to portion size and endless trays of pastries and breads, mousselines and parfaits is nothing short of miraculous. Most will be quickly consumed and the process starts again. Most diners have little idea of what it takes for their food to reach them.

Although originally commencing from need, the practice of producing virtually everything ourselves is now an ingrained way of doing things. We persist, although the practice goes against the growing and economically more viable trend for restaurants to outsource and to use portion-controlled products.

Young qualified cooks who cannot recognise fish species, much less fillet or bone them or break down meats, are an increasing concern. The benefits of doing things in-house are immeasurable.

There are benefits also in our contact with local suppliers. Most of today's young trainee cooks have not grown up in households with chooks and vegetables in their backyards. The fragrance of a just-picked, really ripe pear or a lusciously ripe

tomato is mostly foreign to them. The problem is often exacerbated by their propensity to eat junk food on days off. Developing a discriminating eye and palate for good produce is essential grounding for any culinary career. Some years ago France's Minister of Culture instituted a program whereby an army of travellers bearing perfect produce descended on schools around that nation. The best bread, perfect peaches, tomatoes and cheeses were offered to students as benchmarks. Quite appropriately, the danger of the demise in understanding good food was considered to be of critical cultural importance. Oh, that it would happen here! Our annual Regional Producer's Day, when local vignerons, growers and suppliers converge on Lake House to exhibit their produce, is often a big eye-opener for our newer city recruits.

TO FIDDLE OR NOT TO FIDDLE?

It is a dilemma of course. We chefs like to show off. But for every diner who wants to be challenged and who does not want to pay for something he can cook for himself at home, there is another who wants a plain steak or something similar. In fact one of Australia's wealthiest men and a client of Lake House often orders a burger. No, it is not on the menu and no, we do not trick it up – we just make him a great hamburger.

The thing is, however, there is no denying the craft of the cuisinier. Training new young chefs to bone, to make sauces, mousses and soufflés, to emulsify, to jell, to stuff and to glaze is an essential part of keeping the craft alive. If we all throw some whiting in the pan with a little butter and serve it with an albeit delicious but simple rocket salad with a scattering of capers and a squeeze of lemon, then all of those arduous time-consuming but very special techniques that form our craft will die out.

I sometimes reflect that the continued chorus of the 'only simple is best' brigade is in danger of contributing to a further deterioration in the already considerable lessening of culinary depth in our industry. To take an example, the food of master Australian chef Cheong Liew is anything but simple. It is a carefully considered exercise in the juxtaposition of many complicated textures and flavours and Australia would be considerably poorer without it. Without question there is an artist at work. Complicated, challenging food is only bad when it serves to mask less than good ingredients. In the hands of a great chef, worked food often appears to be intrinsically simple when it lands on the plate. '*Faits simple*,' Escoffier commanded. Refinement should enhance and not obliterate flavour.

Lack of refinement, simplification and, as some would have it, the 'dumbing down' of food is most often financially driven. Nowadays the mouth feel of reductions, emulsions and sauces that have been refined through continual skimming, and passing many, many times through sieves and tamis, is a considerable luxury, just because of sheer economics. Enjoying a beautiful fresh lobster is one thing but eating one bathed in its liquid essence of a jus that has been painstakingly created from its shell raises it to quite a different level. A great sauce has always been a hallmark of culinary brilliance.

And of course there are many customers who expect and want to see the craftsmanship and the flourishes. So for every plain steak and steamed piece of Murray cod we serve – and our menu offers the option of very simple fare for those who want it – we also have rabbit in three guises, spring lamb noisettes stuffed with sweetbreads and kidney served with minted pea foam, and cabbage roll of boned quail stuffed with pork in a spiced broth. A bit of clever and delicious art on the plate has always been part of the challenge for me.

FEEDING BODY AND SOUL: THE SPA EXPERIENCE

The way we enjoy food has changed in many ways over the past two decades. Indulgence nowadays is more about taste and quality rather than quantity. The notion of being oversated with alcohol and food to the point of discomfort after leaving a restaurant makes as much sense as leaving a fine music concert with sore ears. Take a look at the practitioners themselves. Today's successful young chefs are lean, work out, and develop habits to compensate for the physical demands and stress levels induced by their profession. Many will profess to a liking for Japanese food on their days off – a cuisine that has perceptibly altered our understanding of how good food can make you feel.

The movement to fresh food that fulfils its original role of nourishment and sustenance and away from processed foods that can adversely affect our wellbeing is becoming increasingly mainstream.

Over two decades there has been a considerable change in the eating and drinking habits of our own clientele at Lake House. A decade ago, breakfast really did not get going until an hour later than at present and we frequently made up 'morning-after' concoctions for guests who did not emerge until noon after a very big night. There were few early risers. Nowadays meeting guests along the forest tracks while on my morning ramble with the dogs is one of the day's most pleasurable experiences.

Many of our clientele take advantage of our location to enjoy exercise and the wonderful fresh air. Some guests take tai chi and yoga classes with us on the lake foreshore. Some come for weeklong retreats to take time out, re-energise and enjoy our

wonderful spa treatments. For those so inclined we offer an array of Spa Cuisine dishes. For these we utilise the best seasonal produce – as often as possible sourced locally. Suppliers are committed to organic or at least sustainable agricultural practices. What happens to the food before we get it is just as important as what we do with it. Balanced utilisation of ingredients from all the food groups is also essential and we often find that guests are surprised at the versatility and flavour of items generally not common in the Western diet.

However, Spa Cuisine at Lake House is never about denial. When a favourite dish cannot be lightened without appreciably altering its taste and texture, we believe that a small portion of something absolutely wonderful is better than a plateful of something mundane. Fear of food is a worrying trend. Above all at Lake House, we believe that eating something truly delicious has always done wonders for the human spirit.

THE RECIPES

The recipes from the Lake House repertoire that I have chosen for this book were never a foregone conclusion. Many times I selected what I thought might be the final list, only to review it later and feel that it could stand some adjustment. Cooking is much like that. The finetuning is endless and I like to think that there will be readers in whose hands many of our recipes will continue to evolve and change. A book can only offer a snapshot of what seems important to me now at the time of writing. By the time you read this no doubt we will have moved on.

Many of the recipes in this book are for restaurant dishes and

Above all at Lake House we believe that eating something truly delicious has always done wonders for the human spirit.

are directed to an audience of already accomplished cooks. These are not about speed and they require considerable engagement and care. Some recipes are for the most curious of our clientele who are forever asking 'how?'. They are also for the avid amateur and professional collector of culinary inspiration. However, while creative restaurant cooking is not for every day, the basic building blocks in the creation of each dish often stand alone or can be transformed into a meal with the addition of something simple. I offer these suggestions within many of the recipes in the hope that anyone with the slightest inclination to do so can accomplish some pleasing and delicious results. And of course I have not been able to help myself. Commencing with every intention of just showcasing many of our beautiful restaurant dishes, my natural inclinations as a teacher have kicked in and in some cases you will find quite a commentary on produce and cooking methods. And, as I am essentially a country cook, you will also find considerable reference to elderberries, medlars, forest mushrooms, morello cherries and other ingredients you may need to forage for – the effort could prove rewarding and enjoyable.

Much of what I have drilled into my cooks applies equally to the lay enthusiast. Find something you think you will enjoy eating and perfect it through repetition. It is better to repeat the same recipe many times over in a short period than to attempt several recipes. Take a recipe and make it your own. Watch how a difference in the produce yields different results. Taste continually. Trust your palate. Develop confidence to fine tune with a splash of vinegar, cream, wine, liqueur, or a particular spice.

The chocolate I learned to add to tomato sauces when the tomatoes are not as ripe as they should be, the addition of nut-based liqueur to a dressing in a salad containing nuts, the splash of vinegar in a sorbet, Fernand Point's pinch of sugar when sautéing spinach, an extra pinch of salt to bring out the flavour in something sweet, a dash of lemon juice to enhance the flavour of almost anything, are all examples of those sorts of refinements.

TOOLS AND TALES

I would like to be able to say that I still have a favourite knife whittled down to a very thin blade over the years and a trustworthy, non-replaceable pan. That may have been true in the past when steel pans required extra care and curing, and carbon steel knives were dried so very carefully when put away. Working as guest chef or participating in Master Classes in big hotel kitchens, I learned to keep much of my very precious and carefully maintained equipment close by my side.

Nowadays most of my special tools are kept for emotional rather than practical reasons. There is the steel crêpe pan that Larissa learned to flip pancakes in when producing breakfast for restaurant staff at the age of seven. There is a wonderful mushrooming knife with attached brush for removing soil that Rita Erlich once brought back for me from Umbria and which gets a thorough work out each mushroom season. A local woman from Richard Beckett's house brought me a tiny nutmeg grater after he died, saying she thought he would want me to have it. Beckett was the real life incarnation of Sam Orr, the much-feared food reviewer of the *Nation Review*. The dozens of tiny petit fours tins brought back from Denhillerin in Paris in the seventies are still in use in the kitchen. The copper pots brought back at the same time are in desperate need once again of re-lining. But they serve as a reminder of my aspirations as a very young woman.

The surfeit of excellent equipment now available to lay cooks is extraordinary. Most revolutionary are the non-stick pans that sear effortlessly, last a long time and can put up with considerable wear and tear. Mind you, a steel pan will still produce a lacier colouring on crêpes and blinis.

Always ensure your knives maintain their sharpness with the frequent use of a good steel. Periodically they will need a going-over on a whetstone or attention from a professional sharpener. Considerably more accidents happen with dull knives that slip on food. The knives you choose should feel well balanced and comfortable to use, with a blade that continues right through the handle. German steel is by far the hardest but the most difficult to sharpen. Mandolines are wonderful things if you want to achieve those finest of vegetable slices that are essential for many professional-looking dishes. Never use one without its guard. I have lost count of the number of young apprentices I have sat with over the years at the local country hospital waiting for their decapitated fingertips to be dressed. Tamis or drum sieves and a flexible pastry scraper are useful if you are after refined smoothness in meat, fish and vegetable purées.

Always go for heavier gauge pans and especially solid baking trays that do not buckle when heated. Heavy-bottomed pots are also essential and it is useful to remember that copper and aluminium are the best conductors of heat while stainless steel is very poor. Stainless steel pots should always have a base core of either aluminium or copper. Wider topped pots and pans reduce things more quickly because of the larger surface area. Items that double up for both stovetop and oven cooking are a bonus. One of my current favourites is a large non-stick, sloping-sided, quite deep sauté pan with two ovenproof handles and a lid. Its non-stick surface caramelises meats and vegetables beautifully over high heat and its large surface area reduces the liquid rapidly when I am after concentrated flavour. It also doubles up as a terrific roasting dish or, with its lid on, as a perfect receptacle for a slow braise.

Other particularly useful items commonly found in professional kitchens include a swivel-headed peeler, which if you do not already have one will change your life; a pair of ordinary tweezers for pin-boning fish; and a hand-held stick blender, especially if you wish to achieve the frothy texture of many contemporary soups and sauces.

Learn to trust your judgement. Failures by many of my students years ago were often found to be caused by incorrectly calibrated ovens. If something looks too hot – it probably is. An oven thermometer and a temperature probe are useful tools to have.

But any amount of wonderful tools cannot replace the taking of pleasure with your cooking. Even when you perform the most mechanical tasks of slicing, chopping and sautéing, you are connecting with generations of people who have done similar things – all in the pursuit of something delicious or in the act of preparing something nourishing and special for others. Above all, enjoy it. Cooking is a wonderful thing.

Chapter Four

LOCAL FOOD

It seems that there is a sort of rosy Tuscan glow associated with having 'a little country restaurant'. Recently I was joined at our bar by a regular guest. This woman is a walking human dynamo, who juggles a full-time lectureship together with speaking engagements, considerable honorariums and board positions. Over a drink or two and with a dreamy look in her eyes, she confided her desire to eventually run a little '45-seater organic foods café' somewhere in the country.

Well, I almost fell off my bar stool. On the outside I was still all smiles and nods but really I wanted desperately to shriek: 'You want to do what? Are you in a rush to do yourself in? A little 45-seater is not like having a dinner party every couple of months. And what's that about organic?'

I said nothing of course. It always seems churlish to me to express horror at others' aspirations in this industry especially when I sit surrounded by the nicely orchestrated clockwork of a busy restaurant, with the advantage of two decades of systems.

There are romantic notions aplenty about running a regional restaurant. Portrayed with appropriate bucolic imagery, the life of a country chef seems idyllic. Often it is all about local produce, with photographs of chefs leaning on a spade in their vegetable garden or wandering down to their nearest herb farm, basket on arm, to pick up a few bunches of organic basil. It is only now after two decades, with my input being less intensely operational, that I might find the time to do anything of the sort.

The country remains a tough turf to do business in and many industry issues are considerably magnified. If you are trying to run a restaurant in the country for more than love, the chances of spending any time in a vegetable garden raising produce for your table are very remote. To further debunk some myths, the chance of that local herb grower waiting around just in case you and a few other cooks drop by to pick up a few bunches of herbs, is even more remote. That herb farmer is also in business and it is more profitable for him to ship all of his organic basil down to the wholesale market in one hit rather than wait for the locals to decide how many bunches they want. What is more, it is possible the local greengrocer on his buying expedition to the wholesale markets will pick up those very herbs and bring them all the way back into the region to sell in his shop. And with this journey of some 200 kilometres, that basil tells the story of some

The desire to communicate directly with growers and suppliers is demonstrated by the proliferation of farmers' markets right around the world.

of the problems associated with our food supply chains. That story is repeated all over the country where food often cannot be purchased at its source unless it has been trucked to the city markets and back. Yet local regional foods are in demand and creating plenty of interest. The history has been interesting.

When we first opened Lake House there were no small specialty local suppliers or even farms growing food for local tables. Like most rural areas in Australia, our region was characterised by mechanised farming businesses where output was measured in tonnages. Long-haul consumption patterns had developed as a result of improved transportation. We could and therefore we did transport food long distances. Unfortunately not all produce travelled well and as the practice of long-hauling increased so did the trend towards limiting produce grown to high-yield crops with long shelf lives, often engineered to last in cold storage and on supermarket displays. This trend, reflected all over the world, has been followed by a sharp decline in the variety and quality of fruit and vegetables consumed. Now it seems even the economic benefits of those practices are questionable. Local farmers receive a very miserly portion of what consumers spend on food. The rest of the value is captured upstream, mostly away from rural areas, by processors, distributors and global retailers. Often the business of moving food around the world is more lucrative than growing it. All that transporting around also has environmental implications in terms of energy usage. If the true cost of distribution, handling and processing is taken into consideration, local food is the least expensive option for society.

Changes are being encouraged by shifts in consumer and culinary thinking. People are heartily tired of perfect apricots and peaches that travel well but are flavourless. There is considerable and growing demand for diversity and real flavour. The provenance of our food has become important, fuelled by the sometimes well-founded suspicion about what is done to it before it reaches us. The desire to communicate directly with growers and suppliers is demonstrated by the proliferation of farmers' markets right around the world. Our connection with food, lost with the demise of small shopkeepers, is more easily regained when the produce comes from nearby.

As a chef, local food provides me with the opportunity to develop a relationship with suppliers, to understand more about the product and in some cases even influence its characteristics. Eating and cooking with what is local makes sense. Call it Slow Food if you like – I just call it smart.

The move to regional areas by people seeking lifestyle change is also a catalyst. It is often these folk who make up the backbone of the new face of agribusiness. Restoring old vineyards and olive groves planted by the original Swiss-Italian settlers of our region, establishing orchards, vegetable gardens and small-scale food enterprises, they have dedication and passion.

Nowadays it is these small producers who often give me and other local cooks a call to ask what specialty produce we might be interested in. As a result, we occasionally have the opportunity of putting daily specials on our menu that include freshly picked produce that has not yet seen the inside of a refrigerator. Peeling and chopping a freshly picked ripe tomato still warm from the sun, tossing it with some local fromage frais, torn basil and fruity local olive oil through some just made pappardelle – what great indulgence!

But accessing what is local is not a given. Those herbs and everything else will move out of the region to wherever there are guaranteed purchasers. Creating a market takes time and a critical mass of businesses and residents dedicated to purchasing locally. It is time that country chefs often do not have. Putting an order through to a city supplier who has established reliable delivery routes into the region and who guarantees supply is simply quite often the most expedient and safest thing to do.

The produce is certainly there, but do not be persuaded to dwell in some delusional rural fantasy. Its growth, development and availability for local tables need to be fostered, encouraged and nurtured by all of us.

Alongside the burgeoning interest in local food, a new generation of chefs is writing menus where 'organic', 'hormone and chemically free', 'free-range', 'line caught' and 'wild' are frequent food descriptions. In the process, the increased demand is spawning new networks of farmers, livestock producers and fish purveyors to supply ingredients produced in these ways. Who would have thought that restaurants and cooks would be driving a socio-political movement of sorts?

As consumers we stand to benefit of course. None of us is too keen about unwittingly ingesting hormones and antibiotics and most of us will pay a little extra for the privilege of ensuring against it. And there's the rub. Participation in the movement may be destined to be a middle class concern because of increased food gathering and production costs. Concerns about biodiversity and the reduction of the gene pool are much the same. Unlike modern food production methods requiring a one-size-fits-all solution, the specialty handling and feeding practices involved in producing rare breed meats, for example, is costly, especially if they are certified organic. The often-small herd or flock inevitably has personal and passionate individual care and concern from a dedicated farmer.

Cheap food comes from practices where corners are cut. Factory farming remains the most tellingly worrying example. Industrial livestock farming can involve vast abuses that are a serious moral problem. It is a strange contradiction that we can be so appalled by cruelty to a puppy but remain unmoved by cruelty to livestock. And is it some sort of bolshie class distinction that allows us to consume battered and de-beaked battery chickens by the million but balk at the notion of cared for, hand-reared and hand-fed geese used in the production of foie gras by handlers following a centuries-old tradition?

It would seem that what is needed is at the very least a set of elementary standards for animal husbandry and veterinary ethics. In our enjoyment of the bounty of the world's creatures, reason and morality would suggest we owe them at least a good life and an untormented death. But production systems that ameliorate the confinements and mutilations that can characterise the industry will cost more. Just as with the kind of restaurants and culinary industry we may want, having 'clean' food produced and grown in desirable conditions will surely affect our hip pocket. And while there is no doubt we should care about the delivery of good food to all, rather than to the limited and privileged few, perhaps as a society we need to reconsider and raise the value we place on food. Concern with the bottom line should surely not be the only consideration.

In time our local food will be recognised for its regional, climatic and even cultural characteristics. Just as our food at Lake House now has a distinctive style, local food will develop specific qualities related to the people who produce it. Skills and knowledge will be passed on. It is my hope that one day you will know the lamb you are eating has come from the volcanic plains around our area because its flavour will reflect the specific terrain as well as the traditional feeding and handling practices of our region.

Chapter Five

A DAY IN THE LIFE OF THE HOUSE ON THE LAKE

There is a light mist hanging over the waters of the lake. The sun has just touched

the tops of the trees on the far shore ...

Our house on the lake is about people. It is about the people who inhabit it and visit it. The place is lived in and worked in every day of the year. There is a rhythm to it ...

6AM The breakfast team arrives, the coffee machine is switched on and there is the aroma of freshly ground beans. Bread is mixed and left to rise, fruit is poached and batches of jam and marmalade are put on. The restaurant, set by the team the night before, is given a spruce and touch up. Newspapers are laid out. Breakfast cutlery and crockery is polished. Muesli ingredients are mixed, a new slab of fresh honeycomb oozing fragrant golden stuff, poached rhubarb, and sheep's milk yoghurt are laid out on the buffet. The smell of baking croissants, brioche, muffins and crumpets fills the air. Bread is punched, rolled and shaped, porridge bubbles.

7AM The front office opens, logbooks are checked, booking sheets completed. Housekeeping give the foyer floors a final buff. The phones start ringing. House guests arrive for a fresh juice before a morning jog around the lake and through the forest. They will return later with tales of kangaroos and wombats along the trails. In the kitchen local bacon and lamb sausages sizzle, roasted tomatoes are topped with freshly torn basil. Cheese blintzes are crisped in the pan and tiny croque-monsieurs and bread and butter puddings are arranged in the hot trays.

8AM Denise arrives, arms laden with freshly picked roses, peonies and mixed foliage, rich pickings from our acreage and from other local gardens.

9.30AM There is a hum of conversation in the restaurant with a little Brahms in the background. The coffee machine is working overtime. Waiters scramble to reset tables. Some guests are after a rapid refuel before a busy day of retail therapy, visiting galleries and vineyards, and long sessions in the day spa. Outdoors in the sunshine overlooking the lake, regular guests are catching up and the pace is more languid. Miriam and Madelaine, two local artists, have stopped off for an espresso and a chat. There is the 'thunk' of balls from the tennis court. Kookaburras arrive for their morning feed and waterbirds are gathering on the shore below for what they know will shortly be a feast of left-over toast and pastries. The noisiest are the geese: Foie gras 1, Foie gras 2, Foie gras 3 and Bernie.

10AM The remainder of the kitchen brigade arrives for morning briefing. The bread is baked and prep work commences in earnest. Stocks left to simmer overnight are strained, terrines and parfaits are put on to bake. The ice-cream churn commences another long day and everywhere there is skimming, slicing, dicing, chopping and boning.

11AM Penny, the breakfast chef, completes her shift with a final array of goodies set out in the staff room for a hungry grounds, maintenance and front office crew, some of whom have been hard at it since 7am. The spa girls come in and take a pastry or two back with them to their sanctuary. Their day is filled with hot mineral water baths, vichy cocoons and all manner of body treatments booked to the hilt. In the restaurant, tables are being reset for lunch. The front-of-house lunch team arrives and gathers for a briefing on guests, specials and wine-list updates.

12 NOON It is looking to be a very busy day with heavy bookings already. Perfect weather means the outdoor terraces are likely to be full with al fresco diners. A 'long lunch' table for 24 has been booked on the lake foreshore. Later in the afternoon there is a wedding ceremony by the lake with an evening function to follow in the Terrace room. The restaurant dinner sitting is full and a regular guest has booked the cellar room for a private dinner for 14. Head chef Matthew officiates over an organisational meeting with James, our sommelier, and Martin, the restaurant manager. We pause for breath for what seems like a split second before the last coffee drinkers on the terrace depart and the first lunch guests arrive. By the lake, welcome drinks are served to the arriving group. Platters of regional antipasto and ice buckets of wine are being loaded from the kitchen onto food buggies.

These will be followed by trays of Moroccan marinated chicken and quail, with accompaniments of harissa, spiced vinaigrette, salads of chickpeas and roast tomatoes and fresh broad bean falafel. In the kitchen the short staccato of incoming orders is barked by the duty manager.

'One quail, two charcuterie, one pork, one lamb, one Murray cod. One Caesar, dressing on the side, one duck, one kangaroo.'

'Room service! Tomato and chilli linguini, green salad, regional cheeses. One Spa Cuisine!'

The concentration is palpable. In the foyer Shelley, the general manager, welcomes regulars and passes them over to Martin in the restaurant. From behind the bar, mango bellinis and raspberry daiquiris are ferried to outside tables where guests are settling in for what looks like being a long lunch.

4PM Tables are reset for dinner and the first shift of kitchen and front of house leave for a break. New guest arrivals are checked in by the front office and offered a drink. James conducts a wine tasting in the cellar for residential guests. Denise and her crew are busy on the foreshore arranging a flower-bedecked table and chairs for the wedding ceremony. Housekeeping has already set the Terrace room for the function. Staff arrive to finish the bar, chill wine and plate hors d'oeuvres. David, sous chef responsible for running the function kitchen tonight, transports everything needed and sets up for dinner. Four guests in white robes arrive on the restaurant terrace, post spa treatments, and call for chilled champagne. The softening sun turns the lake a molten gold ...

3.30PM Last lunch orders are rolling in. The foreshore lunch group has moved to tables on the lower deck overlooking the pool and lake for shade. Platters of cocktail sandwiches, scones and cake are departing for the guest lounge for the residential guests' regular Saturday arvo high tea. It's quite a gathering in there already. In the restaurant, pear and almond tarts, baked plum cake and other assorted afternoon fare are being served to foreshore walkers popping in for coffee.

6PM The wedding function in the Terrace room is already in full swing and strains of light jazz drift across the gardens. Colourful silk dresses and bare shoulders soak up the early evening glow on the outdoor terrace. Inside, bowers of cascading roses fill the air with scent. Candles are lit. Allan in his black suit is setting up the Saturday night bar for residential guests in the lounge. Remaining staff line up for staff dinner in the kitchen. It is an essential break in a very busy day. Tonight it is penne with braised lamb and olives, salad and goat's cheese tart for vegetarians. The restaurant team takes their dinner to the cellar for the evening's briefing. I join them to discuss some new dishes that have been sent down for tasting. Wine matches are discussed.

7PM In a quick turnaround, the cellar is reset for the private dinner for 14. It is a beautiful evening and early arrivals are ensuring the bar is kept busy with martinis, Americanos and our signature Flying Ducks. Across the lake, cockatoos cover the trees like white exotic blooms. Every now and then a great flock takes off screeching into the sky. The reddening horizon promises another perfect day tomorrow. I take my place on the pass, registering table changes, VIPs, last-minute announcements of special dietary needs, orders and call aways.

8PM The pace picks up.

'One soup, one scallops, two salmon, one pork, one bass, one chicken, one vegetarian.'

'Two DG. *Amuse bouche* away on 23. Table 8, Mr Marks wants to know if we can do the kingfish as he had a month ago – that's Asian salad with crisp shallots.'

'Duck course on cellar DG in 12 minutes.'

'Table 11 mains away. Pre-dessert on 15. Three charcuterie, one eel, one bass, two beef and one lamb, just with mash – no fancies and with side veg.'

'Are we getting table 24 today? It's on 25 minutes already.'

'*Amuse bouche* away on 62, 6, 15. Why are we holding mains on 14?'

'Chef, they're outside having a fag.'

'How long? If he wants his lamb pink – get him back in now.'

The brigade responds in the culinary-lingua franca of kitchens everywhere.

'Oui, Chef', 'Two minutes, Chef', 'On the pass now, Chef' …

There is a blur of black and white through the in and out doors. Apart from the three courses served for guests not having the eight-course degustation – there are *amuse bouche*, pre-desserts and various condiments to silver serve. Then there are additional 'complimentaries' sent out to return guests. Timing is all and concentration cannot and does not lapse.

Meanwhile Ian, our brilliant plongeur of 15 years, is busy answering calls for more pans, more rectangular and circular moulds, more eggcups, as he juggles the incoming tide of hundreds of dishes and the needs of the chefs. He's probably the most crucial man in the kitchen.

Front-of-house commis in long black pinafores and white shirts are setting up trays for inevitable room-service requests for dessert – there is a big rugby game on television tonight. Through the double doors in the dining room soft music plays, all is smooth. The sommeliers take a table through a flight of Heathcote shiraz. There is the clink of glasses, soft laughter and hum of conversation.

10.30PM The kitchen team from the function room returns. Dinner there has been a success and guests are now dancing up a storm. Meanwhile the cellar group request cheese, cognac and cigars in the guest lounge. Shelley calls it a day and catches up with a couple of regulars at the bar. Ian is elbow deep at the sink. A departing guest pushes open the kitchen door with a 'Thanks guys – formidable'.

Outside guests are making their way back to their rooms under an inky black and starry sky. There is a crispness to the air. Laughter can be heard from the bridge spanning the spring-fed creek. Others waiting for taxis are farewelled at the door by Martin and his team. Tables are being reset in the restaurant. Commis are polishing glasses and cutlery.

12.30AM Once 'Elvis has left the building', the restaurant is reset for breakfast. In the kitchen all stove surfaces are left soaking. Stockpots are put on. All the stainless steel is scrubbed, *mise en place* lists written. Staff enjoy a knock-off drink.

2AM By now the function room basic clean is completed, kitchen and bar are spotless. Only tables and chairs remain to be moved by housekeeping tomorrow. Duty manager completes lockdown.

4AM Kitchen hands come in to steam and scour the kitchens.

6AM The breakfast team arrives ...

9.30PM Five resits are enjoying champagne at the bar, waiting for tables. Desserts are going out. A batch of warm, freshly baked madeleines are carried around as this evening's special treat. The telephone rings in the kitchen with a request for more salad greens for the function kitchen. As things slow a degree, two of the kitchen team break off to top up *mise en place* for tomorrow.

BREAKFAST

❧ PENNY'S PORRIDGE ❧
Makes 6 large bowls

This has to be one of our most asked for recipes. There is no magic, it is just that Penny, our breakfast cook, does not use instant oats and can afford the indulgence of cooking the oats long and slow. Soaking the oats overnight can reduce the cooking time. The toppings that follow the porridge recipe are optional but deliciously wicked.

3 cups oats (not instant oats)
3 cups water
3 cups milk
1 tablespoon salt

In a saucepan, bring all the ingredients to the boil over a moderate heat, stirring regularly. Turn the heat down to low so that the porridge just 'plops' along for approximately 30–40 minutes, stirring regularly. Check the consistency near the end as the porridge may need some more liquid to 'loosen' it up.

SERVING OPTIONS

- Near the end of cooking, mix in ⅔ of a cup of raisins that have been soaked overnight in orange juice.
- Top with caramelised bananas. Prepare these by frying thick slices of banana in butter and adding brown sugar and a dash or two of cream at the end.
- Cover with brown sugar sauce, made by boiling cream with brown sugar and a cinnamon stick for 5 minutes.

❧ FRENCH TOAST ❧
Serves 6-8

Called *grenki* in our Russian household, this was one of my favourite breakfast treats and was made from what was then called a Vienna loaf. Use the best day-old white bread you can get. At Lake House we use our house brioche. French toast is delicious with good jams, alongside the Winter Salad of Poached Dried Fruits (see page opposite) and yoghurt or just on its own.

1 loaf day-old unsliced white bread or brioche
1 litre (34 fl oz) milk
4 eggs
60 g (2 oz) caster (superfine) sugar
50 g (2 oz) butter, chopped
50 g (2 oz) additional caster (superfine) sugar, combined with ½ teaspoon ground cinnamon

Trim the ends from the bread or brioche, cut it into slices about 3 cm (1¼ in) thick and remove the crusts. If desired, for easier handling cut each slice in half diagonally. Whisk the milk with the eggs and sugar until the sugar is dissolved. Soak the bread or brioche slices in the mixture. This is most easily done by spreading the slices in a baking pan and pouring the mix over the top. Allow the bread to soak for a minute while melting the butter in a pan over moderate heat. Drain each bread slice before placing it in the pan to cook on both sides until well coloured, then transfer it to kitchen paper. Serve with the cinnamon sugar sprinkled over the top.

❖ Winter salad of poached dried fruits ❖
Serves 6-8

In winter we often serve this poached fruit salad, which utilises dried fruits. Early in the season we might add poached fresh quinces. In late winter and early spring, the addition of poached fresh rhubarb adds a delicious tang. But just as is, this fruit salad served warm or at room temperature is delicious with yoghurt for breakfast or with a steamed pudding for dessert. An added drop or two of rosewater offers an interesting variation.

125 g (4 oz) dried apricots
125 g (4 oz) prunes
125 g (4 oz) dried figs
125 g (4 oz) dried peaches
1.8–2 litres (60–68 fl oz) water
180 g (6¼ oz) Demerara sugar
2 strips lemon rind
4 teaspoons lemon juice
2 cinnamon sticks
2 pieces star anise
3 cloves
30 g (1 oz) blanched almonds, split and toasted
poached pears, rhubarb or quinces and their syrup (optional)

Soak the dried fruit together in the water overnight. Strain the syrup from the soaked fruit, pour it into a saucepan and add the sugar (you may wish to adjust the quantity to taste). Set the soaked fruit aside. Heat the syrup slowly until the sugar is dissolved. Add the lemon rind, lemon juice and spices and boil for about 10 minutes to reduce and thicken the syrup a little. Add the reserved soaked fruit, except the prunes, and simmer gently over a low heat for about 15 minutes or until the fruit is tender. Add the prunes to the warm fruit and allow the fruit to cool. Add the almonds and, if using, the other poached fresh fruit — along with any syrup, for compote-like consistency, or to adjust and enhance flavours. Set aside ready to use or refrigerate for up to 4 days.

❖ COOKED RHUBARB ❖

Serves 6–8 as a breakfast accompaniment

Rhubarb, one of my favourite things, is related to buckwheat and sorrel, two other favourite ingredients – it has to be a coincidence. I indulge my love of this vegetable by using it in pies, chutneys and compotes and we even dedicate a whole dessert to it in the restaurant. Do not cook rhubarb in water as it is too difficult to control and can result in overcooking. The fruit drops sufficient liquid as it is. We simply sugar the rhubarb batons and bake them with a little steam. In the domestic kitchen the best process is to bake the rhubarb in a baking dish tightly covered with foil. The amount of sugar will depend on how sweet you like the finished product.

500 g (1 lb 2 oz) trimmed rhubarb, cut into 5–6 cm (2–2½ in) batons
170–200 g (6–7 oz) Demerara sugar

Preheat the oven to 200°C (400°F). Place the rhubarb in a baking dish and sprinkle with the sugar. Cover with greaseproof paper then tightly with foil (rhubarb and aluminium will react so likewise ensure you never use an aluminium utensil to cook it in). Bake for about 20 minutes. Check the rhubarb towards the end. The batons should be tender while still keeping their shape and some natural syrup will have formed. Allow the fruit to cool. Store in a glass or ceramic bowl, covered with plastic wrap, in the refrigerator. At breakfast the rhubarb is served alongside our Bircher muesli and local sheep's milk yoghurt. We also sometimes add it to our Winter Salad of Poached Dried Fruits (see page 83).

Poached eggs in cheese soufflés
Serves 6

I do these as a special treat. It is a dish of the great Fernand Point of La Pyramide. I give instructions here for individual soufflé dishes but you can use a large dish and bring it to the table for a group brunch. In that case use the grated cheese sprinkled on top to signal where each egg is buried. You should then be able to scoop out portions of soufflé without breaking an egg. I find that gruyère offers the best flavour here.

2 tablespoons butter
3 tablespoons plain (all-purpose) flour
500 ml (17 fl oz) milk, brought to the boil
100 g (3½ oz) freshly grated gruyère
3 egg yolks
salt and freshly ground white pepper
freshly grated nutmeg
5 egg whites
6 small very fresh free-range eggs, poached and drained (see Poached Eggs, page 290) and trimmed to a neat shape
25 g (1 oz) additional freshly grated gruyère

Preheat the oven to 200°C (400°F). Melt the butter in a heavy-based saucepan over a gentle-to-medium heat. Add the flour then stir to combine the mix into a paste. Remove the pan from the heat and add a little of the boiled milk, stirring to dissolve the paste. Continue adding the rest of the hot milk, stirring until it is well combined. Return the saucepan to the heat and, stirring continuously, cook until the milk mixture thickens into a sauce. Take care to ensure it does not catch on the bottom of the saucepan. Remove from the heat and stir in the first quantity of grated cheese. One by one whisk in the egg yolks. Season with salt and pepper and two or three scrapes of nutmeg. In a very clean bowl whisk the egg whites until stiff with a pinch of salt then fold through the still warm mix.

Divide the mixture in half and distribute the first half equally between six buttered soufflé dishes. Arrange a poached egg on top of the mixture in each dish then spoon the remaining mixture onto the top of the eggs. Using the additional grated cheese, sprinkle a little over each dish. Bake in the oven for a couple of minutes then lower the temperature to 180°C (350°F). The soufflés should be served as soon as they have risen and the tops are coloured. This takes around 6–8 minutes. The soufflés should still be a little underdone in the middle and the eggs must remain soft.

PRESERVES

What is breakfast without a decent jam or a real marmalade? Much of the stuff on supermarket shelves nowadays is mostly sugar and very little fruit. The bite of a good marmalade is very hard to find as most of those available have succumbed to the sweetness that pervades so much of our food.

Seasonal fruit is the basis of many of our preserves. Windfalls from local gardens are often proffered through the back door of our kitchen or cadged from friendly neighbours. Many of our preserve recipes have origins in *Windfalls*, a book by local cook Sue Ruchel, which I was delighted to launch many years ago. Our well-thumbed and slightly sticky copy resides in the pastry section of our kitchen and is taken up and scoured each time a glut of some seasonal local fruit arrives.

Our preserves have aficionados as far afield as Hong Kong, where an annual Lake House guest has her raspberry jam sent by mail order. Lake House preserves are also represented on the shelves of Harvey Nichols' wonderful food hall in London.

❦ MEDLAR JELLY ❦
Makes about 500 ml (17 fl oz)

Medlars come to us each year from Pauline and Fred Stapleton's beautiful old garden. The unusual fruit is green, round with pointed calyx segments and comes from trees that bear white flowers and have beautiful autumn foliage. Picked when just starting to go brown, they ripen over a couple of weeks, becoming brown and soft inside (see photograph on page 42). We transform the fruit into a delicious red jelly, which is beautiful taken with tea, Russian style, and sensational spooned around a warm apple tart.

5 cups washed, drained and halved medlars
1 lemon, sliced
1 stick cinnamon
sugar to measure

Place the medlars, lemon and cinnamon stick in a wide heavy-based saucepan. Cover with water and boil until the fruit is soft, which should take 20–30 minutes. Pour the mixture into a jelly bag or well-secured cheesecloth and allow the syrup to drip slowly into a bowl. Do not be tempted to hurry this process by squeezing the jelly bag. When the clear syrup has all passed through, discard the fruit. Pour the syrup into a saucepan and add 1 cup of sugar for each cup of syrup. Stir to dissolve the sugar. Bring to a brisk boil and cook until setting point has been reached (test by putting a little jelly on a saucer and placing it in the freezer for a few minutes – if the jelly wrinkles when the saucer is tilted, the cooking is complete). Remove the jelly from the heat and bottle it in sterilised jars while still hot.

❦ QUINCE & SEVILLE ORANGE JELLY ❦
Makes about 1 litre (34 fl oz)

Some years there is a moment in seasonal crossover when quinces are still around – and are sufficiently fresh to set a good jelly – and the first of the Seville oranges arrive. Few of us can resist a delicious, ruby-coloured and tangy quince jelly. Seville oranges make a much stronger statement in marmalades and jellies and have their own aficionados. But put the two together in a jelly and something truly ethereal is produced. More peach-coloured than ruby, with a beautiful perfume, this jelly is worth waiting for.

1 kg (2 lb 3 oz) quinces, washed
1 kg (2 lb 3 oz) Seville oranges
sugar to measure

Halve, quarter and chop the whole unpeeled and uncored quinces into small pieces. Completely peel the oranges (including pith) and chop roughly. Place the fruit in a saucepan and add water to just cover. Bring to the boil then reduce to a simmer and cook for at least 1 hour or until the quinces are completely soft and pulped. Pour the fruit mix through a jelly bag or well-secured colander, double-lined with muslin, and leave to stand for several hours or until all the liquid has dripped through. Discard the fruit. Add 1 cup of sugar for each cup of liquid and stir to dissolve. Bring to a brisk boil and cook until setting point has been reached (for testing, see method for Medlar Jelly). Bottle and seal.

❧ BLUEBERRY JAM ❧
Makes about 1 litre (34 fl oz)

Nowadays feted for being high in antioxidants, blueberries grow particularly well in our region. Joy Durston and Claude Forell supply us from their small acreage in Glenlyon and often arrive with a just-picked kilo or two when popping in for lunch on the terrace in the height of summer. That sort of freshness is hard to resist. If any are left, they're put to good use in breakfast pancakes, muffins or in this terrific jam.

2 generous-sized punnets blueberries
juice and grated rind of 3–4 lemons
300 ml (10 fl oz) water for tiny berries, less if using large ones
500 g (1 lb 2 oz) sugar

If desired top and tail the berries. Put all the ingredients, except the sugar, into a saucepan. Simmer until the berries are just soft. Add the sugar and stir until dissolved. Boil briskly until setting point is reached (for testing, see method for Medlar Jelly, page opposite). Bottle and seal.

❧ SOUR CHERRY JAM ❧
Makes about 1 litre (34 fl oz)

Cherries do not contain much pectin. Sour cherries have a little more than sweet cherries but setting the jam can still be difficult. Powdered pectin, red currant juice, or lemon juice as in the following recipe, can assist. Russian-style cherry jam, however, is always quite liquid – more a confiture than a jam and is still quite delicious.

600 g (1 lb 5 oz) morello cherries
juice of 2 large lemons
400 g (14 oz) sugar

Pit the cherries, crack the pits with a hammer and tie them in muslin. Simmer the cherries and bagged cherry stones in the lemon juice, and a little water to prevent sticking, for about 20 minutes or until the fruit is tender. Remove the stones. Add the sugar, stirring until it is dissolved, then boil rapidly until setting point is reached (for testing, see method for Medlar Jelly, page opposite). Stand for a few minutes. Stir well so that the cherries do not rise to the top. Bottle and seal.

AFTERNOON TEA

We often create little delicious things for afternoon tea. In warm weather they may be served by the lake with iced teas and cordials.

❧ ELDERFLOWER CORDIAL ❧
Makes about 1.5 litres (51 fl oz)

Elderberries grow profusely in our region, often on the sides of the road and as hedgerows. In late spring and early summer the first fragrant flowers appear. Creamy at first then becoming white, they have a strong sweet perfume. Elderflower syrups, cordials, sorbets and fritters will only be as scented as the original flower. When picking, choose the best creamiest blooms and do not wait until too late in the season. English cook and author Sophie Grigson was a visiting guest chef at Lake House. This is her recipe for a delicious cordial.

20 very large and full elderflower heads
1.8 kg (3 lb 15 oz) caster (superfine) sugar
1.2 litres (41 fl oz) water
2 lemons
75 g (2½ oz) citric acid (available at chemists)

Pick over the elderflowers, discarding any insects, and place in a large bowl. Put the sugar in a pan with the water and bring to the boil, stirring to dissolve the sugar. Pare the zest of the lemons and toss it into the bowl with the flowers. Slice the lemons, discarding the ends, and add the slices to the bowl. Pour the boiling sugar syrup over the flowers and zest and stir in the citric acid. Cover with a cloth and leave at room temperature for 24 hours. Next day strain the cordial through a muslin-lined sieve or a jelly bag. Pour it into thoroughly cleaned glass or plastic bottles, screw on the lids and store in a dark cool cupboard. The cordial will last for several months.

A DAY IN THE LIFE OF THE HOUSE ON THE LAKE

FRIANDES

Makes 18 small friandes

1½ cups icing (confectioner's) sugar, sifted
1 cup almond meal
½ cup plain (all-purpose) flour, sifted
6 egg whites
185 g (6½ oz) butter, melted

Preheat the oven to 170°C (340°F). Combine the icing sugar, almond meal and flour in a bowl. Whisk the egg whites until soft peaks form. Fold the egg whites and the melted butter into the dry ingredients. Place the mix into greased friande moulds and bake for 10 minutes.

VARIATION Add a splash of pure vanilla essence to the mix and set one whole fresh raspberry or blueberry into the centre of each friande before baking.

MADELEINES

Makes 12 large madeleines

2 eggs
110 g (3¾ oz) caster (superfine) sugar
110 g (3¾ oz) plain (all-purpose) flour, sifted
85 g (3 oz) butter, melted

Preheat the oven to 170°C (340°F). Whisk the eggs and sugar together in a bowl. Fold the sifted flour into the egg mix then fold the melted butter into the mix. Put the mixture into greased madeleine moulds. Bake large moulds for 9 minutes, and smaller moulds, if using, for 6 minutes. For a really decadent treat, serve madeleines with a little pot of chocolate sauce to dip into.

VARIATIONS To make citrus madeleines, add the zest of 1 orange or the zest of 1 lime and serve with a little pot of Lemon Curd (see Lemon Charlotte with Citrus Salad, page 258).

❧ Summer rose cupcakes ❧
Makes 16 cakes

In the height of summer when the roses are in bloom we have made these cupcakes for Valentine's Day. Occasionally, we have used them as part of a wedding gateau assembled from many miniature cakes. They are also lovely just with tea. The roses give a very subtle scent to the cakes. You can add a little rosewater to the icing if you like. We garnish these pretty cupcakes with crystallised rose petals. Our fabulous and very large climbing Albertine rose puts on a great albeit brief show each year and is perfect to use.

THE CAKES

125 g (4 oz) softened butter

1 cup caster (superfine) sugar, rose-scented if possible (see Flavoured Sugars, page 293)

1 large egg

½ cup milk

1½ cups plain (all-purpose) flour

1 teaspoon baking soda

½ teaspoon salt

½ cup hot water

CRYSTALLISED ROSE PETALS

32–48 scented pink rose petals

1 egg white, lightly whisked

rose-scented caster (superfine) sugar (see Flavoured Sugars, page 293)

THE ICING

3 cups icing (confectioner's) sugar, rose-scented if possible (see Flavoured Sugars, page 293)

4 tablespoons milk

4 tablespoons softened butter

⅛ teaspoon salt

1–2 drops pink vegetable food colour

1 teaspoon rosewater

THE CAKES Preheat the oven to 170°C (340°F). Line a muffin tray with paper cups. Using an electric mixer, cream the butter and sugar then add the egg and milk and combine well. Add the flour, baking soda and salt and beat to just incorporate. Add the water and beat the mixture until smooth. Divide the batter evenly between the paper cups. Bake for 20–25 minutes or until the cakes have risen and are golden (a skewer inserted into the middle of the cakes comes out clean). Allow the cakes to cool.

CRYSTALLISED ROSE PETALS Brush both sides of the petals with egg white. Sprinkle with some scented sugar and place on a sheet of greaseproof paper in a warm place to dry.

THE ICING Using a hand-held beater, mix all the ingredients in a mixing bowl until smooth and creamy. With a spatula spread the icing onto each cupcake. Garnish with crystallised rose petals while the icing is still very soft on the surface.

Many of the cheeses we serve at Lake House are from small boutique producers.

AFTER-DINNER TREATS

CHEESE WITH FRUIT AND NUTS

Our immediate region is not conducive to dairy farming but sheep and goat's milk cheeses are in good supply. Ann Marie Monda and Carla Meurs of Holy Goat Cheeses have what is probably the happiest and most indulged, organically certified flock of goats in the state. Their Black Silk, an ash-coated fresh curd cheese, is a personal favourite.

Figs are delicious with fresh goat's cheese but they can often be a disappointment nowadays, somehow lacking in flavour, succulence and sweetness. But perhaps my memory of climbing fig trees with fig juice running down my chin is a deceptive fantasy. In any case, I find oven-drying the figs just a little increases the flavour quite a bit.

Blue cheese and ripe pears are always delicious. If the pears are not perfect we concentrate their flavour by making Pear Crisps (see page 291), which we serve with Julie and Sandy Cameron's Meredith Blue, a deliciously creamy cheese redolent with the flavour of spring ewe's milk. The sweetened peppery bite of honeyed spiced walnuts makes for another pleasant accompaniment, as do Crostini (see page 281), made from our fig and aniseed bread.

❖ SLOW-BAKED FIGS ❖

large purple figs, each cut into 6 wedges
icing (confectioner's) sugar, for dusting

Preheat the oven to 175°C (340°F). Place the fig wedges on a silicon-lined baking sheet and dust with icing sugar. Bake for around 30 minutes. The figs should feel dry on the outside but still supple. Place them in an airtight container and store in the refrigerator.

❖ SPICED HONEY WALNUTS ❖

1 tablespoon honey
2 tablespoons olive oil
¼ teaspoon cayenne pepper
1 cup walnut halves
½ teaspoon salt

Preheat the oven to 180°C (350°F) and grease a non-stick baking sheet. Combine the honey, olive oil and cayenne pepper in a mixing bowl. Add the walnuts and toss until they are well coated. Spread the nuts on the baking sheet and bake for 10–15 minutes. Check them every 5 minutes to make sure they do not burn. Stir the nuts after 10 minutes, turning them for even cooking. Season the nuts with salt and let them cool on the baking sheet. Use immediately or store in an airtight container.

❖ COCONUT MACAROONS ❖

If you do a bit of cooking and baking you will usually have excess egg whites. In commercial kitchens there are always buckets of them. They are used up generally for clarifying consommés but we try to have at least one dessert that requires a considerable number of them. Floating islands, pavlova and dishes that require Italian meringue are a good start. These macaroons are simple to make in large quantities and store well in airtight containers.

300 ml (10 fl oz) egg white
600 g (1 lb 5 oz) sugar
¾ cup plain (all-purpose) flour, sifted
3 cups toasted shredded coconut

Preheat the oven to 130°C (265°F). Whisk the egg white with the sugar in a stainless steel bowl over a pot of simmering water, for about 6–8 minutes or until the mix feels warm and is thick, white and has increased in volume. Remove the mix from the heat, scrape it into a mixing bowl and beat at high speed until it is cool and has doubled in volume. The meringue will be thick and glossy. Gently fold in the flour and coconut. Using a 2–3 cm (¾–1¼ in) rosette nozzle, pipe the meringue onto trays lined with baking paper, or non-stick trays. Bake for about ½ an hour until firm. The macaroons should not colour. Remove them from the oven and allow them to cool. They will crisp up further. They are delicious drizzled with or half-dipped in chocolate.

❖ SIENNA CAKE ❖

Makes 20 x 30 cm (8 x 12 in) tray

150 g (5 oz) hazelnuts, skins removed by toasting in oven at 160°C (320°F) for 6–8 minutes then rubbing with a towel
150 g (5 oz) whole peeled almonds
100 g (3½ oz) plain (all-purpose) flour
50 g (2 oz) cocoa
200 g (7 oz) candied peel
1 teaspoon ground cinnamon
1 teaspoon ground mixed spice
160 g (5½ oz) honey
200 g (7 oz) caster (superfine) sugar

Preheat the oven to 130°C (265°F). Place the ingredients, except for the honey and caster sugar, in a large mixing bowl and combine well. Put the honey and sugar in a small saucepan over a gentle heat and stir to combine. Increase the heat and cook until the syrup registers 115°C (240°F) on a sugar thermometer. Pour the hot syrup over the dry ingredients in the bowl. Stir well until completely and evenly incorporated. Spread the mix in a non-stick baking tray and bake for 2–2½ hours until the cake is quite firm.

❧ BISCOTTI ❧

Makes about 100 biscuits

It makes sense to cook a large quantity of biscotti as they keep very well in sealed containers in the cupboard. These ones are full of fruit.

2 eggs
250 g (9 oz) sugar
250 g (9 oz) plain (all-purpose) flour
1 teaspoon baking powder
50 g (2 oz) sultanas
50 g (2 oz) dried apricots, roughly chopped
50 g (2 oz) walnuts, chopped
50 g (2 oz) pistachio nuts
50 g (2 oz) blanched almonds, chopped
50 g (2 oz) hazelnuts, skins removed by toasting in oven at 160°C (320°F) for 6–8 minutes then rubbing with a towel, then chopped
zest of 1 lemon

Preheat the oven to 160°C (320°F). Cream the eggs and sugar then stir in the flour and baking powder. Add the fruit, nuts and lemon zest. Roll the mixture into a log 20 cm (8 in) in diameter. Place on a well-greased baking tray and bake for 20 minutes. The mixture will spread into a flattened loaf shape. Reduce the oven temperature to 130°C (265°F). Remove the tray from the oven and allow the log to cool until you are able to slice it. Cut it into 2 cm (¾ in) slices then each slice into two or three. Return to the oven and continue to bake until the biscotti are dry. Remove them from the oven and allow them to cool completely before storing in airtight containers.

Chapter Six

THE APPLE NEVER FALLS FAR FROM THE TREE

Growing up as a 'new Australian', as we were called in Melbourne in the 1960s, was difficult. I attended a school in the western suburbs populated almost entirely by Anglo-Saxons. I desperately wanted to fit in, which was not easy. My home-made lunches consisted of thick rye bread, home-made dill cucumbers and garlicky sausage. I dreamed of refined crustless white bread sandwiches and birthday parties with cocktail sausages and tomato sauce. I fantasised about having the money to buy a cream bun, oozing mock cream and red stuff.

My father, a shift worker, delighted in taking me to the Footscray delicatessens then recently opened by Polacks, Ukrainians and Germans. All of these seemed to be populated by similar rotund smiling women whose one ambition was to feed you. My father, fluent in five languages, tall and good looking, flirted outrageously, while sampling the latest bloodwurst, presswurst, hams and cheeses. I was never without a cheese pastry or piece of sliced tongue smothered with horseradish in my hand, my cheeks sore from having been pinched and exclaimed over.

In that immigrant-to-immigrant hand over that has invigorated much of Melbourne for generations, the Polacks and other Eastern Europeans eventually moved on, giving way to Vietnamese butchers, greengrocers and cafés. Nowadays of course there are plenty of Anglo-Saxon shoppers out chasing Asian greens and nam pla for their soups and salads.

But back then it was all pretty weird – none of my friends at school did anything like this. Their families shopped at our nearest shopping strip, which in those days boasted a butcher with sawdust on the floor and lots of lamb chops and white sausages in the window, a somewhat dingy fruit and veg shop, and a grocer where sugar, tea, flour and other staples, including a pound of broken biscuits for five pence, were measured into paper bags over an old wooden counter. It was well before the time of supermarkets.

Most Saturdays we travelled all the way to Collingwood so I could attend Russian school. There I learned Russian history, geography and literature as well as the ancient Slavic language still in use for church services. On Sunday the same journey was repeated to attend church. And after the service, in the church hall surrounded by portraits of long-dead Russian aristocrats, we were offered *piróshki*, *blinchiki* and extraordinary cakes with black tea in tall glasses. The hall was very much the hub of Russian cultural life in Melbourne. There were concerts, plays and dances. Hand-kissing was a common form of greeting, sometimes even accompanied with just a small click of the heels. Women wore furs in the winter and smelled of lilac or violets.

On the weekends spent in Daylesford, my father collected mineral water in much re-used soft drink bottles rust-lined with oxidised iron. I was told to drink the evil-smelling stuff for my health. He and his cronies enjoyed hot mineral baths in the rusted tubs of the old Hepburn Springs Bathhouse, which in those days resembled some steamy, smelly and very mysterious place indeed to my friends and me.

Two weeks of every summer holidays between the ages of 6 and 16 were spent at camp. There, every morning we saluted and pledged allegiance to the long dead tsar as the pre-revolutionary Russian flag was raised. All this was, of course, at the height of Soviet power. We took turns in the camp kitchen, hiked many miles and participated in forest games and manoeuvres in case, I suppose, we should ever be called upon to assist with the liberation of the homeland. At night we often sang old White Russian army songs by the huge campfire.

My father, a Muscovite, had led a pre-revolutionary life of privilege in Russia. His father, a colonel in the tsar's army, was executed by firing squad in 1918. But before ill fortune befell the family there had been a French tutor and a French cook.

Russians have always been mad about mushrooming, and their literature is full of stories of mushrooming parties.

My father told stories of military parades, glittering banquets and balls with buffets of feather-decorated partridge and pheasant from the hunt, shimmering aspics and beribboned charlotte Russes.

In front of me in my study are portraits of my grandfather Dimitry, in full uniform, complete with monocle, and my grandmother Fillipina, short-haired and looking every inch the cigar-smoking, card-playing modern woman she must have been. It was probably my father's memories of those Franco-Russian banquets that inspired my earliest journey to France.

My mother, on the other hand, came from a very large and almost entirely self-sufficient but monetarily poor farming family in Kishinev, Bessarabia, now Moldova. Virtually the only item not produced by the household was sugar, an alarmingly expensive commodity, which was bartered for with other goods. My maternal grandmother wove cloth, spun wool, butchered, made cheese, sausages and preserves and cured and smoked pork. She also raised eight children.

I never knew either of my sets of grandparents. Flight from civil war, the ravages of succeeding occupying forces and consequent orphaning and separation from families, left my parents as displaced persons in postwar Europe. With most returnees destined for gulags, the proffered assisted passage to either the United States or Australia was eagerly seized upon by them and thousands of others. Australia won by a narrow margin because football featured prominently in the pamphlets designed to attract migrants. My father was a manic follower of soccer. He had, of course, no idea about Aussie Rules!

For me, growing up in a Russian household meant being absorbed in all the rituals embodied in the task of cooking for people. Setting the table was like some sort of fanfare indicating that whatever had been simmering and issuing delicious smells for hours was about to be served. If guests were coming, the hand-embroidered cloths and best *rumochki* (shot glasses) were put out. Various salads and *zakúski* would already be in the refrigerator in their cut glass dishes.

Sometimes along the way there would be treats. Poaching beef for filling *blinchiki* or *piróshki* meant that at some point the meat and bones would be removed from the simmering liquid, which would then have various vegetables added as the first step towards a nourishing borscht. That poached beef while still warm and the marrow-filled bones were some of my father's favourite treats – and mine. Buttered rye bread topped with warm marrow or a slice of warm poached beef and French mustard were splendid fare that we demolished with glee, irritating my mother with our loud sucking noises as we retrieved every precious bit of marrow from the bones.

Depending on the occasion, sometimes the cooking lasted for days and as each dish was prepared and stored one could pilfer and sample. My mother's cabbage *piróshki* and my father's *holodets*, or *en gelée* as the French would call it – poached chicken or fish with vegetables in a jellied stock, poured into decorative serving bowls and placed in the refrigerator to set – were memorable.

We were a relatively religious family and the principal holy days of the Orthodox calendar were always observed. Easter was the most special of times, a greater celebration than Christmas. Based on the old Julian calendar it often fell outside the Anglican and Catholic Easter period. As the build-up was considerable, I frequently had to take time out of school to help.

First, hard-boiled eggs were coloured and decorated. Then the *kulichi*, or Easter breads, were commenced. These required several provings, including one that lasted most of the night as the dough proved in traditional tall tins on top of the warm stove, covered with feather doonas. No door banging or draughts were allowed. The house was silent for the duration and redolent with the aromas of freshly grated nutmeg and lemon zest.

Pashka, a fruit-filled moulded cheese dessert, was prepared and decorated as were other celebratory dishes destined to be consumed after the midnight church service in the early hours of Easter Sunday. Small portions of everything as well as coloured eggs and whole *kuliches*, topped with tall candles, were placed in a lace-lined basket ready to be taken to church to be blessed just after midnight. The church hall with its rows and rows of highly decorated baskets was a sight to behold.

The feast, consumed well after midnight, marked the end of the forty days of Lent. Lent commenced with the Russian equivalent of Shrove Tuesday – *Maslianitsa* – when blinis made with yeast and buckwheat flour, smothered with sour cream and served with salt herrings, were cooked and consumed by the dozen.

There was a great deal of ritual and folklore in the way things were done. There were family recipes handed down despite the dispersal of people all over the globe. The use of feather doonas

I saw repeated for another dish in another Russian household halfway across the world. In 1979 Allan and I visited my father's sister Irina, then living in Bucharest with Alla, an actress and singer friend. Both already retired, they lived like most expatriate Russians of their generation – as though the revolution of 1917 had never happened. Swanning around in the afternoon in silk *peignoirs*, they played old Russian tangos and foxtrots on the gramophone, drank tea and engaged in ruthless games of canasta, intermittently dispatching shoes at the television whenever the loathed Ceausescu made an appearance.

Both women adored cooking. Rumania, however, had been reduced to the sorriest of states. Despite being the height of summer, the market in Bucharest, previously the showcase for a country known as the fruit bowl of Eastern Europe, was now filthy, mostly empty and depressing. Foraging had taken on a new and different meaning. Armed with packets of Marlboros to be offered as 'additional incentives', Alla, Irina and myself spent the better part of half a day tracking down a reliably fresh chicken, vegetables and fruit for dessert. The afternoon was spent in their kitchen, browning the spices and onions for the pilaf, poaching fruit and roasting the bird. It was at the end of the cooking time for the rice that the enamel pot was removed from the stove and placed in a wooden blanket trunk. A feather doona was placed over it and the trunk was closed. Finishing touches were made to the meal, the table was set on the outdoor terrace under an old canvas awning, and wine was poured. As we sat down to eat, the pilaf was retrieved from the trunk. To this day I remember it for its aroma, perfect texture and the separation of grain from grain.

My aunt assured me that it was all to do with the doona in the blanket box.

Friends in the Russian community visited each other regularly. During most of my childhood few households had telephones and people often arrived without notice. Hence the refrigerator was ever on 'ready' especially on weekends or on special celebration days. If it was someone's birthday or name day a cake was baked because the chances of friends remembering and dropping by was quite good. I can recall my mother getting into a flap at an evening knock at the door on my name day, which we never particularly celebrated as already we were a little more westernised and adhered mostly to birthdays. It was the Russian archbishop, complete with staff and black monk's robes, having come all the way to the western suburbs by train. I have enormously fond memories of that man who had considerable patience with my mischievous habits and already rebellious nature in his classroom. He bore a little religious book as a gift. My mother's consternation was caused by her lack of knowledge of whether or not it was a 'fasting' period when no meat or dairy products were to be consumed. There were plenty of those dates in the Orthodox calendar. Just in case, the ever reliable salted herrings and potato salad with mum's cucumbers were hauled out of the refrigerator for the supper. And another occasion was celebrated.

Guests always brought something, a box of chocolates, roses from the garden or home-grown produce. The gift of a piece of someone's precious 'yoghurt mother' or 'vinegar mother' was always something to talk about. The 'yoghurt mother', kept under milk at room temperature, grew and eventually had pieces pruned off and offered to friends. Used to make a type of cultured milk as well as yoghurt, drunk and eaten daily, these were the age-old precursors to what we now purchase as 'probiotics'. The 'vinegar mother', kept in a crock in a dark, cool place, helped the transformation of left-over wine to an aromatic vinegar.

Herbs had a medicinal purpose as well as being used to add flavour. Caraway and fennel seeds were made into a tea to ease colic or wind. Fresh mint tea was considered to have similar soothing properties. My mother steeped chamomile flowers to assist sleep and brewed valerian from the garden to ease my pre-exam nerves. Our large aloe vera plant provided balm for burns. The state of one's health, digestion and the remedies one was using were discussed almost as much as food and politics. As a child these things were all an embarrassment and did little to help me fit in. Fifty years on, I am constantly amazed by how much I draw on the hidden curriculum of my early years. A long-term association with traditional Chinese medicine has also helped me understand how much these things are a fundamental part of other cultures. We were not really that weird after all.

In my early twenties, in a rebellion of sorts, I turned to French haute cuisine with a vengeance, mentally relegating the food of my upbringing to peasant stodge. Now, much, much later in my culinary career, I am aware of how much the food and cooking of my childhood has influenced the ingredients I use, the preserving I do and the presentation of many of our dishes. Each year in August I celebrate my heritage with a traditional Russian feast

The traditional Russian way for serving tea is in tall glasses in silver stands with a little fruity conserve, for sweetening the tea, on the side. We occasionally fire up the old family samovar replete with its proud medals from the famous factory where it was made.

held in our function room. As it is in the dead of winter, the glow of the open fire and the vodka are welcome warmers. A series of dishes are woven around a recital of traditional and contemporary Russian music performed by a 20-piece balalaika orchestra. Allan does a large beautiful painting of a Russian scene for the wall and the waiters all dress in colourful Russian embroidered shirts. The highly polished family samovar and my mother's embroidered cloths take pride of place. It is always a great night.

The following are not traditional Russian recipes. Rather they are dishes that have evolved from my Russian roots and have been tempered with many other influences and the change in the way people eat today. But they remain recipes that give more than a passing nod to the flavours of my youth. At the end, however, I do offer my mother's recipe for Khvorost, a sugared fried pastry, and her Napoleon torte.

Russian trio

Serves 6

Smoked fish has always been popular with Russians. This recipe celebrates that connection with a combination of jellied smoked eel and smoked trout in a sampling plate of three Russian delicacies.

JELLIED EEL AND SMOKED TROUT
3 saffron threads
600 ml (20 fl oz) clear fish stock, heated
4½ gelatine leaves (gold)
salt and freshly ground white pepper
300 g (10½ oz) boned smoked eel fillet
300 g (10½ oz) boned smoked trout fillet
25 g (¾–1 oz) green peas, cooked

STUFFED EGGS WITH HORSERADISH
6 Hard-boiled Eggs (see page 290)
100 ml (3½ fl oz) Mayonnaise (see page 285)
20 g (¾ oz) Horseradish Cream (see page 289)
salt and freshly ground white pepper

RUSSIAN SALAD
180 g (6⅓ oz) cooked beetroot (beets), cut into ½ cm (¼ in) dice
180 g (6⅓ oz) cooked potato, cut into ½ cm (¼ in) dice
100 g (3½ oz) dill cucumber, cut into ½ cm (¼ in) dice
6 sprigs dill, finely chopped
Lake House Dressing (see page 284)

JELLIED EEL AND SMOKED TROUT Infuse the saffron in the hot fish stock. Soak the gelatine in cold water until soft then drain and squeeze them to remove excess water. Add them to the hot fish stock and stir until dissolved. Allow the liquid to cool over a bowl of ice, stirring frequently until close to the point of setting. Taste and adjust the seasoning with salt and pepper. Cut the smoked eel into batons and the smoked trout into dice. Divide the eel, trout and peas among six moulds (we use sections of PVC pipe with plastic wrap attached tightly to the bottom). Pour the almost-set fish stock on top and place the moulds in the refrigerator until the jelly is set.

STUFFED EGGS WITH HORSERADISH Slice a little egg white off the bottom of each hard-boiled egg to ensure that they will stand upright. Slice off just sufficient egg white from the top of each egg to enable the yolk to be scooped out easily. Combine the yolk, mayonnaise and horseradish cream until smooth then season with salt and pepper. Place the mixture in a piping bag and pipe into the egg whites. Refrigerate the stuffed eggs.

RUSSIAN SALAD Toss the vegetable dice and chopped dill with the dressing until well combined. Refrigerate the salad until ready to use.

TO SERVE Turn out the jellied eel and smoked trout onto individual plates, along with the stuffed eggs. Using a piece of 4 cm (1½ in) diameter PVC pipe, fill it with Russian salad and, with a spoon, push the salad down onto each plate then lift off the pipe. Repeat with the remaining plates.

COULIBIAC, or *kulebiaka*, is the glamorous end of a whole range of savoury, baked, filled pastries that are a staple of the Russian kitchen. Most often called *pirog*, they have assorted fillings including minced poached beef, wild mushrooms, rice, hard-boiled eggs and cabbage. We occasionally prepare a very rich version made with blini that I learned in the kitchens of the Grand Hotel Europe in St Petersburg, but the following recipe, although still the sum of many components, is much less tricky and time-consuming. If you are having friends to dinner it is a beautiful sight served whole and sliced at the table. Although this is not a traditional coulibiac, its flavours echo that of the original. Rather than use plain rice, I find the nuttiness of wild rice a better texture to have as a pastry filling. In season we use local wild forest mushrooms (see introduction to Ragout of Wild Mushrooms, page 136) but ordinary cultivated mushrooms will do. Traditionally encased in a yeast dough, this recipe utilises puff pastry. As time for baking depends on the thickness of the salmon fillet, a temperature probe is a useful piece of equipment here. The number of serves suggested is generous and allows for breakages and scoffing the end bits before anyone notices.

Coulibiac

Serves 10

We serve coulibiac with warm poached cucumbers and tangy Sauce Beurre Blanc (see page 287), sprinkled with chopped dill.

300 g (10½ oz) puff pastry
plain (all-purpose) flour for dusting
100 g (3½ oz) butter
300 g (10½ oz) mushrooms, finely chopped
300 g (10½ oz) Wild Rice, cooked (see page 281)
4 large stalks of dill, finely chopped
100 g (3½ oz) fresh breadcrumbs
1 egg
salt and freshly ground pepper
6 x 15 cm (6 in) Plain Crêpes (see page 283)
1 x 700 g (1 lb 9 oz) cleaned, skinned and pin-boned side of salmon
additional egg for egg wash

Roll the pastry into a rectangle a few centimetres (approximately 1 inch) longer than your salmon fillet and just over two times wider than the widest part. Dust the pastry lightly with flour and fold it over like a parcel. Chill pastry in refrigerator.

Melt the butter in a pan and add the chopped mushrooms, cooking over a medium heat. The mushrooms will initially drop some juices. Continue to cook until the liquid has evaporated and the mushrooms are cooked through. Combine the mushrooms, wild rice, chopped dill, breadcrumbs and the egg. Mix to combine and add seasoning to taste.

On your work surface, lay a sheet of plastic wrap at least as large as your puff pastry, and place the pastry on top. Cover the pastry with crêpes, overlapping them where necessary. Centre a 2 cm (¾ in) thick layer of mushroom mix, approximating the shape and length of your salmon fillet, down the middle of the crêpes and pastry. Lay the salmon fillet on top. Using the plastic wrap to assist, wrap up tightly, with the crêpes and pastry creating a seal at the top – in the middle of the fillet. Trim off excess pastry and crêpes and seal both ends of your pastry. Turn your pastry package over and place it on a baking tray, with the join underneath and the mushroom layer on top of the fish. Glaze the pastry with egg wash and decorate by scoring with a knife or cutter over the surface of the pastry. Take care not to cut right through the pastry layer. (You can refrigerate the coulibiac at this point for a couple of hours.)

Preheat the oven to 190°C (375°F). Bake the coulibiac for around 30 minutes or until a temperature of 45°C (115°F) is achieved in the middle of the fillet. Remove the coulibiac from the oven and allow it to rest for at least 10 minutes in a warm place. The resting time allows for finishing off a sauce or vegetable accompaniment. When serving, cut coulibiac into 5–6 cm (2–2½ in) slices with a serrated knife.

❧ Blinchiki with chestnut soup ❧

Serves 6

Blinchiki, or Russian crêpes, have many fillings including minced poached beef and cottage cheese. They are wrapped parcel-fashion and refried. The beef variety is delicious with French mustard, the cheese crêpes we often serve for breakfast dusted with sugar or alongside blueberry or sour cherry jam. This recipe offers a filling of wild rice, chestnuts and local forest mushrooms and we serve the dish with chestnut soup, served in a demitasse cup. The beef filling variation is a great way of using up left-over beef after making the Borscht Terrine (see page 119).

WILD RICE, CHESTNUT AND MUSHROOM FILLING

1 cup cleaned and chopped mushrooms
30 g (1 oz) butter
1 shallot, finely diced
1 cup Wild Rice, cooked (see page 281)
½ cup cooked chestnuts, roughly chopped (see Cooking Chestnuts, page 295)
salt and freshly ground pepper

THE CRÊPES

12 Plain Crêpes (see page 283)
300 g (10½ oz) ricotta or soft fresh goat's cheese (optional)
1 egg white, lightly whisked
oil for cooking
50 g (2 oz) butter

WILD RICE, CHESTNUT AND MUSHROOM FILLING If you are using wild forest mushrooms, follow the method for cleaning and trimming in Ragout of Wild Mushrooms (see page 136). Heat the butter, add the diced shallot and cook over medium heat to soften. Increase the heat, add the mushrooms and sauté, stirring or tossing for about 6–8 minutes until they are cooked through. Combine the rice, chestnuts and mushrooms then season with salt and pepper.

FILLING AND COOKING THE CRÊPES Lay out the cooked crêpes. If using, smear 20–30 g (¾–1 oz) of your chosen cheese on the middle section of each crêpe. Place 1½–2 tablespoons of filling at one end of each crêpe. Roll each crêpe as you would a parcel, folding the sides in first. Use a little whisked egg white to seal the ends and place side by side on a plate as you complete each one. Refrigerate the filled crêpes until ready to finish and serve.

Heat sufficient oil to moisten the base of a large non-stick pan. Add the 50 g (2 oz) of butter and melt over medium heat until foaming. Place all the crêpe parcels in the pan, side by side, and cook over medium heat until they are browned and crisp on one side. Using tongs, carefully turn the parcels over by one-third. When browned, continue with one more turn and cook until most of the surface of each parcel is golden and crisp. Carefully remove the crêpes from the pan with tongs and drain them on kitchen paper. Serve with a cup of chestnut soup alongside.

»

~ recipe continued ~

BEEF FILLING VARIATION

500 g (1 lb 2 oz) cooked beef

1 tablespoon butter

1 medium-sized onion, chopped

2 hard-boiled eggs, diced

6 sprigs flat-leaf parsley, finely chopped

10 sprigs dill, finely chopped

salt and freshly ground pepper

sour cream or mustard for serving

CHESTNUT SOUP

75 g (2½ oz) butter

2 shallots, finely chopped

1 kg (2 lb 3 oz) fresh chestnuts, peeled (see Cooking Chestnuts, page 295)

⅓ cup porcini powder (available from specialty stores or grind dried porcini to powder in processor)

1 tablespoon balsamic vinegar

2 tablespoons dry sherry

4 cups water

500 ml (17 fl oz) thickened cream (35% butterfat)

1 tablespoon black truffle olive oil (optional)

salt and freshly ground pepper to taste

BEEF FILLING VARIATION Mince the cooked beef. Melt the butter and cook the onion until it has softened. Add the onion, egg and herbs to the beef. Combine well and season. In this case, spread a thin layer of filling all over each crêpe. Fold in the sides and roll up, parcel fashion, sealing the ends with whisked egg white. Cook as described and serve hot with sour cream or mustard.

CHESTNUT SOUP Melt the butter in a large soup pot. Add the shallots and cook until they are soft. Add the chestnuts, raise the heat and cook, stirring, until the chestnuts are golden. Stir in the porcini powder, vinegar, sherry and the water. Add the cream and stir, scraping any sediment from the bottom of the pot. Lower the heat and simmer for 20 minutes. Purée the soup in a blender and, if using, stir in the truffle oil. Reheat the soup — it should be warm, not piping hot. Season with salt and pepper if necessary. Blitz with a hand-held blender to create a frothy texture and serve in demitasse cups (12 serves) alongside the plated blinchiki, or bowls (6 full serves).

Borscht terrine
Serves 12

This dish put together by David, my sous chef, not long after our annual Russian feast, was inspired by the flavours of the traditional borscht that had been served. The beef shin adds to the depth of flavour in the borscht and although not part of the final dish can be used in something else, such as the beef filling for Blinchiki (see page 114). If you want a vegetarian dish, omit the beef and cook 2–3 chopped tomatoes with the other vegetables and add a little chilli to the finished borscht liquid. The salt herring and dill cucumber garnishes are traditional ingredients of Russian *zakúska*. It is a lovely dish.

1 kg (2 lb 3 oz) large beetroots (beets), peeled (use gloves)
500 g (1 lb 2 oz) carrots, peeled
8 shallots, peeled
1 teaspoon caraway seeds
1 bay leaf
200 g (7 oz) beef shin, fat removed
2 large leeks, white part only, halved lengthways and washed
8 gelatine leaves (gold)
salt and freshly ground pepper

GARNISHES
150 ml (5 fl oz) Horseradish Cream (see page 289)
150 g (5 oz) salt (schmaltz) herring, drained and cut into slivers
2 small, preferably homemade, dill cucumbers, cut into fine batons

Place all the ingredients, except the leeks, gelatine, salt and pepper, in a pot. Cover with water and bring to the boil. Skim then reduce the heat and simmer until the beetroots are cooked, skimming frequently. Strain, reserving the liquid and the beetroots, shallots and carrots. Keep the poached beef for another use as suggested above. Bring the reserved liquid to the boil and reduce it to 500 ml (17 fl oz). Meanwhile separate the white leek strips and blanch in boiling water until they are tender enough to cut with a knife. Drain the leek strips.

Soften the gelatine leaves in cold water, wring them out and add them to the hot liquid, stirring to incorporate. Allow the liquid to cool. Line a 1.5 litre (51 fl oz) terrine with plastic wrap, then with slightly overlapping slices of the cooked leek, ensuring that there is enough overhang of leek and plastic wrap to encase the contents of the terrine entirely. Slice the cooked beetroots, shallots and carrots (lengthways) and season with salt and pepper.

Check the cooled 'borscht' liquid for seasoning and adjust. When on the point of setting, pour a layer of the liquid into the lined terrine. Add a layer of sliced beetroots. Add more liquid and top with a layer of carrots and shallots. Repeat the procedure until all the liquid and vegetables are used, finishing with a layer of the jellied 'borscht'. Fold over the overhanging leek slices and plastic wrap to cover completely. Refrigerate overnight.

TO GARNISH AND SERVE Invert the terrine onto a cutting board, remove the plastic wrap and cut the terrine into 2½ cm (1 in) slices. Place a slice in the centre of each plate then spoon a small quenelle of horseradish cream on top of each. Garnish with slivers of herring and dill cucumber.

Napoleon torte

Makes 1 x 20-22 cm (8-8½ in) diameter cake

This cake made an appearance at our house virtually every birthday or when guests were coming. Simply a version of mille-feuille, pastry cream lightened with whipped cream is interspersed between layers of baked puff pastry (which my mother made herself). Crushed off-cuts of pastry decorate the top and sides. To temper the sweetness and richness, my mother added cooked apple purée or sour cherry jam between the layers. The cake improved in flavour and was easier to cut after a day's refrigeration. Many Russian households we visited had their own version of this torte, served as a dessert or with tea.

PASTRY
450 g (1 lb) good-quality puff pastry
plain (all-purpose) flour for dusting

PASTRY CREAM
500 ml (17 fl oz) milk
1 vanilla bean
125 g (4 oz) sugar
5 egg yolks
40 g (1½ oz) plain (all-purpose) flour
200 ml (7 fl oz) thickened cream (35% butterfat)
40 g (1½ oz) icing (confectioner's) sugar

TO SERVE
150 g (5 oz) stewed apple purée, drained in a sieve for 10–15 minutes

PASTRY Preheat the oven to 220°C (430°F). Divide the pastry into three and return it to the refrigerator. Lightly flour your work surface. Take out one piece of the pastry and roll it into approximately a 24 cm (9½ in) square sheet, about 2 mm (⅛ in) thick. Brush a suitably sized baking sheet with water and lay the rolled pastry on it. Prick it evenly all over with a fork. Place it in the refrigerator for 5–10 minutes while repeating the process with the remaining two pieces of pastry. Bake the pastry sheets in the oven for 18–20 minutes until crisp and browned then allow them to cool, preferably on wire racks. When cold, place the pastry sheets on a firm flat work surface. Using a plate, or similar circular guide, with a diameter of approximately 22 cm (8½ in), cut the sheets into three circles. Reserve the pastry trimmings.

PASTRY CREAM In a saucepan, heat the milk with the vanilla bean and 1 tablespoon of the sugar then set aside to infuse. In a bowl beat the egg yolks and remaining sugar together until creamy then gradually beat the flour into the mix. Return the milk to the boil. Remove the vanilla bean (you can wash, dry and reserve it for another use).
Pour the hot milk in a stream over the egg mixture, stirring continuously. Return this mixture to the saucepan and cook over medium heat, continuing to stir until it comes to boiling point. Pass through a sieve into a bowl and allow to cool. Place a piece of damp greaseproof paper on the surface of the mixture to stop a skin from forming. When cool, you can store the pastry cream in the refrigerator for up to two days.

When ready to complete, whip the thickened cream with the icing sugar until it has the consistency of soft peaks. Fold the cooled pastry cream into the whipped cream with a whisk to aerate and keep the mixture as light as possible.

TO ASSEMBLE AND SERVE I use unsweetened apple purée, but sweeten it if you prefer. Place one pastry circle on a serving board or plate. Using a spatula, spread half the apple purée evenly over the pastry then spread about one-third of the pastry cream on top in an even layer. Top with the next pastry circle and repeat the process, finishing with the last pastry circle. Very gently apply a little pressure with your hand to the top circle to ensure that it is horizontal. Spread the remaining pastry cream over the top and sides of the cake, to conceal all the layers. Crush the reserved pieces of pastry into crumbs with a rolling pin and scatter the crumbs over the top of the cake and press onto the sides. Remove any excess from around the cake. Chill very thoroughly in the refrigerator for at least 12 hours. To serve, slice into wedges.

❧ KHVOROST ❧
Makes at least 2 dozen pastries

Most cuisines have some sort of recipe for sweet fried dough. The French have *bugnes*, the Italians have *crostoli*, the Swiss have *merveilles* and the Russians have *khvorost*, or *khrustiki*. These pastries are twisted or knotted, fried, drained and showered with icing sugar.

3 egg yolks
30 g (1 oz) sugar
100 ml (3½ fl oz) vodka
2 cups plain (all-purpose) flour
½ teaspoon salt
oil for deep-frying
icing (confectioner's) sugar for dusting

Beat the egg yolks with the sugar then stir in the vodka. Sift the flour and salt into a bowl, make a well in the centre of the flour and pour in the egg mixture. Gradually work the flour into the liquid, mixing it in to form a stiff dough. Roll out on a floured board to about ½ cm (¼ in) in thickness. Cut into strips about 10 cm long and 3 cm wide (4 x 1¼ in). Make a slit lengthways in the middle of each strip and pull one end through. Deep-fry the pastries in hot oil. Put 3 or 4 pastries in at one time and deep-fry until golden brown. Drain the pastries on kitchen paper and cool. Sift icing sugar over them and store them in a dry airtight container.

Chapter Seven

FROM THE SOIL

My early experiences of restaurant kitchens in Australia did little for my knowledge in this area. Vegetables were an afterthought added to every plate. In the home they were considered to be nutritionally necessary but treated with little care, generally overcooked and piled on the plate as accompaniments to large slabs of meat. The sorcery of frozen foods was a tempting novelty. Even then, we were already looking for the convenience of 'fast food'.

At the time we opened Lake House in the early 1980s, there was an expectation that all 'real' meals should come with three vegetables. In most restaurants the same vegetable garnish was used with every dish. Salads were inevitably made with iceberg lettuce, often still wet with washing water. Dressings used brown and white vinegars. I remember the fiery expletives of chefs when the rare order for a vegetarian meal was called for by a hapless cowering waiter.

My earlier experiences in French kitchens were another matter. Meat dishes rarely came with vegetables. They were frequently a separate course. Specialty vegetable produce was highly prized and vegetarian degustation menus were not uncommon.

Interestingly, the embrace of nouvelle cuisine by Australian restaurants seemed often to translate into, among other things, undercooked green vegetables. Perhaps as a backlash after years of drab, overcooked grey and khaki greens, we ate squeaky green beans, crisp broccoli and asparagus. These were frequently under-seasoned as well. Luckily it was a passing fad.

There were other fads that have affected the enjoyment we experience with vegetables. In the 1990s, in our rush to embrace the much-touted healthier olive oil-based diet of the Mediterranean, we denied ourselves the pleasure of a marriage made in heaven. Well-cooked and well-seasoned vegetables, given a little love in the best butter you can find, are truly sublime. A spring-summer mix of peeled broad beans, baby peas, zucchini and asparagus, all pre-blanched, refreshed, well-drained and then tossed off simply with butter in a pan and a grind or two of pepper, is simply delicious. If my cooks are on a break on a summer afternoon I will often raid their vegetable *mise en place* and make just that, for a quick late lunch, perhaps crumbling a little goat's cheese over the top. Mind you, I am not averse to the oil thing either. Late at night I am sometimes caught raiding the preserving jars for our roasted tomatoes, mopping up the garlicky, herby oil with a chunk of crusty sourdough and adding a little fresh pancetta. There is no shortage of fast-food options at our house on the lake. And vegetables play a large part in them.

Other food fads have included the still-prevalent mania for very expensive tiny vegetables. Not all vegetables are at their best when small. Some require some size before their flavour fully matures. It irritates me, for example, that nowadays it can be difficult to get thick asparagus. Thin asparagus, the choice of the minute, has little of the appropriate full, fleshy flavour. And the ratio of flesh to coarse outer fibres is considerably less. With thick asparagus, you can snap off the woody bottoms, peel as necessary and still have plenty left. Tiny leeks are another example where the normally delicious creamy nature of the vegetable is completely foregone for the sake of visuals. Frightfully expensive, they look suspiciously like the surplus vegetables most gardeners throw away when thinning out the leek patch.

At my family home, vegetables were treated with considerable reverence. Frequently they were home-grown or came from someone else's garden. Mind you it was not about tiny green beans cooked to the precise second – the sort of thing

we labour to get just right in the restaurant. But it was about using things in season. The summer beans from the garden quite often found themselves in hot-pot-style casseroles, braised with meat, other vegetables in season, herbs and garlic. Even though considerably cooked down, they were still delicious having both absorbed and contributed flavour to the surrounding stew. And appropriately at season's end when no longer available, they were replaced with dried borlotti or cannellini beans and plenty of root vegetables.

Eggplant, especially in the form of baba ghanoush (in Russian, literally 'eggplant caviar', *baklazhannaya ikra*), was often part of *zakúska*, or starters. Mushroom season was eagerly anticipated every year, my parents and their friends returning from mushroom-gathering expeditions with bootloads of boxes laden with slippery jacks and pine mushrooms. The tiny ones were most in demand, the chore of trimming, cleaning and chopping often a group effort around the kitchen table at our family country house (*dacha*). Australian neighbours frequently voiced concerns about them being poisonous. Pine mushrooms had to be processed quickly as they turn green when cut. Blanched and pickled with vinegar, bay leaf and peppercorns they make a fine *zakúska* to accompany vodka. My father prepared the hot pickling liquid and jars for them while the women sliced around the table.

Particular methods of pickling and salting cabbage, tomatoes and cucumbers were household specialities – recipes varying with the inclusion of more or less sugar, salt, vinegar chilli or garlic. Never known to arrive empty handed, my parents and their friends exchanged jars of these preserves when visiting. 'Your dill cucumbers are exceptional,' remains in my memory as one of my mother's most eagerly anticipated compliments – quite often proffered in a flirtatious way. A good-looking woman who also made great dill cucumbers had to be pretty special.

Of course food was always one of the Russians' most favoured topics, running second only to politics. Subtle nuances of recipes were discussed with great interest at the table. Successful special additions were harboured as family secrets and arguments raged over authenticity.

Beetroot was often on our table – in a Russian salad or poached, sliced and served with sour cream. It also always figured in my father's magnificent borscht. It was only considerably later that I discovered the reputation this vegetable has as a liver cleanser and wondered at the possible connection to the fondness the Russians have for drinking to excess.

There was always sorrel in the garden and I have some planted at Lake House from my mother's original patch. The lovely lemony leaves were the basis of a summer soup of greens and rice that Russians call *zelyonie* (green) *shchi*. Tomatoes were another staple. Warm and fragrant, just picked from the vegetable garden, thickly sliced onto buttered chunks of rye bread and salted, they were the best of summer treats. As were baby radishes dunked into soft spreadable butter and sprinkled with salt or sliced into thick sour cream and topped with chives.

Tomatoes were never refrigerated but lived on windowsills, ripening. Each autumn the last tomatoes were taken from the garden, still on the vine, before the first frosts came. They were hung upside down in the garden shed and left to ripen alongside the drying bunches of dill seed pods. That heady scent of tomatoes and dill to this day transports me to the dark warmth of my parents' potting shed. Dill, incidentally, was always the herb of choice. My father stored the seeds in a jar and religiously planted them out every season. When eventually unable to tend a large vegetable garden, my mother still always grew a couple of pots of tomatoes and dill.

As far as favourite vegetables are concerned, for me as a cook it is once again about anticipation and the annual rediscovery of pleasures available for a limited time. At Lake House the first asparagus, artichokes, local fungi, chestnuts, squash blossoms and many more ingredients available only seasonally are planned for each year with a brand new set of dishes. Even if you are not a gardener as well as a cook, thinking about food from the perspective of planting and the rhythms of the seasons changes how you cook. There is real pleasure to be had in that sense of being at one with the eternal order of things. Broad beans for example – those late winter arrivals and always a welcome new addition to the menu – signal that spring is not far away. Cooked, twice peeled and tossed with slivers of a hard sheep's milk cheese like pecorino or manchego and a bit of olive oil and black pepper, they are a well-known treat. For the keen gardener they offer a harvest when there is little else around. Once all the beans are harvested, digging the plants back into the soil provides nitrogen for the garden bed, which can then be used for a summer crop of tomatoes, peppers or zucchini once the frosts have gone. In the Daylesford region tradition decrees that to be after Melbourne Cup day – the first Tuesday in November.

We use a lot of carrots at Lake House, partly because of the availability of wonderful organic carrots from just down the road. The Chambers at Fernleigh Farm export organic carrot juice to Japan and supply us with as much of the vegetable as we can use. Carrots are often the poor cousins of restaurant kitchen repertoires, mostly relegated to mirepoix and the like. In our kitchen, having the sort of succulence and fragrance of something just taken from the ground, carrots are constantly used for sauces, mousses and soups.

Daylesford lies in the middle of potato-growing country. The potato dishes we offer often reflect the local variety that is in season. New season's Pink Eyes, available around March, are simply steamed and served with a herb and garlic butter. Bisons, Desirees and Colibans are great for boiling and mashing and are particularly useful for things like gnocchi. Nicolas are beautiful boiled and crushed – écrase-style as the French would say – and served under fish with a drizzle of the best local olive oil. Red Pontiacs make a great potato salad as do varieties such as Patrones and Kipflers that hold their shape when cooked. Bintjes, Sebagos and Kennebecs make the best fries. I include the use of potatoes in several of the recipes. To do them real justice would require another book or two.

In the last decade there has been a considerable turnaround in vegetable appreciation with particular interest in growing practices and the expansion of available varieties. Our vegetarian degustation menu is chosen by an increasing number of Lake House guests. Creating vegetarian dishes with vegetables is a joy.

SALADS

At Lake House an uncomplicated salad of selected leaves dressed with our house dressing is served with main courses. Guests are asked whether they would prefer to enjoy the salad from the same plate and mop up any remaining juices or on a fresh plate as a palate freshener. If you have ever roasted a chicken and eaten it drizzled with its sticky pan juices and scraped up bits of skin, you will know how delicious mopping up the last bits of jus or sauce with a well-dressed salad leaf or two can be.

Our salad mix is composed of leaves selected for their flavour and texture combination and their ability to withstand our fairly robust dressing. Butter, red and green oak and lamb's lettuce often feature, with the addition of some small leaves of Belgian witlof and occasionally a little baby frisée. We resist the temptation to embellish what is essentially designed to be an enhancer.

Mostly the salad leaves come from whole lettuces. Be wary of some of the ubiquitous salad mixes and pre-cut leaves available in supermarkets. Unless you have an excellent purveyor who understands the notion of mesclun, the former are often full of stalky rubbish. If choosing the latter, check that the cut ends are not rust-coloured, a sure sign they have been harvested some time ago. Once again freshest, and therefore from not too far away, and most recently cut is best. Always wash leaves with great care and spin dry in small batches. Bruised leaves will spoil a salad. Fragile leaves should be soaked only for a few minutes. Firmer leaves benefit from longer soaking and can be revived if a little wilted. Washed lettuce is best stored wrapped in a cloth in the refrigerator.

Salads become dishes at Lake House with the addition of other leaves such as watercress, dandelion, purslane, rocket, mizuna, cos and tatsoi as well as vegetables, cheeses, eggs, nuts, meat and fish. Australians now find a composed salad served even as a main course perfectly acceptable. Sometimes the greens might be lightly wilted with the addition of a warm dressing or even a vinaigrette 'split' with a warm meat jus. In the domestic kitchen similarly the possibilities are endless. Leftovers matched with a judiciously chosen dressing and garnishes can often very successfully stretch a cooked meal.

Witlof salad with hazelnuts and blue cheese crostini

Serves 4

Also known as Belgian endive and chicory, crunchy witlof leaves have a mild bitterness to them, offering a refreshing foil for creamy cheeses and a conduciveness to the sweetness of caramelisation (see page 297). The classic dish of witlof baked with ham under a creamy cheese sauce and topped with breadcrumbs is one of our favourite household treats. Baby witlof leaves make a perfect receptacle for filling and using as canapés. In this salad, curls of sliced prosciutto are an optional but delicious addition. See page 130 for a photograph of this salad.

BLUE CHEESE CROSTINI

50 g (2 oz) creamy blue cheese such as Meredith Blue or Gorgonzola, mashed to spreading consistency with a little cream

8 small Crostini (see page 281)

THE SALAD

24 hazelnuts, skins removed by toasting in oven at 160°C (320°F) for 6–8 minutes then rubbing with a towel

3–4 small heads witlof

4 cooked kipfler potatoes, peeled and sliced

16 baby green beans, trimmed and blanched

1 quantity Hazelnut Dressing (see page 284)

salt and freshly ground pepper

CROSTINI Spread the cheese thickly on the crostini and set aside.

THE SALAD Split or coarsely chop the hazelnuts then return to the baking tray. Trim the base from the witlof and separate the leaves. Wash and dry the leaves. Re-warm the hazelnuts. Place the witlof leaves, sliced potato and green beans in a bowl together with two-thirds of the dressing. Toss well to ensure all the ingredients are evenly coated. Adjust seasoning.

TO ASSEMBLE AND SERVE On each plate arrange the sliced potatoes in the centre and begin layering and building the witlof leaves in a circle, radiating out from the centre of the plate. Place the dressed green beans at the centre of the leaves. Sprinkle the warmed hazelnuts over the top and garnish with the cheese crostini. Drizzle over remaining dressing.

Beetroot carpaccio with fetta and walnuts

Serves 4

If you have never thought about eating beetroot raw, this salad should convince you. You really do need a mandoline or special vegetable slicer to achieve the wafer-thin beetroot slices. Dunked in a lemony dressing, beetroot is very more-ish this way. The rest of the salad is simplicity itself. As is often the case with ingredients that are in season together, the ones here combine beautifully. I am very fortunate to have Julie Cameron as a local supplier. We use her sublime Meredith fetta and sheep's milk yoghurt for this recipe.

300 ml (10 fl oz) plain yoghurt

¼ teaspoon salt

2 fresh chives, finely chopped

freshly ground pepper

20 x 2 cm (¾ in) cubes firm fetta

200 g (7 oz) plain (all-purpose) flour

4 eggs, beaten

200 g (7 oz) fine dried breadcrumbs

2 medium-sized beetroots (beets), peeled and sliced very finely on a mandoline

60 ml (2 fl oz) Basic Vinaigrette (see page 284)

1 good handful rocket (arugula) leaves, washed and dried

1 handful walnuts, toasted

2 ripe pears, very finely sliced

Combine the yoghurt and salt and leave to drain in a coffee filter or hang in muslin overnight in the refrigerator. Next day combine the drained yoghurt with the chives and pepper. Set aside.

Preheat the oven to 200°C (400°F). Dredge the fetta cubes lightly with the flour and coat them with the egg then the breadcrumbs, shaking off the excess. Place the crumbed fetta cubes on a non-stick baking tray and bake for 10 minutes or until golden brown all over. Keep warm while assembling the remainder of the salad.

Dress the beetroot slices with vinaigrette and arrange them on the plates as with a carpaccio. Toss the rocket and walnuts in the vinaigrette and centre them in a mound in the middle of the beetroot. Add a few sliced pears to the top, then a good dollop of yoghurt and then a couple of the nicest pear slices on top as a garnish. Divide the cubes of warm fetta around and over the salad. Add a grating or two of pepper.

Asparagus, broad beans and globe artichokes form a trinity of special vegetables that come together in spring. Precooked and refreshed they simply need a bit of love in butter to make a delicious warm spring salad. If you like, add the crunch of a tempura-battered baby zucchini and its blossom. The tarragon aïoli glistens as it slides off the warm vegetables. We serve this salad with asparagus velouté topped with parmesan foam.

Spring salad with asparagus velouté and parmesan foam

Serves 6

SPRING SALAD

100 g (3½ oz) butter

3 shallots, diced

6 artichokes, cooked and quartered (see Preparing Artichokes, page 293)

250 g (9 oz) broad beans, cooked and peeled (see Preparing Broad Beans, page 294)

12 asparagus spears, peeled and cooked until tender (see Preparing Asparagus, page 294)

salt and freshly ground pepper

50 g (2 oz) baby spinach leaves, stemmed

6 baby zucchini (courgettes), with flowers attached

1 quantity Tempura Batter (see page 280)

vegetable oil for deep-frying

plain (all-purpose) flour for dusting

tarragon aïoli (see Aïoli/Variations, page 285)

ASPARAGUS VELOUTÉ

500 ml (17 fl oz) thickened cream (35% butterfat)

500 ml (17 fl oz) milk

5 sprigs thyme

30 g (1 oz) butter

1 onion, chopped

3 cloves garlic, chopped

1 kg (2 lb 3 oz) asparagus stalks, sliced (use tips elsewhere)

1 handful spinach, just wilted in pan with a little warm butter (optional)

salt and freshly ground pepper

1 quantity Parmesan Foam (optional; see page 283)

SPRING SALAD Melt the butter in a pan and cook the shallots until soft but not coloured. Add the artichokes, broad beans and asparagus and toss on high heat or lift and turn them gently on moderate heat until the vegetables are warmed through. Season well. Add the spinach leaves and toss them through until glossy with butter and wilted. Adjust the seasoning. Set aside and keep warm while cooking the zucchini. Make the tempura batter and keep it chilled.

In a deep-fryer or a tall pot heat the oil to 170°C (340°F). Dust the zucchini and its flower in a little plain flour, dip it in the batter and deep-fry until golden brown, turning to ensure even cooking. Remove with a slotted spoon, drain on kitchen paper and season with salt and pepper.

ASPARAGUS VELOUTÉ Combine the cream and milk, heat to a simmer then add the thyme. In a separate pot melt the butter and fry the onion and garlic until soft then add the asparagus. Increase the heat, stir and as the ingredients are on the point of colouring strain the milk mixture into the pot. Continue to cook until the asparagus is tender enough to purée. Purée the contents of the pot in a blender. Adding the wilted spinach during the blending process will increase the colour of the soup without perceptibly altering the asparagus flavour. Pass the soup through a sauce sieve or fine tamis. Taste, season and pour into demitasse cups, and top with parmesan foam, if using.

TO SERVE Place a mixture of the warm vegetables and crisp zucchini, topped with tarragon aïoli, on individual plates and serve with asparagus velouté on the side.

Ragout of wild mushrooms
Serves 4-6

In autumn our local forests yield slippery jacks (*Boletus luteus*), and saffron milkcaps (*Lactarius deliciosa*) otherwise referred to as pine mushrooms. Nearby paddocks offer field mushrooms. Fresh morels are not in season with autumn mushrooms but in spring they are found in the sandier and more gravelly soils of local bushland. In good years we string up morels to dry and have them on hand throughout the year. A few of any kind of dried mushroom will add a depth of flavour to a mushroom ragout. Unless you are a skilled mushroom gatherer it is inadvisable to go gathering. This recipe will work just as well with cultivated mushrooms.

500 g (1 lb 2 oz) fresh wild autumn mushrooms
100 g (3½ oz) dried morels or other dried mushrooms, soaked for 20 minutes in very hot water and squeezed dry (retain the water)
90–100 g (3¼–3½ oz) butter
2 medium-sized shallots, finely chopped
1 cup chicken stock or retained mushroom soaking water passed through a fine sieve
salt and freshly ground pepper
60 g (2 oz) additional butter or sour cream (optional)
chopped chives for garnishing

Cultivated mushrooms generally require only trimming and brushing. Wild mushrooms, if they need to be washed at all – where a great deal of dirt and grit is visible – must never be soaked. A quick splash should suffice. The only exception is fresh morels. The conical sponge caps can harbour insects as well as sand. They often require washing in several changes of water.

Brush clean any field mushrooms and cut them into quarters. Slippery jacks any larger than 4 or 5 cm (1½ or 2 in) in diameter will need peeling. Trim the stems and cut into 1–2 cm (½–¾ in) slices. Discard any overlarge saffron milkcaps or any that are waterlogged from rain. Brush off pine needles and dirt then trim and slice.

In a sauté pan melt about one-third of the butter. Sweat the shallots for 3–4 minutes then add the dried morels and cook slowly for 2–3 minutes. Add the stock or strained mushroom water and simmer, partly covered, for about 15 minutes until the morels are tender. Remove from the heat and allow the pan contents to cool. In another pan, heat a little of the remaining butter over medium heat and sauté the fresh mushrooms in batches, for 5 minutes at a time, or until cooked through. Add to the morels and their juice. Season to taste with salt and pepper.

When ready to use, reheat and serve as is, or swirl in extra butter or sour cream. Stir through, adjust seasoning, serve and garnish with chopped chives. This simple recipe can be enhanced with the addition of garlic or tarragon as desired, depending on its final use. It is delicious with polenta or stirred through pearl barley. We use the latter quite often as the bed for a rich roast chicken or pheasant (see Butter-poached Pheasant Breast, page 199).

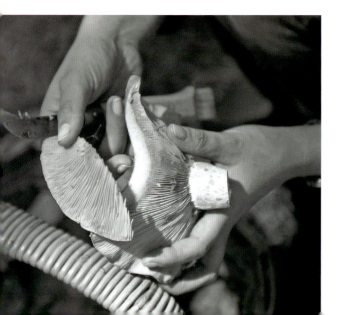

Spiced roasted tomatoes with fresh soya beans and broad bean falafel

Serves 6

Use tomatoes only in season and choose the best you can find. Try farmer's markets or barter for some from a friend's garden if you are interested in getting hold of some of the thinner-skinned varieties, long abandoned by the long-term storage requirements of the grower–supermarket relationship. Keep tomatoes at room temperature even if they are ripe. They are never at their best after refrigeration. Tomatoes purchased very late in the season when the growers have ceased irrigating are usually not only less expensive but have a less watered down flavour.

SPICED ROASTED TOMATOES AND FRESH SOYA BEANS

1 quantity Slow-roasted Tomatoes (see page 297), but with following spices added before roasting:
½ teaspoon ground cumin
½ teaspoon ground coriander
½ teaspoon ground ginger
100 g (3½ oz) freshly podded soya beans
1 quantity Spiced Dressing (see page 285)

BROAD BEAN FALAFEL

250 g (9 oz) broad beans, podded but not peeled
125 g (4 oz) chickpeas, soaked overnight and ground in a processor
½ bunch coriander (cilantro), washed, dried and chopped
½ bunch flat-leaf parsley, washed, dried and chopped
1 small onion, chopped
1 small chilli
1 clove garlic, peeled
1 teaspoon cumin seeds, toasted and ground
1 egg
plain (all-purpose) flour, if necessary
salt and freshly ground pepper
vegetable oil for frying
½ quantity Cucumber Raita (see page 289)

SPICED ROASTED TOMATOES AND FRESH SOYA BEANS Add the spices to the tomato mix before roasting. After roasting the tomatoes, while still warm, combine them with the soya beans and drizzle over sufficient of the dressing to give a light coat.

BROAD BEAN FALAFEL Cook the broad beans in salted boiling water until the skins are tender, which can take up to 8 minutes. Drain and cool the beans. Place the ground chickpeas, coriander, parsley, onion, chilli, garlic and cumin together in a bowl.

Blend the broad beans in a processor until broken down. Add the egg and combine. Add the chickpea mix and process to a coarse paste. Add a little flour if the mix is a bit wet then season to taste. Allow the mixture to sit for ½ an hour. Form the mixture into quenelles or patties and fry in hot vegetable oil, turning to ensure a good colour all over. Remove the patties from the pan with a slotted spoon and drain on several layers of kitchen paper.

TO SERVE Place three falafel beside a mound of spiced roasted tomatoes and fresh soya beans and spoon some raita alongside.

Ripe tomato salad, fried green tomatoes and buffalini
Serves 4

This is a dish inspired by late summer when there are plenty of magnificent ripe tomatoes around but the vines are also heavy with green fruit. The chopped tomatoes are macerated with herbs and coriander seed and are used as a bed for green tomatoes dusted with polenta and lightly fried. These are interleaved with slices of fresh buffalo mozzarella. The dish is topped with a dollop of salty tapenade and the flourish of a basil 'pesto' emulsion. The ripeness of the tomatoes and their temperature are crucial to this assembly. The fried green tomatoes add to the warmth and can even begin to soften the buffalini.

TOMATO SALAD

1 tablespoon coriander seeds, roasted and crushed
1 tablespoon extra-virgin olive oil
1 tablespoon white wine vinegar
1 clove garlic, very finely chopped
2 tablespoons very finely diced red onion
2 tablespoons chopped flat-leaf parsley
2 tablespoons chopped chives
1 tablespoon chopped basil
6 ripe tomatoes, skinned, seeded and diced
salt and freshly ground white pepper

FRIED GREEN TOMATOES

3 large green tomatoes, cut into 1¼ cm (½–⅔ in) slices
1 cup polenta
½ cup vegetable oil

TO SERVE

8 buffalini, each cut into 4 slices
1 quantity Tapenade (see page 289)
1 quantity 'Pesto' Emulsion (see page 288)
grissini sticks to garnish (optional)

TOMATO SALAD As soon as you have toasted and crushed the coriander seeds, put them in a bowl and add the olive oil then prepare the remaining salad ingredients. When preparation is complete, add all the remaining ingredients to the bowl, season with salt and pepper, and stir to amalgamate. Stand at room temperature for 1 hour to allow the flavours to meld.

FRIED GREEN TOMATOES Dredge the tomato slices with the polenta. Heat the oil and fry the tomato slices over medium heat for 2–3 minutes on each side or until they are tender but still have some firmness. Drain the slices on kitchen paper and keep warm until they are all fried.

TO SERVE Taste the tomato salad, adjust the seasoning and spoon the salad onto individual plates. We use a metal cutter to keep the tomato in a contained shape on the plate. Lay four slices of buffalini on top of each salad mound. Place overlapping slices of fried green tomato on top of the buffalini, alternating with more buffalini slices. Place a spoonful of tapenade in the middle of each assembly. Spoon 'pesto' emulsion around, and garnish with grissini sticks, if using.

Zucchini custard, summer herb tortellini and sauce Jacqueline

Serves 6–8

In this dish the fragrantly herbaceous tortellini, light zucchini custard, crisp fried flower and the colour of the sauce combine to make a summery plate. Tackle the components individually – the zucchini custard is a lovely appetiser with the sauce. Use small zucchini not only for flavour but also for the greater skin to flesh ratio, which produces a better-coloured custard. The summer herb tortellini has a very time-consuming filling and is for dedicated cooks with time on their hands. The result is worth it for the intense summery flavour. The goat's cheese tortellini is a more manageable alternative. Sauce Beurre Blanc (see page 287) can replace the sauce Jacqueline.

ZUCCHINI CUSTARD

zest of 1 orange, very finely chopped

¼ tablespoon finely chopped ginger

30 g (1 oz) butter

¼ onion, very finely chopped

280 g (10 oz) small zucchini (courgette), roughly chopped

100 ml (3½ fl oz) thickened cream (35% butterfat)

2 eggs

salt and freshly ground white pepper

SUMMER HERB FILLING

vegetable oil

1 medium-sized onion, thinly sliced

1 clove garlic, very finely diced

½ teaspoon finely chopped fresh rosemary

1 teaspoon fresh thyme leaves

1 litre (34 fl oz) container moderately packed small chard leaves, de-stalked and deveined

1 litre (34 fl oz) container moderately packed small rocket (arugula) leaves

1 litre (34 fl oz) container moderately packed stemmed and deveined baby spinach leaves

½ teaspoon freshly grated nutmeg »

ZUCCHINI CUSTARD Cover the chopped orange zest and ginger with boiling water in a small bowl. Steep for a couple of minutes then drain well. Melt the butter in a frying pan then lightly fry the onion and add the zucchini and ginger–zest mix. Cook for a few minutes but do not allow to brown. Add the cream and continue to cook until the ingredients are just tender. Set aside to cool. Grease the moulds.

Preheat the oven to 170°C (340°F). Combine the cooled zucchini mix with the eggs until well blended. Season well and distribute the mixture among 6–8 x 200 ml (7fl oz) dariole moulds. Place the moulds in a bain-marie, covered well with greaseproof paper and foil, and with sufficient hot water to reach halfway up the sides of the moulds. Bake in the preheated oven. Custards should take about 30 minutes and are cooked when slightly risen and firm to touch. They can be cooled and reheated in a microwave when required.

SUMMER HERB FILLING This filling requires a dedication to searching out the best herbs and leaves. Spread a film of vegetable oil over the base of a small pot and place over medium heat. Add the onion and garlic, stirring and cooking for about 1 minute until they are just translucent. Do not allow them to burn. Add the rosemary, thyme and nutmeg, just cover with water and cook gently until the water has evaporated and the onion is completely tender. Remove from the heat and set aside.

Before blanching the chard, rocket, spinach and watercress, wash all the leaves very well. Bring a large pot of water to the boil. Have a bowl of iced water, a skimmer and a colander ready. Blanch each of the leaves successively for 1 minute in the boiling water, except for the chard, which will require 2 minutes. After blanching, refresh each lot in the iced water, drain it and spread on kitchen paper to dry. »

✲ recipe continued ✲

½ bunch watercress
½ bunch basil
¾ bunch chervil
½ bunch dill
½ cup fresh tarragon leaves
½ bunch coriander (cilantro)
100 g (3½ oz) ricotta
50 g (2 oz) mascarpone
salt and freshly ground pepper

TORTELLINI
½ quantity Basic Pasta Dough (see page 290)
a little beaten egg
rice flour for dusting

VARIATION: GOAT'S CHEESE FILLING
250 g (9 oz) goat's cheese
125 g (4 oz) cottage cheese
1 egg yolk
salt and freshly ground white pepper

TO SERVE
½ quantity Sauce Jacqueline (see page 287)
zucchini flowers in Tempura Batter
   (optional; see page 280, for method see page 135)
blanched zucchini ribbons for garnishing (optional)

Pick over all the herbs then wash and dry. To finish the herb filling, blend the sweated onion mix together with the washed fresh herbs, until smooth. Add the blanched and dried salad leaves, blending until smooth. Add the ricotta, mascarpone and salt and pepper to taste. Place in a muslin-lined colander over a bowl and leave in the refrigerator for a couple of hours or overnight. Taste and adjust the seasoning once again before using to fill the tortellini.

PASTA Divide the dough into three. Pass each piece through the pasta machine until the last setting is reached. Hang the pasta sheets over a wooden dowel for a few minutes.

TO ASSEMBLE TORTELLINI Cut the pasta with a round cutter, 5 cm (2 in) in diameter, and glaze with egg wash. Place small teaspoonfuls of filling onto the lower half of each pasta circle. Fold the upper half of each pasta circle over the lower half, pressing the edges together and removing any air bubbles. You should now have semicircles of pasta, filled with herb mixture. Draw the outer ends of each half circle together, pressing the dough firmly. Store the completed tortellini on a tray, sprinkled with rice flour, until ready to cook.

TO COOK If desired, the tortellini can be blanched quickly in plenty of salted boiling water, chilled in iced water, drained and set aside for reheating when needed. Otherwise cook it to order in boiling salted water for 2 minutes.

VARIATION To make the goat's cheese filling, combine the ingredients either by hand or very gently with an electric mixer. Do not process as the mixture will break down and become too sloppy to use. Refrigerate until required. Proceed to fill and cook the tortellini as described above. They may be used as part of this dish but are also delicious on their own – cooked, tossed in a little virgin olive oil and sprinkled with freshly ground black pepper and shaved parmesan.

TO ASSEMBLE AND SERVE Turn out a zucchini custard into the middle of each serving plate. If using, garnish each with a tempura-battered zucchini flower. Arrange the warm tortellini around each custard and spoon the sauce around. Garnish with blanched zucchini ribbons if desired.

Chapter Eight

WATERY CREATURES

Daylesford is some 100 kilometres from the nearest stretch of coastline. Although methods of catching and delivering fish have improved considerably over the past twenty years, the issue of food miles remains a consideration.

FROM INLAND WATERWAYS

We are blessed with an increasing number of local folk who pursue the fishing of eels or who have become aquaculture specialists in the farming of Murray cod, trout and yabbies. All four products are regularly showcased on Lake House menus, quite often in combination with each other.

EELS

Eels have a special place in my heart because they remain food from the wild. They cannot be farmed. They can be caught and held in a lake or dam until they are large enough to harvest but otherwise they persist every year with their migration to their spawning grounds.

Annually, as if on some prearranged signal, eels emerge from lakes and rivers and travel up the east coast of Australia to an area in the northern Coral Sea near New Caledonia. There they spawn and die. The emerging baby eels nourish themselves on the carcasses before beginning their momentous journey south again. Incidentally, these baby eels, or elvers, are a great delicacy in many cultures.

Smoked eel was a frequent specialty on my Russian family's *zakúska* table. My father regularly swapped my mother's green dill tomatoes and cucumbers for eels freshly smoked by a Hungarian gentleman who ran a boarding house not far from my parents' dacha in Daylesford.

Braise of fresh eel with tomatoes and olives

Serves 6-8

I served this dish at a luncheon for local suppliers and vignerons at a huge shared table under the birches by the lake at the bottom of the Lake House garden. I have adapted my mother's method of burying fish in a dense vegetable or tomato sauce to braise. Her tomato-based sauce included carrots and celery. It is a good cooking technique for types of fish that toughen or go rubbery easily and require very gentle cooking. Mum's fish was served cold in its sauce, mopped up with fresh bread. It was a good picnic dish, ideal for gatherings where every household brought food for the shared picnic table.

TOMATO STEW

150 ml (5 fl oz) olive oil

1 onion, finely chopped

1 leek, white part only, sliced

2 shallots, finely chopped

1 clove garlic, finely chopped

3 tablespoons anise-flavoured liqueur (Ricards or Pernod)

½ teaspoon fennel seeds

500 g (1 lb 2 oz) very ripe 'cooking' tomatoes, peeled, seeded and chopped

2–3 sprigs flat-leaf parsley

1 sprig fresh thyme

1 bay leaf

2 thinly peeled strips orange rind

300 ml (10 fl oz) fish stock

300 ml (10 fl oz) dry white wine

pinch of saffron strands, steeped in 2 tablespoons boiling water

salt and freshly ground pepper

120 g (4 oz) pitted small black olives

4 tablespoons vegetable oil

fresh eel, skinned and filleted to provide about 1.2 kg (2 lb 10 oz) flesh, cut into 5–8 cm (2–3 in) pieces

TOMATO STEW In a large wide pan heat the olive oil and add the onion, leek, shallots and garlic and cook until softened. Do not brown. Add the anise liqueur and fennel seeds. Cook rapidly to drive off the alcohol. Add the tomatoes, herbs and orange rind. Stir in the fish stock, wine, saffron and its liquid, salt and pepper. Bring to the boil then simmer for 30–40 minutes. The result should be a flavoursome, thickish-textured tomato stew. If there is still too much liquid, bring the stew to the boil and continue cooking to evaporate excess liquid and achieve a good sauce consistency. Stir occasionally to prevent the mixture from catching. Add the olives, stir through then adjust the seasoning. Cool and store the stew, covered, in the refrigerator until ready to use.

TO COOK THE EEL Heat the vegetable oil in a frying pan and colour the eels in it over low-to-medium heat for no more than 3–5 minutes. As soon as the eel pieces have stiffened and are starting to colour, remove them from the pan and drain on kitchen paper.

TO FINISH Heat the tomato stew in a broad-based pan. Ladle out the top one-third of the mixture. Lay the pieces of eel on top of the remaining stew in the pan and season with salt and pepper. Pour the remaining tomato stew back in the pan, 'burying' the eel pieces. Bring to a gentle simmer. Cover with a couple of layers of greaseproof paper and continue to cook very gently for 10–15 minutes. Check to see that the eel pieces are sufficiently cooked through. They should be moist and tender and not too firm. If necessary, continue to cook for a further 5 minutes. Serve with crusty bread and grilled vegetable salad.

SMOKED EEL RILLETTES
Serves 6 (about 50 g each)

1 leaf gelatine (gold)
150 ml (5 fl oz) fish stock, heated
300 g (10½ oz) smoked eel, skinned and boned
3 tablespoons soft butter
salt and freshly ground pepper

Soak the gelatine in a little cold water then drain and squeeze it dry. Add the gelatine to the warmed fish stock and stir to dissolve. Place the smoked eel meat in a processor and pulse to break the meat down but do not purée it completely. Gradually add the warm stock and continue to pulse until completely absorbed. Allow the mixture to cool then place it in a bowl and beat in the soft butter with a wooden spoon. Season then refrigerate in a covered container. Remove from the refrigerator and allow the rillettes to lose its chill before serving.

At the restaurant we have served this as part of a platter of tastes from the local waterways. But the rillettes is just delicious piled onto warm grilled ciabatta, drizzled with virgin olive oil and sprinkled with freshly ground black pepper. A salad of ripe tomatoes, served at room temperature, is all that is needed for a quick and simple lunch.

MURRAY COD

Murray cod is now on the endangered species list in Australia and there are strictly enforced regulations to limit fishing for it in the wild. We are fortunate to have Tony Butler growing this beautiful fish for us nearby. I am able to source it at its peak and at the size I want. As is the case with many other farmed fish, such as barramundi, fish that are too small will not have developed much texture and the result is disappointingly mushy when cooked. Murray cod over 2 kg (4 lb 6 oz) have had the opportunity to develop some 'muscle tone', especially if they have had to swim against introduced currents. The cod lends itself to simple steaming and serving with Asian-inspired accompaniments and we also occasionally pan-fry it in a jacket of finely sliced potatoes.

Ceviche of Murray cod and steamed yabbies in coconut dressing

Serves 6

This dish combining Murray cod with yabbies is served in an oversized martini or cocktail glass in a sort of retro celebration of the ubiquitous seafood cocktail of my youth. The coconut dressing is lovely just served alongside any grilled or pan-fried fish finished with a squeeze of lime. The yabbies are simply steamed over lime and ginger.

1 quantity Coconut Dressing (see page 286), chilled

CEVICHE

1 x 600 g (1 lb 5 oz) skinned and boned piece Murray cod (or other firm-fleshed white fish)
600 ml (20 fl oz) lime juice
1 teaspoon fish sauce

YABBY DRESSING

3 teaspoons lime juice
1 teaspoon fish sauce
1 small knob palm sugar
4 mint leaves

STEAMED YABBIES

12 live yabbies
½ lime, thinly sliced
3 kaffir lime leaves, bruised
2 stalks lemongrass, roughly chopped and bruised

TO FINISH AND GARNISH

½ iceberg lettuce, washed and dried
1½ limes, cut into quarters
6 small red chillies, sliced lengthways twice through to stem and placed in iced water
approximately 24 rice noodles, fried in hot oil until puffed and crisp, drained and seasoned

CEVICHE Slice the fish diagonally across the fillet into even slices approximately 5 mm (¼ in) thick. Blend the lime juice with the fish sauce and coat the fish with this dressing, ensuring a good overall coverage. Place the fish slices in a plastic, glass or ceramic tray. Pour any remaining dressing over the fish, cover and refrigerate for 2 hours. Drain the lime juice from the marinated fish and coat the slices generously with cold coconut dressing. Reserve some coconut dressing for the final assembly of the dish.

YABBY DRESSING Combine ingredients to make a dressing.

STEAMING THE YABBIES First anaesthetise the yabbies over ice or place them in the freezer for a few minutes. Scatter the lime, kaffir lime leaves and chopped lemongrass over the base of a steamer basket and set it to fit over a saucepan of boiling water. Steam the yabbies, a few at a time, in the covered basket for 3 minutes per batch. Immediately afterwards plunge them into iced water. When cooled, keeping them in their shells, proceed as described (see Cooking Yabbies, page 161) to degut, peel back the shells and crack the claws. Dry the yabbies well and toss them in a bowl with the yabby dressing.

TO SERVE Choose 6 large lettuce leaves to line the cocktail or martini glasses. Shred the remaining lettuce into strips, or chiffonnade, and lightly coat with the coconut dressing. Distribute a little of the dressed chiffonade among the cocktail glasses. Top with slices of ceviche. Repeat with another layer of lettuce then ceviche. Hang a couple of dressed yabbies over the rim of each glass. Garnish with a lime quarter and the sliced chilli and puffed rice noodles. Serve immediately.

Murray cod in a potato jacket with asparagus and morels
Serves 4

Paul Bocuse's wrapping of red mullet in crisp potato slices, *Ecailles de Pomme de Terre*, has inspired many dishes including this one. Because it is fairly time-consuming to prepare, we usually serve it with the simplest of seasonal garnishes. Here it comes with asparagus and morels finished with a little cream and mustard.

3–4 very large potatoes, peeled, rounded sides sliced off and discarded
50 g (2 oz) butter, melted
salt and freshly ground white pepper
4 sprigs fresh tarragon
4 x 180 g (6 ⅓ oz) skinless Murray cod fillets, or other firm-fleshed white fish, trimmed into rectangular shape
butter and olive oil for cooking

ASPARAGUS AND MORELS IN MUSTARD CREAM
salt
500 g (1 lb 2 oz) thick asparagus spears, bottom ⅔ removed
400 g (14 oz) fresh morels, washed several times and squeezed to remove excess water
100 g (3½ oz) butter
1 large shallot, peeled and finely diced
1 teaspoon finely chopped fresh thyme leaves
2 tablespoons dry sherry
300 ml (10 fl oz) pure cream (45% butterfat)
1 tablespoon seeded mustard

Cut the straight-sided potatoes into long thin slices using a mandoline then toss the slices in the melted butter and seasoning. Place a 20 cm (8 in) square of plastic wrap on your work surface and arrange 8–10 slightly overlapping potato slices side by side in the middle. Place a tarragon sprig in the middle of the potato slices and centre a fish fillet on top and season. Fold the potato over to wrap the fish completely. Wrap the potato-enclosed fish in the plastic wrap. Repeat with all the potato and fish then refrigerate the parcels to set for 1 hour.

ASPARAGUS AND MORELS IN MUSTARD CREAM Fill a large deep pan two-thirds full of water and bring to the boil. Add salt then drop the asparagus tips in and cook for about 4–6 minutes until tender (test with a small sharp knife). Drain asparagus and drop into iced water. When the asparagus is cool, quickly remove, pat dry and store on kitchen paper. Place morels on kitchen paper to drain and dry – give them a gentle turn in the salad spinner if you wish. Heat a non-stick pan over high heat and, when hot, add the morels and some salt, stirring until morels drop their juices. Cook until liquid has evaporated. Add the butter, shallot and thyme and cook and stir. Add the sherry and allow it to evaporate. Add cream and mustard and cook over medium heat. Add asparagus tips, heat through and cook until the sauce is viscous and creamy. Adjust the seasoning and keep warm.

TO COOK FISH PARCELS Preheat the oven to 200–220°C (400–430°F). Melt a little butter with a drizzle of olive oil in a non-stick pan. Cook the parcels on medium-to-hot heat for 3–4 minutes on each side until coloured. Do not crowd the pan. Finish cooking in the hot oven for 4–5 minutes. Test for readiness remembering the fish will continue to cook for a couple of minutes after being removed from the oven. Arrange the parcels on plates with the vegetables in mustard sauce alongside.

TROUT

Locally caught brown speckled trout arrive in our kitchen from guests who go fly fishing at one of the local waterways with Colin, our groundsman. We are always delighted to prepare and serve them. Supplies of farmed trout, from down the road at Tuki Springs, arrive daily ready to be smoked, marinated or simply pan-fried whole *à la meunière* for our daily Express Lunch menu.

Escabèche of freshwater trout with remoulade-style salad

Serves 4

This is a delicious method of marinating fish, here using local trout but it works well with many other fish especially sardines and fresh anchovies. Cooking time varies with the fish variety – in some cases just the hot marinade poured over the fish is sufficient. Once you have mastered the process, experiment a little. The remoulade here is an adaptation of the original. Its chief ingredient is still celeriac, but the addition of apple offers sweetness that tempers the light acidity of the marinated trout. The capers and dill cucumber add extra textures as well as salt.

MARINADE

3 shallots, diced
1 clove garlic, diced
800 ml (27 fl oz) olive oil
4 peppercorns
1 bay leaf
3 sprigs thyme
3 tablespoons caster (superfine) sugar
200 ml (7 fl oz) white wine vinegar

TROUT

2 x 300 g (10½ oz) trout
salt and freshly ground white pepper
olive oil for cooking

REMOULADE-STYLE SALAD

1 small celeriac, peeled and cut into julienne
5 tablespoons Mayonnaise (see page 285)
1 teaspoon Dijon mustard
2 stalks celery, cut into julienne
1 medium-to-large crisp apple, cut into julienne
2 small dill cucumbers, cut into julienne
1 tablespoon salt-packed baby capers, rinsed and dried
salt and freshly ground pepper

MARINADE In a heavy-based stainless steel saucepan on a low heat, sauté the shallots and garlic in 1 tablespoon of the olive oil until they are translucent. Add the rest of the olive oil then the peppercorns, bay leaf and thyme and gently heat. In a bowl whisk the sugar and vinegar until they are well combined then add to the warm olive oil mix. This marinade can be made in advance, refrigerated and re-warmed when necessary.

PREPARING AND MARINATING THE TROUT Have your supplier clean, fillet and pin-bone the trout. Season the four fillets with salt and pepper. Heat a non-stick pan and coat it lightly with olive oil. Place the trout fillets in the moderately hot pan, skin side down, and cook for 1 minute. This should be sufficient time to turn the edges of the fillets opaque while their centres remain uncooked. Carefully remove the fillets from the pan and place them in a ceramic or glass dish. Pour the warm marinating mixture over the fish (see photograph on page 34). Cool, cover and refrigerate for 8 hours. After this time the fillets are ready to be drained, cut into appropriately sized pieces and used in a variety of ways.

REMOULADE-STYLE SALAD Drop the julienne of celeriac into acidulated water while preparing the other salad ingredients. Drain and dry the celeriac. In a bowl, combine the mayonnaise and mustard then add all the remaining ingredients and toss well.

TO SERVE Mound the salad onto plates or shape it using a round cutter. Place three pieces of marinated trout on top of each salad.

❖ Smoked trout sausage and smoked eel with potato pancakes ❖

Serves 6 or more

This is a dish of several components. The smoked trout sausage can stand alone steamed or lightly grilled and served with salad greens or a warm potato salad with mustard dressing. The potato pancakes are delicious served warm, topped with Gravadlax (see page 173) or smoked salmon, crème fraîche and dill. With either component, it is worth making extra and the recipe allows for this. The dish is reminiscent of the smoked fish and blini combination that was so much a part of my Russian childhood. The photograph shows an appetiser version of this dish using one pancake per person.

SMOKED TROUT SAUSAGE

300 g (10½ oz) salmon fillet, pin-boned, trimmed and chopped

1 x 180 g (6 ⅓ oz) smoked trout, skinned, boned and diced

1 egg white

200 ml (7 fl oz) thickened cream (35% butterfat)

1 tablespoon chopped chives

salt and freshly ground pepper

butter for cooking

SMOKED TROUT SAUSAGE Chill the processor and blade. Have the fish, egg white and cream well chilled. Working quickly, process the salmon to a fine purée in the processor. Add the egg white and blend until the mixture is well combined. Gradually blend in half the cream. Place the mixture in a stainless steel bowl and fold in the diced smoked trout. Combine well then place the mix in the refrigerator for ½ an hour. Remove from the refrigerator and fold in the rest of the well-chilled cream. Add the chopped chives, season with salt and pepper then return to the refrigerator.

Cut some aluminium foil into 15 cm squares. Place 2–3 heaped tablespoons of the trout mousse on each square. Roll each square into a sausage shape and twist both ends of foil tightly to finish the sausage neatly and to ensure that the mousse is completely sealed. Refrigerate for at least 1 hour.

Simmer the sausages gently in water for 2–3 minutes. If not using them immediately, slip the sausages out of the foil and place them on a tray to cool, then cover and refrigerate. If you are assembling the whole dish, you will have extra sausage that can be refrigerated for reheating and enjoying later. If you are serving the sausages on their own, gently pan-fry them in a little butter until they are lightly browned and warmed through, or coat them in butter and heat them in a preheated oven at 160°C (320°F) for about 8–10 minutes.

»

~ recipe continued ~

POTATO PANCAKES

150 g (5 oz) dry mashed potato

1 whole egg

1 tablespoon self-raising flour

70 ml (2 ⅓ oz) milk, warmed

salt and freshly ground pepper

1 egg white

butter for cooking

EEL AND PANCETTA

400 g (14 oz) smoked eel, skinned and boned (about 300 g/10½ oz net)

6 thin slices pancetta, cut in half

GARNISH AND DRESSING

90 g (3¼ oz) baby salad leaves

Basic Vinaigrette (see page 284)

Horseradish Cream (see page 289)

Beetroot Relish (see page 294), optional

POTATO PANCAKES Warm the potato then add in the whole egg, beating it in by hand until there are no lumps. Sift the flour and fold it into the potato mix. Whisk the warm milk in and season to taste. Whisk the egg white until stiff then fold it through the potato mix. Gently pan-fry 20 g (¾ oz) quantities of the mixture, each spread into a circle about 7 cm (2¾ in) in diameter (the mixture makes about 15 pancakes). Turn the pancakes over halfway through the cooking, ensuring that both sides are golden coloured. Remove from the heat and store on absorbent kitchen paper. When cool, trim each pancake with a 7 cm (2¾ in) diameter cutter.

EEL AND PANCETTA Cut the skinned and boned eel flesh into pieces approximately 4 cm (1½ in) long. Place the pancetta slices on an oven tray and bake in a low oven (150°C/300°F) until crisp.

TO FINISH Preheat the oven to 160°C (320°F). Slice the cold smoked trout sausage. You will need 4–5 slices per person. Place the slices on a baking tray together with the eel pieces and two potato pancakes per person. Warm these components gently in the oven for about 6–8 minutes or until they are all warmed through. Meanwhile dress the salad leaves with the vinaigrette.

TO SERVE Place a pancake on each plate, top with two or three slices of sausage, a piece or two of smoked eel, a little of the dressed greens, a half piece of pancetta and the second pancake. Repeat the process omitting the pancetta and finishing with the salad greens. Drizzle any remaining dressing over and around each salad. Spoon a quenelle of horseradish cream onto the top of each lot of greens then garnish with the remaining pancetta. If desired, serve with beetroot relish.

❖ Smoked trout custards ❖

Makes 7 half-cup moulds or 14 eggcups

These custards are often offered as an *amuse bouche* in the restaurant. They are particularly good served warm, in which case omit the mayonnaise garnish. This is a useful recipe if you have boned your smoked trout and used most of the flesh in another way, perhaps tossed through some warm pasta. However, the greater the quantity of smoked trout flesh you have to use the better the flavour of the custards.

1 small leek, white part only, washed and diced
1 clove garlic, sliced
2 shallots, sliced
2 tablespoons butter
bones, skin and flesh trimmings from 2 smoked trout
300 ml (10 fl oz) thickened cream (35% butterfat)
200 ml (7 fl oz) milk
salt and freshly ground white pepper
5 eggs
'soldiers' (see Croutons and Crostini, page 281) for garnishing

GARNISH (OPTIONAL)
Mayonnaise (see page 285)
salmon roe
sprigs of dill

Sauté the leek, garlic and shallots in butter until they are tender. Add the trout bones, skin and trimmings and continue to sauté for 1 minute. Add the cream and milk and simmer over a low heat for ½ an hour. Remove from the heat and leave to infuse for a further 1 hour.

Preheat the oven to 165°C (325°F). Season the infused mixture with salt and pepper and pass through a fine strainer, pushing on the skins, flesh and bones to release the maximum amount of flavour. Allow the mixture to cool. Whisk in the eggs then pour the mixture into moulds or eggcups. Set the moulds in a deep oven dish and pour in sufficient hot water to reach halfway up the sides of the moulds. Tightly cover the oven dish with foil and bake for 10–15 minutes, or less time if you are using eggcups. The custards should be firm around the perimeter but slightly wobbly in the middle. Allow them to cool slightly in the water before removing and serving with crisp 'soldiers'. Alternatively allow the custards to cool completely and garnish with mayonnaise, salmon roe and a sprig of dill.

YABBIES

Yabbies are Australia's own freshwater crustacean. Regularly caught in dams and rivers, simply boiled quickly and served with crusty bread, good mayonnaise, plenty of freshly ground pepper and lemon juice, they are common fare at country picnics.

However, the farmed yabby is a much superior beast – large, perfectly formed and purged for several days, it is now frequently exported. Some country aficionados will tell you that a yabby is not a yabby without that special muddy taste of the wild but I have yet to be convinced.

I admit that I am unable to come at gutting yabbies while they are still alive, the way I was taught, by twisting off the tail. What follows is a process that we use in our kitchen, which I am happier with. In some sort of desire for karmic balance, I also have three or four yabbies released back into our creek with every box that arrives. If nothing else it pleases the kids sinking smelly meat on strings much further downstream.

COOKING YABBIES

Keep live yabbies anaesthetised by layering them with ice. Bring a large pot of salted water to a rolling boil and have a large bowl of ice and water ready. Throw about 10 yabbies into the pot at a time and, if wishing to reheat them or use in any further cooking process, cook for 2 minutes to just 'set'. Otherwise cook each batch for 4 minutes. Remove the yabbies from the boiling water with a skimmer ladle and put them straight into the bowl of iced water to stop the cooking process. Remove them from the chilled water as soon as they have cooled and allow them to drain well.

If serving the yabbies in the shell, slit along the back of the tail carapace with sharp scissors and remove the intestinal tract with a small knife. Peel back the shell a little to help expose the flesh. Crack the claws. If you have deliberately undercooked the yabbies, store them covered in the refrigerator until ready to use. They can be thrown in their shell onto the barbecue or into a pan for a couple of minutes. Otherwise shell them, take out the tails and remove the intestinal tract with a sharp knife. Reserve the shells for yabby oil or bisque. Toss the tails with butter in a pan over medium heat for a few minutes and serve over a simple salad like baby rocket leaves and finely shaved fennel dressed with fruity olive oil, lemon juice and freshly ground pepper. Otherwise stir the tails through a risotto or use as suggested in the following recipe.

~ Sautéed yabbies with pea ravioli and pea tendril salad ~
Serves 6

This recipe uses ravioli made with wonton wrappers. The result is silky and fine, good with delicate dishes and is best with fillings that require heating through rather than cooking. These ravioli, made with peas, are paired with sautéed yabbies. They are also wonderful with spring lamb, with a little chopped mint added to the filling. The recipe may produce more ravioli than you need. Enjoy them with a little melted butter and freshly ground pepper as you cook. Making a filling with less than one cup of peas is hardly worth the effort. We use three ravioli per appetiser serve for the complete dish.

PEA RAVIOLI
40 g (1½ oz) butter
1 cup shelled fresh peas
1 teaspoon chopped fresh tarragon
100 ml (3½ oz) water
salt and freshly ground pepper
36 wonton wrappers (makes 18 ravioli)
1 egg, beaten with 1 tablespoon water
rice flour for dusting

24–30 large live yabbies (minimum 80 g/3 oz each)

WHITE WINE SAUCE
25 g (1 oz) butter
1 leek, white part only, sliced
2 shallots, finely chopped
1 sprig thyme
1 clove garlic, crushed
100 ml (3½ fl oz) Pernod
300 ml (10 fl oz) dry white wine
300 ml (10 fl oz) fish stock
200 ml (7 fl oz) pure cream (45% butterfat)
salt and freshly ground white pepper

PEA RAVIOLI Melt the butter in a pan over medium heat. Add the peas and tarragon and cook until warmed through. Add the water and continue to cook until the peas have slightly softened then drain, reserving any remaining liquid. Transfer the peas to a blender and purée. Pass through a tamis for a smooth filling, using just a little of any reserved liquid to assist, or leave the purée coarse if desired. Season then leave the purée to cool.

TO ASSEMBLE THE RAVIOLI Lay out half the wonton wrappers on your work surface. Place a heaped teaspoon of pea purée in the centre of each wonton and brush the edges of the wrapper with the egg wash. Top each with another wrapper and firmly press the edges to seal, creating a small round in the centre as you push out as much air as possible. Cut with a round cutter. Put the ravioli in a tray on baking paper lightly dusted with rice flour. Refrigerate uncovered for up to 1 day until ready to use. Alternatively freeze the ravioli on the tray, then transfer them to a covered container and keep frozen for up to two weeks.

TO COOK THE RAVIOLI Bring a large pot of water to the boil. Generously salt the boiling water and slip in the ravioli. Immediately turn the heat down, so that the water just simmers, and cook the ravioli for 3–4 minutes. With a slotted spoon, remove the ravioli to a tray lined with kitchen paper and allow them to drain. Set aside and keep warm.

TO FINISH

small knob of butter for frying

12 snow peas, topped, tailed, strung, blanched for 10 seconds and refreshed, cut into thin julienne

salt and freshly ground white pepper

60 g (2 oz) fresh pea tendrils

1 tablespoon Basic Vinaigrette (see page 284)

20 g (¾ oz) additional butter for finishing sauce

TO PREPARE YABBIES See Cooking Yabbies (page 161) Cook the yabbies for 2–3 minutes in rolling boiling water then drain, remove the tails and clean. Set the yabby tails aside and reserve the shells.

WHITE WINE SAUCE Melt the butter in a saucepan and sweat the leek, shallots, thyme and garlic for 5 minutes. Do not allow the ingredients to colour. Add the yabby shells, crushing them with a spoon. Continue to cook for a further 3–4 minutes. Pour in the Pernod and cook over a high heat to cook off the alcohol. Add the wine and fish stock, reduce to a medium heat and cook until the liquid has reduced by half. Add the cream and continue to cook over medium heat for a further 10 minutes. Strain through a chinois, pressing hard on the solids, then strain through a very fine sieve and season. Keep warm while finishing the yabbies and snow peas.

TO FINISH If necessary, place the ravioli in the top of a steamer and reheat over simmering water for 2 minutes. Remove the pot from the heat and set aside. Melt the knob of butter in a pan and when just foaming, add the snow pea julienne and yabby tails. Toss to heat through and season with salt and pepper. Toss the pea tendrils in the dressing. Place the additional butter in the warm wine sauce and blitz with a hand-held blender.

TO SERVE Place three pea ravioli in the base of each of six large bowls. Pile 4–5 cooked yabbies on top and scatter the snow pea julienne around. Spoon the white wine sauce over the top and around. Garnish the yabbies with a small cluster of dressed pea tendrils.

FROM THE SEA

In the early days of the restaurant we rarely used any sea fish. Deliveries were erratic, and fishing and holding practices of the time left a lot to be desired. We have a lot to thank our Japanese chefs for in Australia. They have been in the vanguard of creating a demand for best practice fishing and delivery.

The need for sustainable fishing practices is becoming more critical as whole species previously abounding in our oceans are fished out. The messages we consumers get, however, are frequently mixed and it is hard to keep up with what is in decline where and what is recovering. Things will not be solved in a hurry but we do have the power to send a message to our suppliers. Ask for line-caught fish rather than trawled. It is often best to select a whole fish and ask for it to be filleted. When you see the whole fish, its intact scales will tell you that it has not been trawled, battered and bruised. The consequent quality of the flesh will reflect the way the fish has been treated. It is essential that we support fishermen who use sustainable practices. Paying a little extra encourages those who are attempting to do the right thing and reinforces the message that the lowest price is not always the priority.

Peppered and herbed seared tuna with cucumber and buckwheat

Serves 6

1x 500 g (1 lb 2 oz) piece sashimi-grade tuna (no bloodline or sinew), 10 cm (4 in) across in diameter and trimmed to a cylinder shape
cracked pepper
4 tablespoons chopped flat-leaf parsley
4 tablespoons finely chopped chives
4 tablespoons chopped chervil

WASABI CRÈME FRAÎCHE

½ cup crème fraîche or sour cream
½ tablespoon freshly grated wasabi
¼ teaspoon salt

BUCKWHEAT VINAIGRETTE

4 tablespoons rice wine vinegar
2 teaspoons soy sauce
2 teaspoons lemon juice
salt and freshly ground pepper
4 tablespoons olive oil
4 tablespoons grape seed oil
½ small cucumber, peeled, seeded and diced
12 tablespoons cooked Buckwheat (see page 280)

Roll the tuna in the cracked pepper and sear it all round in a very hot pan for about 10–15 seconds on each side. Combine the parsley, chives and chervil and roll the tuna in the mix. Wrap the tuna tightly in plastic wrap to retain the cylindrical shape and refrigerate for at least 2 hours. Before serving, remove the plastic wrap and slice the tuna into 5 mm (¼ in) slices.

WASABI CRÈME FRAÎCHE Combine all the ingredients and store, covered, in the refrigerator.

BUCKWHEAT VINAIGRETTE Combine the vinegar, soy sauce, lemon juice and salt and pepper. Combine the oils then whisk slowly into the vinegar mix. Place the diced cucumber and cooked buckwheat in a bowl and add the dressing.

TO SERVE Mound the dressed cucumber and buckwheat onto plates or use a cutter to form a circular shape for these ingredients. Smear some wasabi crème fraîche on the tuna slices. Arrange the tuna slices on the buckwheat, using 3–4 slices per serve depending on size and with the crème fraîche side down. Brush a little of the vinaigrette over the tuna slices. We garnish this dish with extra wasabi crème fraîche and slivers of fried bean curd skin. If desired, drizzle plate with a little Herb Oil (see page 285).

Confit of tuna in a salad niçoise with salsa verde

Serves 4

Although most preparation for this dish can be done in advance, with the ingredients refrigerated and then assembled when ready to serve, the result would be a pale imitation of a dish put together virtually as it is cooked. With the potatoes and even the soft-boiled egg retaining some warmth and the tuna just cooled from cooking, but still at room temperature, it is something else altogether.

SALAD NIÇOISE

350 g (12 oz) baby green beans

750 g (1 lb 10 oz) kipfler potatoes, scrubbed

4 medium-sized ripe tomatoes

1 clove garlic, crushed and very finely chopped

2 teaspoons white wine vinegar

4 tablespoons olive oil

salt and freshly ground pepper

24 small black olives, pitted

½ soft green lettuce such as mignonette, leaves separated, washed, dried and torn into small pieces

4 anchovy fillets, halved lengthways

3 Soft Eggs For Salads and Dressings (see page 290)

CONFIT OF TUNA

4 x 100 g (3½ oz) tuna fillets, 4–5 cm (1½–2 in) thick

salt and freshly ground pepper

4 cups olive oil

Salsa Verde (see page 288) for finishing

SALAD NIÇOISE Bring a large pot of water to the boil, add salt and cook the beans at a rolling boil until tender. Plunge them into iced water, drain immediately and place in a bowl. Place the kipflers in a saucepan, top with cold water and bring to the boil. Reduce to a simmer and cook until tender. Peel the potatoes and cut them into 1 cm (½ in) thick slices and add to the beans. Blanch and peel the tomatoes, cut them into quarters, seed and trim, retaining only the exterior flesh in the shape of 'petals'. Cut each of these lengthways into four or five strips and add to the beans and potatoes. Combine the garlic with white wine vinegar then slowly whisk in the olive oil. Season with salt and pepper and use a little of this mix to dress the vegetables. Add the olives to the bowl.

CONFIT OF TUNA Season the tuna fillets with salt and pepper. Place the fillets in a saucepan so they sit side by side. Add olive oil to cover the fish by at least 1½ cm (¾ in) then place on high heat. Bring the temperature of the oil to 90°C (190°F). Remove the saucepan from the heat and leave the fillets to sit for 5 minutes for rare tuna or up to 8 minutes for medium–rare. Remove the tuna from the saucepan and place it on several layers of kitchen paper to drain. Strain the cooking oil and reserve it for making dressings for fish dishes or for cooking fish.

TO ASSEMBLE AND SERVE Dress the salad leaves with some of the remaining dressing and season. Cut the tuna fillets into slices or break them into chunks and season. Arrange the potato slices on each of four plates. Layer the leaves and other ingredients over the potatoes, interspersing with slices of tuna and two strips of anchovy fillet. Arrange three egg quarters around and drizzle any remaining dressing over the salad. Drizzle salsa verde around the plate.

Cauliflower panna cotta with oyster fritters

Serves 8

We use a sheet of hemisphere moulds for the panna cotta in this dish. The creamy texture of the oysters within the crisp batter works well with the creamy rich-flavoured panna cotta. Black bean dressing provides salt with depth and contrasting colour. Truffle oil, although suffering from frequent abuse, works very well in tiny amounts with the right ingredients. Cauliflower is one of them.

CAULIFLOWER PANNA COTTA

2 shallots, sliced

1 clove garlic, sliced

½ head (about 500 g/1 lb 2 oz) cauliflower, cut into florets (toughest stems discarded) and roughly chopped

3 sprigs thyme

170 g (6 oz) butter

30 ml (1 fl oz) Pernod

30 ml (1 fl oz) vermouth

900 ml (30 fl oz) thickened cream (35% butterfat)

500 ml (17 fl oz) milk

1 teaspoon salt and freshly ground white pepper

¼ teaspoon truffle oil (optional)

8 leaves gelatine (gold), soaked in cold water until soft

OYSTER FRITTERS

24 oysters

seasoned flour for dusting

1 quantity Tempura Batter (see page 280)

oil for deep-frying

salt and freshly ground pepper

Black Bean Dressing (see page 284) for serving

CAULIFLOWER PANNA COTTA Sauté the shallots, garlic, cauliflower and thyme in the butter for 1 minute. Add the Pernod and vermouth then cook until almost no liquid remains. Add the cream and milk and simmer for 20 minutes or until the cauliflower is tender. Transfer the mix to a blender and purée until very smooth. Season with salt and pepper to taste and add the truffle oil if using. Pass the purée through a fine strainer into a bowl. Drain the gelatine, squeeze dry and add it to the warm cauliflower purée and stir until dissolved. Taste and adjust seasoning. Pour the purée into greased or latex moulds and allow it to set in the refrigerator for a minimum of 4 hours.

OYSTER FRITTERS Shuck the oysters, remove them from the shells and place them on kitchen paper to dry (you can reserve the oyster juice for another use). Pat the oysters dry, lightly dust them with the seasoned flour and drop them in the batter. Turn them around to ensure they are completely coated. Lift each oyster from the batter with a fork, allowing the excess to drain off. Deep-fry three or four at a time in hot oil, preheated to 180°C (350°F), turning the oysters with a slotted spoon and cooking until golden and crisp. Drain the oysters on several layers of kitchen paper and season well.

TO SERVE Turn out the panna cottas onto plates and place three oyster fritters on top of each. Drizzle with black bean dressing and serve.

THERE ARE some things that regular guests demand to see on our menu. We have always cured our own salmon and it is always on the menu in one guise or another. It is one of those very versatile staples. The way we cure it varies although generally we use less salt and a longer cure than most recipes. It may not be fashionable but I love Caesar salad. Just having a container of the dressing in the refrigerator and some washed cos leaves provides for an instant snack. In the following recipe the salad is alluded to rather than playing the dominant part in the dish. The texture of the croutons, a feature of the original salad, is present in the crisp bread container. The parmesan cheese is present in the form of crisps. The bacon is omitted altogether. The poached egg is crumbed and fried. The external crunch and the runniness of the yolk combine with the Caesar dressing and the sweet saltiness of the cured salmon in quite a delicious way. If you are going to cure a side of salmon, a large one will be no extra work. You will have some delicious salmon left over to slice and eat on hot toast or to serve on warm Potato Pancakes (see page 158), or try it with Remoulade-style Salad (see page 155).

Gravadlax with flavours of Caesar and crisp crumbed poached egg

Serves 6

Play around with this recipe, adjusting the salt–sugar ratio and curing time. Experiment with other spices. Fennel seed and a little Pernod produce an intriguing flavour and will give you sliced salmon that is lovely with a shaved fennel salad. However, using other fish that lack a high oil content is generally a waste.

CURED SALMON

300 g (10½ oz) coarse salt

450 g (1 lb) caster (superfine) sugar

1 x 1.2 kg (2 lb 10 oz) side of salmon, boned, trimmed and skin left on

150–200 ml (5–7 fl oz) brandy or vodka

½ cup finely chopped dill

½ teaspoon freshly ground white pepper

SALAD AND OTHER GARNISHES

6 Bread Rings (see page 281)

4–5 baby cos (romaine) leaves per serve

1 quantity Caesar Dressing (see page 286)

6 Crisp Crumbed Poached Eggs (see page 290)

1 quantity Parmesan Crisps (see page 283), cut into 3 cm (1¼ in) squares

2 teaspoons baby capers, washed, dried and crisp-fried in a non-stick pan

1 teaspoon finely chopped chives

1 teaspoon fine julienne of anchovies

CURED SALMON Mix the salt and sugar thoroughly. Place half the mix in a narrow non-reactive tray large enough to hold the salmon. Place the salmon, skin side down, on top of the salt mix. Drizzle the brandy or vodka over the salmon then sprinkle it with dill and pepper. Place the remaining salt mix over the top of the salmon, spreading it all over the surface. Cover with plastic wrap, refrigerate and leave to cure for 48 hours. Once cured, rinse off the salt mix and pat dry. The salmon is best stored in the refrigerator wrapped in a damp towel and will keep that way for up to a week. When ready to serve, slice into very thin slices down towards the skin with a sharp flexible-bladed knife. Just before you get to the skin, flatten the blade to a horizontal position. As more slices are cut you will find that you are eventually cutting the salmon almost horizontally to the skin.

SALAD AND OTHER GARNISHES Place the salmon slices, slightly overlapping, on serving plates. Position a croûte ring in the centre of the salmon. Dress the baby cos leaves with Caesar dressing and arrange upright inside the croûte. Place the crumbed poached eggs on top of the cos. Garnish the salmon with parmesan crisps, dollops of Caesar dressing, fried capers, chives and tiny slivers of anchovy.

❖ Spiced blue eye with eggplant relish, sweet curried mussels ❖ and chickpea chips

Serves 6

The separate components of this dish can stand alone but also come together very nicely. Try dusting the spice over snapper, trevally or kingfish and serve with a salad. Add the smoky eggplant purée to enhance and you get something special. The method for cooking mussels will stand you in good stead and the curry sauce is finger-licking delicious with roast chicken and a salad of Asian leaves. This will make more eggplant relish than you need to serve with the fish. It will keep in a covered container in the refrigerator and is excellent with roast lamb.

MUSSELS

18 black mussels

1 tablespoon olive oil

2 cloves garlic, crushed

2 shallots, chopped

1 cup white wine

FISH SPICE

2 tablespoons coriander seeds

4 tablespoons ground cumin

2 tablespoons fennel seeds

16 black peppercorns

2 tablespoons turmeric

¼ tablespoon salt

pinch of ground nutmeg

THE FISH

6 x 180 g (6⅓ oz) fillets blue eye

salt and freshly ground pepper

25 ml (1 fl oz) vegetable oil

25 g (1 oz) butter

MUSSELS Place the mussels in a bowl of cold water (I can never cook so few as they are delicious straight from the pot with a glass of wine while you are putting together the rest of the dish). With a clean nylon scourer or brush scrub the shells, removing any weed or barnacles. De-beard with a knife, pulling off any weed protruding from the shell. Discard any mussels that have opened but will not close when pressed.

Heat oil in a large pot and add mussels, garlic and shallots, stirring over high heat. Add the wine and stir or shake the pot to ensure quick and even cooking. As soon as the mussels have opened — the signal that they are cooked — remove the pot from the heat. Remove mussels with a slotted spoon and place in a bowl until just cooled enough to handle. Strain the cooking juices through a very fine sieve and reserve for another use. The juice will freeze well and is a wonderful addition to fish sauces. If you are going to use it later, check for salt as mussels vary considerably in salinity.

Once mussels are cool enough to handle remove the top shell from each, leaving the mussel nestled in the half shell. Use at once or refrigerate covered until ready to use. Place in a steamer over simmering water for a few seconds to reheat.

FISH SPICE Toast the first four spices in a non-stick pan over moderate heat until they release their aroma (approximately 1 minute). Combine with the remaining ingredients in a mortar and pestle or small grinder and grind to a fine powder. This spice can be made in advance and stored in a small screw-top jar.

»

~ recipe continued ~

ACCOMPANIMENTS

1 quantity Smoky Eggplant Purée (see page 295)
1 quantity Eggplant Relish (see page 296)
1 quantity Fried Chickpea Chips (see page 280)
1 quantity Curry Sauce (see page 288)

COOKING FISH Salt and pepper all sides of the fillets and coat well in spice mix, including the skin. Either use a pan that is oven-proof and will eventually hold all six fillets comfortably or use a smaller pan and have an oven tray ready. Preheat the oven to 200°C (400°F). Film some oil over the base of the pan and place over high heat with half the butter. Cook the fish two to three fillets at a time depending on your pan size, skin side down, for about 2 minutes until golden. Set aside until remaining fillets are cooked, using a little additional oil and butter as required. When all fillets are crisp and browned on the skin side, turn them over and either return to the pan and put into the oven or place onto the baking tray and into the oven. Bake for 6–8 minutes until fillets are cooked through.

TO SERVE Place a mound of warm eggplant relish on each plate, top with cooked fish with a tablespoon eggplant purée on each fillet. Arrange 3 warm mussels on the half shell on each plate and a stack of four chickpea chips. Drizzle the curry sauce over the mussels and a little close by the fish.

Snapper and oysters with cucumber, sorrel and champagne

Serves 6

I am a sucker for sorrel. My mother always grew it. The lemony flavour is perfect with fish. But many recipes do not warn that it turns into a 'gloopy' brown mess if cooked for more than an instant. In this recipe, add the sorrel to the sauce after the oysters, just as you are ready to spoon the sauce around the fish. The crunch of the cucumber pieces and the creamy oysters in the rich sauce are a good foil for the crisped snapper fillet. I enjoy the yeasty flavour that champagne brings to the dish but a fine dry wine will do just as well.

THE SAUCE

18 oysters
30 g (1 oz) butter
2 shallots, finely chopped
150 ml (5 fl oz) dry white wine
1 sprig fresh thyme
350 ml (11½ fl oz) pure cream (45% butterfat)
200 ml (7 fl oz) fish stock
300 ml (10 fl oz) champagne
salt and freshly ground white pepper

THE FISH

50–70 ml (2–2⅓ fl oz) vegetable oil
6 x 200 g (7 oz) snapper fillets
salt and freshly ground pepper

TO FINISH

1 medium-sized Lebanese cucumber, peeled, seeded and cut into julienne
12 large sorrel leaves, rolled and cut crosswise into fine strips

THE SAUCE Shuck the oysters and remove them from their shells, catching the juices over a bowl. Set the oysters aside. Pass the juices through a fine sieve and reserve. Melt the butter in a saucepan, add the shallots and cook without colouring for 2–3 minutes. Pour in the white wine, add the thyme and cook to evaporate all the liquid. Pour in the cream and the fish stock, lower the heat and simmer slowly until reduced by half. This could take up to 15 minutes depending on the size of your saucepan. Strain the liquid through a fine sieve into a clean saucepan. In a smaller saucepan, place the reserved oyster juices and champagne and reduce by half over medium heat. Add to the reduced cream mixture. Bring to the boil and lower the heat to a bare simmer. Adjust the seasoning.

THE FISH Preheat the oven to 200°C (400°F). Heat the oil over medium heat in either an ovenproof pan that will eventually be large enough to hold all the fillets, or use a smaller pan and have a baking tray ready. Season the fillets on both sides then sear them, two or three at a time, for about 2 minutes on each side until lightly browned. Transfer the pan or baking tray with all the fillets to the oven and roast for about 3–5 minutes until the fish is cooked. Remove the fillets from the oven and set aside, tented with foil, to keep warm while you finish the dish.

TO FINISH AND SERVE Add the cucumber to the warm sauce to heat it through then take the sauce off the heat. Add the oysters and chopped sorrel at the last moment and for no longer than 1 minute. Place one fish fillet in each of six warm shallow bowls. Spoon the sauce with the cucumber, sorrel and oysters over and around the snapper and serve.

Chapter Nine

PLUCKY BIRDS AND GAME FRIENDS

I grew up always having chooks in the backyard. My mother would bring the eggs inside when they were close to hatching and place them in a cottonwool-lined box under a heat lamp. Watching the chicks emerge was always a special treat. The demise of the hens and old boilers destined for the pot at the other end of their lives was not as pretty. Lopping heads had apparently been at some time decreed a man's job. My father, a shift worker and as such one of the few men available to do the job during the day, was frequently called out to neighbouring houses to perform the deed. Striding down the street axe in hand, he was quite a sight. Often he would return with some special home-baked slice or cake as payment of sorts.

CHICKEN

There's nothing like a free-roaming chicken for producing a delicious roast bird. Always try to buy the best you can. Mind you, 'free-range' can be a little misleading. Hens that are kept loose indoors might be labelled as such and are a great improvement to the battery hens kept in cages. But they are still usually very densely stocked and a long way from naturally grazing hens free to peck about eating grasses, seeds and grubs or those that feast on vegetable leftovers, scratch around, have dust baths and enjoy plenty of shell grit.

Demanding real free-range hens should eventually increase the breed varieties that are available. With the revival of commercial free-range farming, farmers have found battery breeds to be too inactive and aggressive to be let loose. Having been bred to have shorter legs, they find walking exhausting and frequently turn cannibal when left free to roam with other birds. As we the consumers show concern through our purchase choices about where our food is coming from and how it is harvested and raised, producers and retailers will listen. No doubt old breeds will be revived or crossbred to provide the traditionally more docile, happy, leggy hens of the past.

~ Assiette of chicken with summer herb bouillon ~

Makes 6 large portions

This dish looks like a chicken version of pot-au-feu but it is not. Rather than a robust broth in which various ingredients are poached, here the broth is refined, and the dish is served in summer when herbs are at their peak. The aroma of the herbed broth poured over the other ingredients at the table is an appetising precursor to the dish. The separate bits bathed in the broth are delicious but you can also serve the broth in a cup alongside. All the elements – herbed chicken, cabbage roll, sausage and herbed broth – can be cooked and enjoyed separately.

ROAST HERBED CHICKEN

6 sprigs tarragon, chopped

6 basil leaves, chopped

6 sprigs chervil, chopped

4 cloves garlic, peeled and chopped

salt and freshly ground pepper

3 tablespoons olive oil

6 'kieved' chicken breasts, skin on, all bones removed except first wing joint

50 ml (2 fl oz) oil for cooking

30 g (1 oz) butter for cooking

CHICKEN CABBAGE ROLLS

½ cup finely diced onion

1 tablespoon butter

450 g (1 lb) raw chicken leg and thigh meat, chopped

60 g (2 oz) chopped rindless Kaiser fleisch or bacon

1 teaspoon salt

freshly grated nutmeg

freshly ground white pepper

1 cup chilled thickened cream (35% butterfat)

½ cup fresh breadcrumbs made from good-quality day-old bread, crusts removed

ROAST HERBED CHICKEN Blend the herbs, garlic, salt and pepper in a mortar and pestle, add the olive oil and blend to a paste. Place a spoonful of the paste between the breast and skin of the chicken, spreading it over the breast. Place the breasts on a tray covered with plastic wrap and refrigerate for 12 hours. To cook the chicken, preheat the oven to 160°C (320°F) and season the chicken fillets. Heat the oil and butter in a pan and sear the breast skin over medium-to-high heat until nicely browned. Transfer the chicken to a shallow roasting dish and roast in one layer, skin side up, for 10–12 minutes or until the meat feels springy to the touch. Transfer the chicken to a warm platter and tent it with foil for a few minutes before serving.

CHICKEN CABBAGE ROLLS The suggested quantity makes about 10 small rolls or 6–8 larger ones. Ensure the mixture in this recipe remains cold throughout its preparation. Sweat the onion in the butter over gentle heat until soft then allow it to cool. Combine the raw chicken meat and bacon and sprinkle with the salt, 4 or 5 gratings of nutmeg and pepper. Add the cooled onion, combine well then chill. Pass the meat mixture through the medium plate of a mincer or divide the mixture in three and pulse each batch in turn in a processor until an even grind is achieved. It is important not to process the mixture into a paste. Ensure the mixture is cold before continuing.

Add half the cream to half the breadcrumbs and leave for a few minutes. Add this to the meat, beating it in with a wooden spoon. Beat the whisked egg into the mixture. If using, add the diced truffle and stir it through. Form a small patty and fry in a pan. Taste and adjust the seasoning. If the texture is too crumbly, add more crumbs and cream (you may not need the full quantity) using the process above.

1 egg, whisked with pinch of salt

10–15 g (½ oz) finely diced black truffle (optional)

12 large cabbage leaves (or sufficient medium-sized leaves to wrap number of rolls being made)

½ quantity Chicken Sausages (see page 245)

SUMMER HERB BOUILLON

1 kg (2 lb 3 oz) chicken wings, finely chopped (see method)

3 tablespoons oil

4 chicken carcasses, finely chopped

1 medium-sized onion, peeled and finely chopped

1 leek, white part only, finely chopped

100 g (3½ oz) button mushrooms, finely sliced

1 clove garlic, peeled and finely crushed

125 ml (4 oz) dry sherry

1.3 litres (44 fl oz) water

½ tablespoon tomato paste

6 black peppercorns, crushed

1 bay leaf

2 sprigs thyme

salt and freshly ground pepper

FRESH HERB GARNISH

6 sprigs tarragon, each divided into three

6 sprigs chervil, each divided into three

To finish the rolls, blanch the cabbage leaves for up to 5 minutes in boiling water then drain and refresh them in cold water. Flatten out any large veins with a rolling pin. Place each leaf on a square of plastic wrap and put 2 tablespoons of chicken farce on each. Roll each leaf into a ball shape using the plastic wrap. Twist and tie the ends, expelling as much air as possible. Place the cabbage rolls in the refrigerator to chill. This can be done up to a day in advance. When ready to serve, steam the rolls with the chicken sausages over a pot of boiling water for 5 minutes.

SUMMER HERB BOUILLON The ingredients only make about 750 ml (25 fl oz) of strongly flavoured broth so adjust quantities if you need more. To chop the chicken wings, use a cleaver or position a large cook's knife on the bones and tap its upper edge with a meat mallet. (When making the bouillon, I do a little preliminary browning and use tomato paste to add some colour. If you prefer you can sweat the ingredients in a saucepan without colouring and omit the paste.)

Preheat the oven to 220°C (425°F). On the stovetop, heat the oil in a large roasting dish over high heat. Add the chopped chicken wings and carcasses in batches, browning each batch for at least 5–6 minutes. As they are browned, transfer them to a large bowl. When all the chicken and bones are browned, place the onion, leek, mushrooms and garlic in the roasting dish and cook for 5 minutes until coloured. Return the chicken and bones to the dish with the vegetables and roast in the very hot oven for 16–18 minutes until they turn a rich brown. Remove from the oven and using tongs, transfer all the bones and vegetables to a large saucepan.

Tilt the roasting dish and spoon out any excess fat and discard. Add the sherry and 100 ml (3½ fl oz) of the water and scrape up any caramelised bits from the bottom of the dish and pour them into the saucepan. Add the tomato paste, peppercorns and herbs. Stir, cover with the remaining water and bring to the boil. Skim then simmer for 40 minutes, continually skimming during this time. Allow to cool a little then strain off and reserve the liquid. Discard the solids. Cool and refrigerate the bouillon. Remove and discard any fat from the surface. Pour into a clean saucepan and reduce to about 3 cups to intensify the flavour. Add salt and pepper.

TO SERVE Using six bowls, place one roasted herbed breast in each, along with a cabbage roll and two to three slices of sausage. Divide herbs among bowls and serve. Pour over hot bouillon at the table.

❧ Chicken sausage and chicken wings with sweet corn sauce ❧

Serves 6

This is a dish inspired by something I recently enjoyed at Alain Ducasse's Mix in Las Vegas. It is best done in late summer and early autumn when corn is at its delicious peak. Cooking the corn in this manner also produces a very flavoursome soup. Use a little additional stock or water to provide the appropriate consistency. A little truffle oil works well with the corn. The chicken wings are cooked confit-style. Duck fat is available from specialty poultry shops or make your own (see Duck Confit, page 189).

SWEET CORN SAUCE

2 cups fresh corn kernels, obtained from 6–8 ears of corn (see method)
50 g (2 oz) butter
2 cups water or chicken stock
150 ml (5 fl oz) thickened cream (35% butterfat)
¼ teaspoon white truffle oil
salt and freshly ground white pepper

CONFIT CHICKEN WINGS

10 coriander seeds
10 white peppercorns
4 teaspoons salt
3 cloves garlic, finely chopped
3 sprigs thyme
12 chicken wings, middle joint only
500 ml (17 fl oz) duck fat, melted

SWEET CORN SAUCE Shuck the corn and remove all the silky fibres. Hold the corn upright at an angle and run a serrated knife down the sides of the cob to release the kernels. Rotate the corn as you go. In a pan melt the butter over a low heat and add the corn, sautéing gently for 4–5 minutes. Do not allow to brown. Add the water or stock, bring to the boil and simmer for about 5 minutes until tender. As soon as it is cool enough, process the corn mix in a blender and pass through a fine tamis to obtain a fine purée. When ready to serve, reheat the purée with the cream. Add the truffle oil and season to taste.

CONFIT CHICKEN WINGS Grind the coriander seeds and peppercorns in a small grinder and combine with the salt, garlic and thyme. Rub the mix over the chicken wings then refrigerate them, covered, for at least 2 hours. Briefly rinse the salt mixture off the chicken wings and pat them dry. Place the wings in a small saucepan, cover with the melted duck fat and bring to a simmer. Reduce the heat to the lowest possible temperature and cook below a simmer for 2 hours. If it is impossible to achieve a low enough heat on your stovetop to ensure the liquid is not moving, transfer the wings and liquid to a pot then cover and bake in the oven at 125°C (255°F) for up to 3 hours. Cooking on the stovetop allows you to check more easily if the wings are done – they are ready when it is possible to slip the bones out with no effort.

Using tongs, remove the wings from the fat and allow them to cool. Remove the bones and cartilage. Place the wings on a tray, cover with another tray, weighed down with two or three cans, and refrigerate. Pass the duck fat through a fine sieve and refrigerate in a covered container for another use (see Duck Confit, page 189). To finish the chicken »

❖ recipe continued ❖

MUSHROOMS AND SAUSAGE

30 g (1 oz) butter

4 medium-sized fresh shiitake mushrooms, finely sliced

1 shallot, finely diced

salt and freshly ground pepper

1 quantity Chicken Sausages (see page 245), sliced

wings, preheat the oven to 200°C (400°F). Place the wings on a baking tray and roast in the oven for 5 minutes or until they are starting to colour. Reduce the heat to 175°C (340°F), turn the wings over and cook for about 4 minutes until crisp and golden. Drain the wings on a double thickness of kitchen paper then season and keep warm.

MUSHROOMS AND SAUSAGE Melt the butter in a pan over high heat. When foaming, add the sliced mushrooms and sauté for 2–3 minutes. Add the diced shallot and continue to cook for another 2 minutes. Season the mushrooms with salt and pepper. Add the sliced chicken sausage and gently heat through.

TO SERVE Spoon a pool of corn sauce onto six plates. Alternate three slices of sausage and two chicken wings on the sauce. Top with shallots and mushrooms. If desired, thin remaining sauce with a little stock. Adjust seasoning. Blitz with a hand-held beater and spoon over mushrooms.

DUCK

There has always been duck on Lake House menus. In the early days it was difficult to sell as Australian diners had suffered a surfeit of badly cooked duck. The problem was that 'high end' cooking in those days inevitably involved classic French dishes highly unsuited to the duck breeds then available in Australia. It was nigh impossible to produce a glorious rare duck breast with what was available. The available duck breeds were better suited to a braise or a confit. This was especially so for the occasional locally supplied free-range birds. These were very flavoursome but generally scrawnier and stringier than farmed ducks. All that foraging made for a leaner bird. Duck braised with figs and port was the duck dish with which we opened in 1984. Confit duck re-roasted in many guises followed.

Eventually crossbreeds of Pekin and Muscovy ducks were produced with generous-sized breasts approximating the highly desirable French *magret*. This extension to available varieties has meant considerable growth in our repertoire of duck dishes. Duck quite often outsells everything else on our menus.

CONFIT

Many recipes for confit are generally ignored. All that puddling around with fat! The result could not be any good for you. I remember demonstrating a dish involving duck confit for a television program that resulted in a deluge of letters asking whether the dish could be completed in some 'leaner' manner. I must have been a dismal presenter or perhaps it was the editing, but clearly the essence of what a confit was about had been lost on the audience. Although the confit process involves considerable amounts of both salt and fat, the end product should be neither oversalty nor fatty. The meat first salted and set aside, then rinsed, dried and simmered in fat until tender, retains excellent flavour and succulence.

Originally a way of preserving meat when refrigeration was not available, confit can become a good cook's fast food.

If you've embarked on the confit process (see following page) and now wish to use it for a quick meal, remove the container from the refrigerator and place it somewhere warm. It is best to have the fat soft in order to retrieve your duck pieces. Using clean hands, reach into the fat and remove the pieces you need, scraping excess fat from the duck and your hands. If there is more confit left you can return it to the refrigerator as long as it is used within the week. Otherwise remove all remaining pieces, place in a clean container, reheat the fat and strain it over the duck once again.

The removed duck pieces can be seared, skin side down, in a large heavy pan for at least 6–8 minutes until they form a lovely crust, and then finished slowly in the oven on a low heat (140°C/280°F) while you prepare any accompaniments. Alternatively all the cooking may be done in the oven at 200°C (400°F) for 15 minutes until the duck is crisp. Served with potatoes and a simple green salad, you have a delicious and quick dinner on a work night. For something a little more special roast the duck meat as described, but sit it on the Witlof Salad (see page 132) topping the Crostini with our Duck Liver Parfait (page 238) instead of the blue cheese.

The term 'confit' is now used to refer to a slow-cooking process (rather than a preserving process) that utilises fat or even oil as the medium. You may have come across references to confit tomatoes and garlic. Elsewhere in this book there are recipes for Confit Chicken Wings (see page 185) and Confit of Tuna (see page 168).

Duck confit

Serves 6

This recipe is for 4 duck legs but I suggest you do more and have that wonderful bounty in the refrigerator. If, on the other hand, you have bought a couple of big-breasted birds, do not waste the breasts with all their wonderful succulence. Pan-sear and oven-roast them using the method in Glazed Roast Duck Breast (see page 195) and confit the legs. The amount of duck fat required will depend on the size of saucepan used. It is essential to have the meat completely covered with fat while cooking. Rendered duck fat can be purchased from good poultry shops.

4 large duck legs (leg and thigh)
⅔ cup coarse salt
1 teaspoon black peppercorns, crushed
½ teaspoon juniper berries, crushed
2 sprigs fresh thyme
2 cloves garlic, crushed
1 litre (34 fl oz) duck fat (or about 500 ml/17 fl oz duck fat to 500 g/1 lb 2 oz meat)

Rinse the duck legs and pat them dry. Combine the salt, crushed peppercorns and berries and rub the mix into the duck pieces. Place a little of the salt–spice mix in the base of a glass, ceramic or enamel dish with the thyme and garlic. Lay the duck pieces, skin side down, on top and sprinkle with the remaining salt mix. Cover with plastic wrap and refrigerate for 12 hours, turning the duck pieces over after 6 hours. Rinse the duck pieces under running water but do not soak. Dry thoroughly with a clean towel or kitchen paper.

In a saucepan large enough to fit the duck pieces in a relatively crowded fashion, melt the duck fat and immerse the duck pieces, ensuring they are completely covered in fat. Cook at a bare simmer for about 1 hour until the duck is tender but still has some spring. Overcooking will produce a dry texture. Using tongs, remove the duck pieces from the fat. You can choose to store the duck legs boned especially if you are not fussed about whether you eventually serve the legs intact or just as duck meat. If so, allow them to cool enough to handle and carefully remove all the bones. These will come out with a little tugging and twisting. Discard the bones and place the duck portions (4 legs and 4 thighs) into a sealable, scrupulously clean or sterilised jar or crock.

Let the pot of duck fat sit for a little to allow any meat juices to fall to the bottom. It is important that these juices are not combined with the preserving fat. Ladle out the fat carefully through a sieve onto the duck pieces, without stirring up any of those meat juices from the bottom. Continue until the duck pieces are entirely covered with fat to a depth of at least 2 cm (¾ in). Cover and refrigerate until needed. The confit will keep for up to 2 months.

❧ Duck broth ❧

Makes about 750 ml (25 fl oz)

If you are doing the duck thing anyway – go the whole way. Pick up those extra duck necks to make the cracklings from the skin (see page opposite) and ask for a couple of extra carcasses. Chicken soup may be the medicine of many cultures but a rich dark nourishing duck broth lends itself to the addition of wonderful spices and aromatics. Once it is done slip in some noodles, bok choy and a little duck confit or some Duck Neck Sausages (see page 246) and you have a sublime and quick meal.

700 g (1 lb 9 oz) duck neck bones and carcasses, chopped, and wing tips, carcasses and any meat scraps well washed and dried
2–3 tablespoons clean duck fat
1 carrot, peeled and chopped
1 onion, peeled and chopped
1 celery stalk, chopped
1 cup dry white wine
1.3 litres (44 fl oz) chicken stock
2 cloves garlic, crushed
1 bay leaf
fresh thyme

Preheat the oven to 230°C (445°F). Place the duck bones and trimmings together with the duck fat in a heavy roasting pan over a high heat. Brown the bones, adding the carrot, onion and celery about halfway through. Place the pan in the hot oven and continue to roast for about 20 minutes, stirring the contents of the pan from time to time and do not allow them to burn. Remove the roasting pan from the oven, spoon the contents onto several layers of kitchen paper to drain then place them in a clean saucepan.

Pour off any fat remaining in the roasting pan. Place it on the heat, add the wine and cook, scraping up any caramelised bits. Boil and cook for 5 minutes then pour into the saucepan with the vegetables and bones. Add the stock, garlic and herbs. The contents should be covered by liquid, otherwise add a little water. Bring to a simmer, skimming any foam that rises to the surface. Continue to cook uncovered for 1½–2 hours, until the stock is a good colour and well flavoured. Strain immediately, refrigerate to cool then remove any fat. Bring to the boil and reduce to increase the flavour. Season appropriately and use as desired. Ginger, a little star anise and even orange zest make pleasant infusions.

DUCK SKIN CRACKLINGS

If you have been dealing with a whole duck you will be left with the neck. If the process of making crackling appeals to you it is worth asking your poultry supplier for a few extra necks when you are purchasing your duck. The process is simple and the result is delicious. The cracklings are a great addition to duck salads as well as being useful in some of the duck dishes featured on the following pages.

6–8 duck necks
cold water
salt

Remove the skin from the necks. The bony necks can be saved for the Duck Broth (see previous page), but if not my dogs always make short shrift of this special treat. Chop the neck skins into small pieces and place in a pot. Add sufficient cold water to just cover by a finger width then simmer over low heat. The simmering process softens the skin and as the water slowly evaporates the duck fat is rendered from the skin. After about 30 minutes of gentle cooking you should be able to strain off the clear golden fat. Strain and reserve it for confit or just for cooking (if you have not tasted potatoes cooked in a little duck fat, you are in for a treat). Continue to cook the skins in a pan until browned and crisp. Drain off any excess fat and strain and reserve it as before. Drain the cracklings on several folds of kitchen paper and salt while still warm.

Roasted confit duck in coriander crêpe

Serves 6

Here crêpe-wrapped re-roasted confit duck draws on the notion of Peking duck. The sweet–sour caramelised sauce, a gastrique, carrying a touch of orange, nods to the classic duck à l'orange. The dish works well for large dinners as the sauce can be made in advance and the warm crêpe-wrapped duck can be held in the oven while you finish the vegetables. We serve it with a little cup of spiced Duck Broth (see page 190) as a digestif. The method for the Orange Gastrique is worth conquering, even for the domestic kitchen.

1 quantity Orange Gastrique (see page 287)

THE CRÊPES
½ quantity crêpe batter (see Plain Crêpes, page 283)
1 teaspoon finely chopped coriander (cilantro)

THE VEGETABLES
2 medium-sized carrots, finely sliced on mandoline and cut into julienne
2 medium-sized leeks, white part only, split, washed and cut into julienne
100 g (3½ oz) butter
2 shallots, finely chopped
small knob of fresh ginger, peeled and very finely chopped
3 small zucchini (courgettes), finely sliced on mandoline and cut into julienne
salt and freshly ground pepper

THE DUCK
6 confit duck legs (leg and thigh), boned (removed from under fat, see Duck Confit, page 189)

GARNISH (OPTIONAL)
Candied Orange Rind (see page 291)
Citrus Powder (see page 291)

THE CRÊPES Just before frying the crêpes stir through the chopped coriander then proceed to cook as described. Set the crêpes aside until ready to use.

THE VEGETABLES Bring a saucepan of water to the boil and add salt. Blanch the carrot julienne for 1 minute then drain and refresh in iced water. Drain again and dry on kitchen paper. Repeat this process with the leeks.

THE DUCK Cook the duck pieces (you should have 12 in total, 2 from each leg) as described on page 189. When crisp on the outside and heated through wrap two pieces in each coriander crêpe and return to a warm oven (150°C/300°F) to hold.

TO FINISH THE VEGETABLES Heat the butter in a pan over moderate heat and when foaming add the shallots and ginger. Cook to soften but not colour. Add the zucchini and toss to coat it well in butter. Add the blanched vegetables, cook without colouring for 2–3 minutes then season.

TO ASSEMBLE Place a mound of gingered vegetables on each plate. Place a coriander crepe containing duck confit on each. Spoon a little of the gastrique around. If desired top the crêpe with some candied orange rind and sprinkle with citrus powder.

Glazed roast duck breast with duck and potato galette

Serves 6

This dish utilises the large duck breasts suitable for roasting rare as well as confit duck legs. The split-style sauce, or broken vinaigrette, is deliberately not emulsified and separates into beads of colour when spooned onto the plate. Duck and potatoes have a natural synergy. Add a little garlic and you are in seriously memorable territory. The layered duck and potato galette, made in advance, is caramelised to a golden brown before serving. Although part of a more elaborate recipe here, it makes a nice casual lunch dish with the addition of a little well-dressed salad.

DUCK AND POTATO GALETTES

3 confit duck legs (leg and thigh), boned
    (see Duck Confit, page 189)
salt and freshly ground pepper
1 kg (2 lb 3 oz) peeled potatoes
200 g (7 oz) butter or duck fat
2 cloves garlic, crushed
3 sprigs thyme

GARNISH AND ACCOMPANIMENTS (OPTIONAL)

Walnut Crumble (see page 282)
Duck Skin Cracklings (see page 191)
Caramelised Witlof (see page 297)

DUCK AND POTATO GALETTES Chop the duck confit leg meat, divide it into six portions and season with a little salt and pepper. Set aside. Slice the potatoes into 2 mm ($1/8$ in) slices, preferably with a mandoline. Melt the butter or duck fat in a pan over moderate heat with the garlic and thyme sprigs. Add the potatoes in batches, coating them in butter or fat and cooking until just translucent. Remove each batch from the pan with a slotted spoon and put into a colander to drain off any excess butter or fat. Discard the thyme and garlic. Season the potatoes well with salt and pepper and mix through.

Preheat the oven to 170°C (340°F). Set six 10 cm (4 in) diameter ring moulds on non-stick baking trays. Distribute one-third of the potato slices among the rings, spreading a layer in the base of each. Top each potato layer with half a portion of duck meat. Cover with another third of the sliced potatoes and the remaining half portion of duck. Cover with remaining potato slices. You should have three layers of potato and two layers of duck in each galette. Press to seal and straighten the surface. Cover with foil and put in the preheated oven for approximately 30 minutes. Take off the foil, remove the rings and press the galettes overnight under a light chopping board or similar. »

DUCK GLAZE

1½ teaspoons ground star anise
1 cinnamon stick
4 cloves
½ cup freshly grated ginger
1 cup rice wine vinegar
2 cups reduced salt soy sauce
2 cups pomegranate molasses
4 cups orange juice
1 cup honey
6 x 200 g (7 oz) duck breasts, boned

SALAD GARNISH

1 very ripe pear, cored and finely sliced
60 g (2 oz) small rocket (arugula) leaves
1 tablespoon Basic Vinaigrette (see page 284)
120 ml (4 fl oz) additional Basic Vinaigrette

❧ recipe continued ❧

DUCK GLAZE In a large saucepan combine the star anise, cinnamon stick, cloves and ginger and warm over medium heat, stirring for 2 minutes. Stir in the rice wine vinegar, soy sauce, pomegranate molasses, orange juice and honey. Bring to a simmer, reduce the heat to low and simmer for 45 minutes or until reduced to just over 1 cup. Strain the glaze through a chinois or fine mesh and set it aside until needed.

COOKING DUCK BREASTS AND GALETTES Preheat the oven to 160°C (320°F). Place the galettes on a non-stick baking tray and reheat for 15 minutes, increasing the temperature to 180°C (350°F) for a further 5 minutes. Score the duck breasts in a crosshatch pattern, making sure the marks cut through the fat but do not penetrate the meat. Season then pan-fry the breasts, skin side down, for 2½ minutes. Turn the breasts over and sear for 1 minute. Generously brush both sides of the breasts with the glaze. Reserve the remaining glaze. Place the breasts, skin side down, on a baking tray and roast at 180°C (350°F) for 4 minutes (rare). You can roast the breasts together with the galettes if you wish. Transfer the breasts to a warm plate and rest for 3 minutes.

SALAD GARNISH Toss the pear slices and rocket leaves with the tablespoon of vinaigrette. Add sufficient warmed duck glaze to the vinaigrette to make a syrupy 'split' sauce.

TO FINISH Place a caramelised potato and duck galette on each plate. If using, place a piece of caramelised witlof on top. Slice the warm duck breast thinly and arrange on the witlof. Garnish with the pear salad. Sprinkle the crumble over the top and spoon the split dressing around the plate.

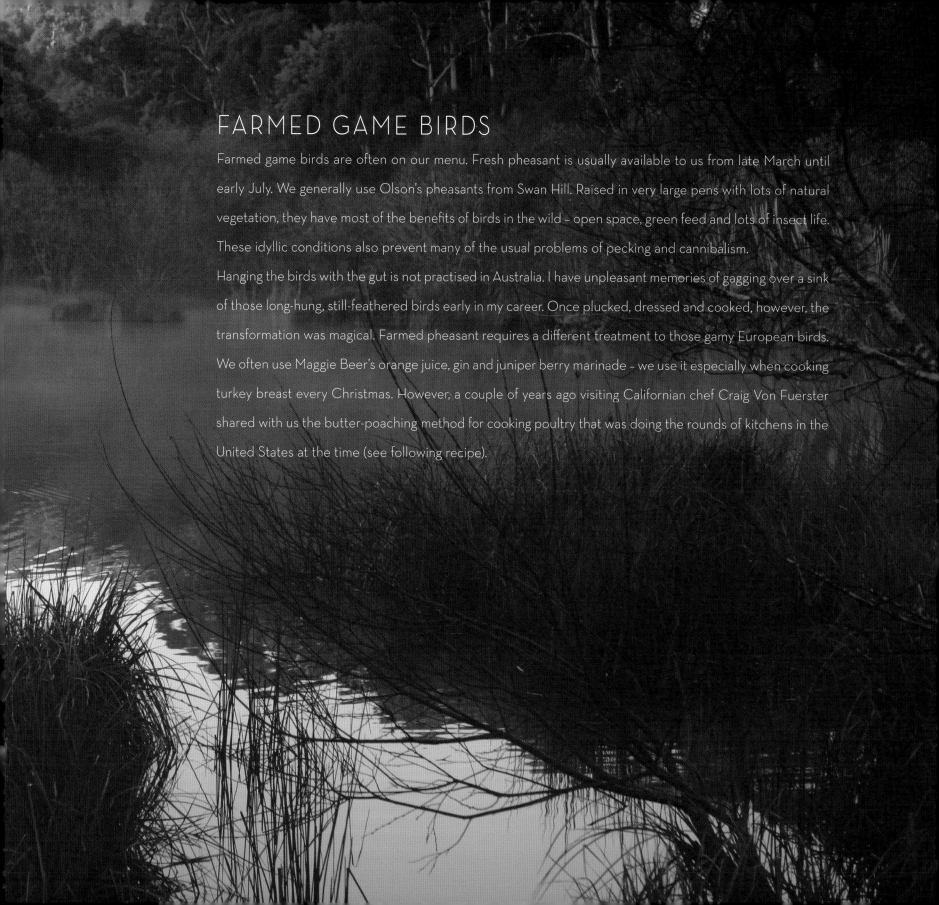

FARMED GAME BIRDS

Farmed game birds are often on our menu. Fresh pheasant is usually available to us from late March until early July. We generally use Olson's pheasants from Swan Hill. Raised in very large pens with lots of natural vegetation, they have most of the benefits of birds in the wild – open space, green feed and lots of insect life. These idyllic conditions also prevent many of the usual problems of pecking and cannibalism.

Hanging the birds with the gut is not practised in Australia. I have unpleasant memories of gagging over a sink of those long-hung, still-feathered birds early in my career. Once plucked, dressed and cooked, however, the transformation was magical. Farmed pheasant requires a different treatment to those gamy European birds. We often use Maggie Beer's orange juice, gin and juniper berry marinade – we use it especially when cooking turkey breast every Christmas. However, a couple of years ago visiting Californian chef Craig Von Fuerster shared with us the butter-poaching method for cooking poultry that was doing the rounds of kitchens in the United States at the time (see following recipe).

With this dish, if you rigorously stick to the timing and required temperature you will get a perfectly moist and succulent result every time. The quantity of butter needed to keep the breasts submerged depends on the size saucepan you use. A small one that still manages to fit two breasts side by side is ideal. The method for producing a crisp pheasant skin delivers a delicious touch otherwise lost when you are not roasting the bird. Pearl barley combined with mushrooms is a good seasonal foil for the pheasant. The intense mushroom emulsion that garnishes the dish provides added depth of flavour.

Butter-poached pheasant breast with barley and mushrooms

Serves 4

BARLEY AND MUSHROOMS

1 cup pearl barley, cooked (see Cooking Barley, page 280), combined with:
   1 cup Ragout of Wild Mushrooms (see page 136)
   1 teaspoon freshly chopped tarragon
1 quantity Mushroom Emulsion (see page 287), prepared to the stage just prior to adding chilled butter, and kept warm

THE PHEASANTS

2 x 1.2 kg (2 lb 10 oz) pheasants or
   4 pheasant breasts
salt and freshly ground pepper
½ cup water
2 kg (4 lb 6 oz) butter
3 sprigs thyme
30 g (1 oz) duck fat

THE PHEASANTS If using whole pheasants, detach the wing tip and first wing joint from the birds. Slice down along the breastbone of each bird to detach the breasts. Pull the skin off the breasts and reserve it. Hold the wing bone remaining in each breast and scrape it clean of meat, trimming its length French-style, with poultry shears. You should have four skinless breasts with the first wing bone cleaned and protruding. Season the breasts with salt and pepper and set aside. (The pheasant wings, legs and carcasses can be reserved for another use. The legs, which tend to be lean and stringy, are best cooked confit style. The meat picked off can be used in ravioli as a garnish. Any remaining pheasant bits can be added to stock.)

In a saucepan, heat the water over medium heat then add the butter, one piece at a time, whisking constantly until all the butter is incorporated. Season with salt and pepper and add the fresh thyme. Keep this beurre fondue at 80–85°C (175–180°F).

Preheat the oven to 175°C (340°F). Brush the reserved pheasant skin with the duck fat and season with salt and pepper. Lay the skin flat between sheets of baking paper and place between two flat baking trays. Place in the oven, cook for 20 minutes then remove the skin from the oven and keep warm.

Slip the breasts into the beurre fondue, two at a time, and cook for 10–12 minutes. Remove the breasts with tongs and keep warm, tented with foil, while cooking the other two breasts. Season the breasts again before serving. (The beurre fondue can be strained after using and kept in the refrigerator for sautéing meat, mushrooms or other vegetables. The extra flavour imparted is akin to using chicken stock.)

TO ASSEMBLE Combine cooked barley, mushroom ragout and tarragon in a saucepan and heat through. Finish the mushroom emulsion with the chilled butter, as described, and blitz with the hand-held blender to emulsify. Spoon some mushrooms and barley into individual flat bowls. Slice the pheasant breasts and place on top. Spoon a little mushroom emulsion over and around. Top with crisp skin.

Spiced quail with noodle cake and Asian salad

Serves 6

Farmed quail are succulent and delicious little birds that require very little cooking and easily take on the flavour of a marinade. If we are butterflying quail we part-bone it, leaving in the leg and wing bones to preserve some shape but also to encourage picking of the delicious morsels of meat from around the bone.

1 quantity Aromatic Carrot Emulsion (see page 286)
6 large quail, each split in half with ribcage, spine and wingtips removed

QUAIL MARINADE

¼ cup orange juice
¼ cup sugar
¼ cup red wine vinegar
1 tablespoon tomato paste
2 tablespoons light soy sauce
2 tablespoons fish sauce
1 piece star anise
1 large clove garlic, peeled and chopped
1 tablespoon chopped ginger

NOODLE CAKES

200 g (7 oz) buckwheat noodles
½ cup coriander (cilantro) leaves
4 large spring onion (scallion) tips, finely sliced on the diagonal
1 teaspoon freshly grated ginger
1 clove garlic, peeled and chopped
2 teaspoons rice vinegar
salt and freshly ground pepper
6 tablespoons vegetable oil

QUAIL MARINADE Combine all the ingredients. Place the quail halves in a shallow non-reactive dish and coat evenly with the marinade. Stand overnight or for at least 6 hours.

NOODLE CAKES Blanch the noodles in salted boiling water until tender, drain then refresh in iced water. Drain again immediately. In a large stainless steel bowl combine the noodles, coriander, spring onion, ginger, garlic and rice vinegar and season to taste. Place well-greased 6 cm (¾ in) wide metal rings in a non-stick pan. Put 1 tablespoon of vegetable oil in the base of each ring, followed by enough noodle mixture to fill three-quarters of the ring. Place the pan on a moderate heat and cook the cakes for 4 minutes on each side, until crisp on the outside but tender and soft on the inside. Remove the cakes, in their rings, from the pan and place them on kitchen paper. Remove the rings from the cakes once slightly cooled. Repeat the process until all the noodle mixture is used. The cakes can be reheated in the oven at 170°C (340°F) for 5 minutes.

QUAIL SALAD DRESSING

100 g (3½ oz) palm sugar

½ piece star anise

½ small chilli, seeded and finely chopped

pulp and zest of 1 orange, roughly chopped

50 ml (2 fl oz) water

2 teaspoons lime juice

1 teaspoon fish sauce

salt and freshly ground pepper

QUAIL SALAD

1 carrot, peeled, finely sliced on mandoline then cut into julienne

1 daikon, peeled, finely sliced on mandoline then cut into julienne

200 g (7 oz) snow peas, cut into julienne

1 spring onion (scallion), sliced

2 tablespoons coriander (cilantro) leaves, washed and chopped

4 mint leaves, cut into julienne

QUAIL SALAD DRESSING Combine the palm sugar, star anise, chilli, orange and water in a small pan and bring to the boil. Lower the heat and simmer until the liquid has a syrupy consistency. Remove from the heat and strain. Add the lime juice and fish sauce. Taste and adjust the seasoning then allow the dressing to cool.

TO COOK QUAIL Preheat the oven to 175°C (340°F). Remove the quail from the marinade and drain it for a few minutes on several layers of kitchen paper. Pat dry then season with salt and pepper on both sides. Spread a thin film of oil over the surface of a large non-stick pan, heat and put in as many quail halves, skin side down, as can be accommodated without crowding. Cook for 2 minutes over medium-to-high heat to ensure the quail is crisp and coloured but not burned. Turn the quail over and sear the other side for 30 seconds. Place the seared quail halves, skin side up, on a non-stick baking tray. Repeat the pan-frying process with the remaining quail. Place the baking tray with all the quail on it in the preheated oven and cook for a further 3 minutes.

QUAIL SALAD Combine all the ingredients and toss with the salad dressing.

TO ASSEMBLE Reheat the noodle cakes if required. Reheat the carrot emulsion over medium heat and emulsify with a hand-held blender. Place a noodle cake on each plate. Place two quail halves on top, overlapping each other in a crisscross fashion. Top each with a small amount of the dressed salad, drizzle carrot emulsion around and serve.

Cabbage roll of boned quail with pork farce and roasting juices

Serves 8

Larissa tells me that there is something very proletarian about my always wanting to put things into cabbage rolls. It is certainly a harkening back to my parents' cooking. Both of them made fabulous cabbage rolls. This dish is inspired by a course offered us by friend, colleague and renowned Australian chef Jacques Reymond for our splendid Two Decades Dinner. His was much more glamorous, held together by pandanus leaves and had a different farce. Mine is absolutely the more proletarian version.

THE FARCE

2 cups stock (or sufficient to cover)

2 cloves

1 star anise

2 cloves garlic, peeled and crushed

⅓ teaspoon chopped chilli

4 peppercorns

3½ tablespoons soy sauce

zest of 1 orange

500 g (1 lb 2 oz) boneless belly pork, skin removed

4 tablespoons hoisin sauce

⅓ bunch coriander (cilantro), well washed and finely chopped

½ tablespoon very fine julienne of ginger

1 tablespoon finely diced shallot

¼ teaspoon fine julienne of chilli

½ tablespoon olive oil

8 large cabbage leaves (or sufficient medium-sized leaves to wrap quail)

8 large boned quail

salt and freshly ground pepper

sautéed sliced shiitake mushrooms for garnishing (optional)

THE FARCE Preheat the oven to 200°C (400°F). Combine the stock, cloves, star anise, garlic, chopped chilli and peppercorns with 1½ tablespoons of the soy sauce and half the orange zest. Place the pork belly in a snug-fitting, shallow baking dish and pour the poaching liquid over it. Place the dish in the preheated oven and after 15 minutes reduce the heat to 190°C (375°F) and continue to bake for a further 1¾ hours or until the pork is completely tender. When cooked, remove the pork from the liquid and allow to cool. Reserve the liquid, cool then chill and remove any fat that rises to surface. Chop the pork into small pieces and combine with the hoisin sauce, coriander and remaining soy sauce and orange zest. Combine the ginger, shallot, julienne of chilli and olive oil in a pan over medium heat and sweat until the ingredients have softened. Add the contents of the pan to the pork mix.

WRAPPING THE ROLLS Blanch the cabbage leaves for up to 5 minutes in boiling water. Drain and refresh in cold water. Flatten out the large veins of the cabbage leaves with a rolling pin if necessary. Place 8 x 20 cm (8 in) squares of plastic wrap on your work surface. Lay the cabbage leaves in the centre of each square. Spread a boned quail on each, skin side down, and season with salt and pepper. Place a tablespoon of farce in the centre of each quail. Pull up the corners of the plastic wrap, taking the quail and cabbage leaves with them and forming a ball shape. Twist the plastic wrap at the top and tie, expelling as much air as possible from the roll. Refrigerate until ready for cooking. »

❖ recipe continued ❖

COOKING AND SERVING Preheat the oven to 200°C (400°F). Pour the reserved degreased pork cooking liquid into a baking pan (large enough to hold the eight quail rolls snugly) and place in the oven to heat the liquid. Meanwhile steam the quail rolls, in plastic wrap, over boiling water for 5 minutes or until just set. Remove the rolls with tongs and remove the plastic wrap. Tie two foil ties around each roll to help keep it intact. Place the rolls in the hot baking pan and cook in the preheated oven for 18 minutes. Remove from oven, remove foil from rolls and serve each one, seam side down, in a flat bowl. Taste the cooking liquid and adjust seasoning if required. If using, add the sautéed sliced mushrooms to the bowl. Pour a little of the strained cooking juices over the top of each quail.

RABBIT AND HARE

Years of drought and various government initiatives have substantially reduced the easy procurement of wild rabbit in Australia. Introduced by the early settlers rabbits soon reached plague proportions and became a staple diet of Australians during the depression. Hence the lack of its popularity during the evolution of what is now Modern Australian cooking. With no such personal predisposition, for me the flavour of wild rabbit remains a firm favourite in a simple stew or in a pie. My father told tales of collecting rabbits by tearing down country lanes with the headlight protectors off his car in the years of rationing in war-torn Europe. Bagging the road kill he would stop at nearby farms to barter the meat in exchange for a little flour, pork fat, sugar or some other necessity. When I was young, his fricasseed rabbit with white wine was a frequent treat.

Nowadays our local Daylesford butcher alerts us to the availability of 'a bit of bunny'. Farmed rabbit is another beast altogether. Much larger and yielding considerably more meat, it lacks the distinctive flavour of its cousin in the wild.

Rich dark hare meat is another favourite. Whenever I braise rabbit or hare I remove the fillets and reserve them for another use. Just as with the breast meat on birds, the fillets require a different style of cooking.

❖ Rabbit rillettes ❖

Makes up to 1 kg (2 lb 3 oz)

Rabbit rillettes were on my very first menu, served at the table out of a large white porcelain rabbit-shaped terrine with toasted house-made brioche and baby cornichons. Nowadays it is often part of a rabbit assiette or our Changing Plate and is even used as a filling for ravioli. In the earliest incarnations my rillettes relied mostly on the richness of pork fat to provide the requisite moistness in the dish. In this recipe the cooking liquid is enhanced with veal bones and reduced almost to a jellied consistency to produce rillettes that are just as satisfyingly moist and with good flavour.

3–4 small-to-medium-sized wild rabbits (the farmed variety will not provide the flavour here)
300 g (10½ oz) lean fresh belly pork, cut into pieces
3–4 veal knuckles
3 sprigs thyme
1 bay leaf
3 whole cloves garlic
2 parts water to 1 part white wine, to just cover
3 additional sprigs thyme
3 cloves garlic, finely chopped
salt and freshly ground pepper

Remove the fillets from the rabbits (reserve for another use). Remove and discard the lungs, heart and liver. Remove the forelegs, hind legs and belly flaps and place them in a heavy saucepan with the pork, veal knuckles, thyme, bay leaf and cloves of garlic. Chop the rabbit carcass in two and add to the pot. Cover with the water and wine and cook over a very gentle heat at a bare simmer, until the pork is tender and the rabbit meat comes away from the bones easily. Remove the saucepan from the heat and allow the meat to cool in the liquid. Strain through a colander and place the liquid in the refrigerator. Discard the rabbit carcasses and veal bones.

Pick the rabbit and pork meat from the bones and shred it with your fingers until all the meat is in fibres and no lumps remain. Cover the meat with wet greaseproof paper to stop it from drying out. Skim any fat that has set at the top of the chilled poaching liquid. Pour the liquid into a saucepan with the chopped thyme leaves and chopped garlic, bring to the boil, skim and reduce by half. Add the shredded rabbit and pork and cook very gently for about 10 minutes, adding salt and pepper, and allowing the seasonings to be redistributed. During this time the meat will reabsorb the well-flavoured reduced rabbit juices.

Put the meat into glass or porcelain containers. If desired, seal the top from air with melted duck fat or butter. The flavour of the rillettes improves with time. Refrigerated and kept sealed with butter or fat they may be stored, if untouched, for at least a month.

❦ Spiced rabbit with Tunisian pastry and harissa ❦

Serves 6

This recipe yields a flavoursome rabbit braise in a russet-coloured sauce, which can be served simply with couscous or soft polenta. Braising can be done on your stovetop or in the oven as long as the cooking is slow and steady. The thickening of the braising juices is achieved through reduction, and puréeing the onions cooked with the meat. The fillets, packaged in pastry turnovers, are fried and served with the braise. A little harissa and a parsley salad are added embellishments.

3 medium-sized rabbits

RABBIT FILLET MARINADE

6 sprigs coriander (cilantro)
1 teaspoon ground cumin
1 teaspoon ground coriander seeds
2 tablespoons vegetable oil

RABBIT BRAISE

1 teaspoon ground toasted cumin seeds
1 teaspoon ground toasted coriander seeds
pinch of dried ginger, ground cinnamon, cayenne pepper, ground cloves and ground turmeric
vegetable oil for cooking
50 g (2 oz) butter
2 large brown onions, finely sliced
½ whole head of garlic
500 ml (17 fl oz) rabbit stock (if made from the carcasses) or chicken stock
300 ml (10 fl oz) tomato juice

RABBITS The rabbits need to be jointed, with the fillets removed and reserved to use in the marinade. The foreleg and hind leg pieces are used in the braise. (The hearts, lungs and livers are removed and discarded. The carcasses can be chopped and used to make the stock if desired.) You can use farmed rabbits here but they tend to be much larger so two are likely to be sufficient — you will need to make adjustments for this in the method. Many suppliers sell fillets of rabbit, in case you need extra of those.

RABBIT FILLET MARINADE Chop the fresh coriander sprigs finely and add the ground cumin and coriander seeds. Remove the shiny membrane from the rabbit fillets and discard. Drizzle the fillets with a little oil and roll them in the spice–coriander mix. Cover and leave to marinate in the refrigerator.

RABBIT BRAISE In a bowl, combine the toasted cumin and coriander with the ginger, cinnamon, cayenne, cloves and turmeric. Roll the rabbit forelegs and hind legs in this spice mix. Spread a film of oil on the base of a deep pan and heat. Add the butter and fry the spiced rabbit leg pieces until browned on all sides. Set the rabbit aside.

Add a little more oil to the pan if necessary and sauté the sliced onions, stirring frequently to scrape up any spices, until the onions are softened and beginning to caramelise. Return the browned spiced rabbit leg pieces to the pan, placing them on top of the onions. Add the half head of garlic, rabbit or chicken stock to just cover and simmer gently for about 45 minutes or until the rabbit is cooked but is just holding onto the bone on the back legs. Remove the rabbit and set aside. Remove the garlic and discard.

Add 50 ml (2 fl oz) of the tomato juice and any remaining stock to the pan. Bring to the boil, reduce the heat and continue to simmer, stirring occasionally to ensure »

✧ recipe continued ✧

RABBIT PASTRIES

24 Tunisian (brik) pastry rounds (if unavailable use filo pastry; see Variation)

2 egg whites, whisked with a pinch of salt

2 tablespoons finely chopped fresh coriander (cilantro)

salt and freshly ground pepper

vegetable oil for frying

GARNISH

Parsley, Pine Nut and Currant Salad (see page 297)

Harissa (see page 289)

the onions do not catch. Continue to reduce the liquid to concentrate the flavour and break down the onions, adding a little more tomato juice if the level drops too low. Once you have a thickish, aromatic, rusty caramel-coloured braise pass it through a tamis or fine sieve and return it to the pan. Adjust the seasoning.

While the rabbit legs are still warm, strip the meat from the bones in large pieces. Store the meat, moistened in some of the sauce and tightly packed in a container, under wet greaseproof paper to avoid it drying out. The meat can be reheated in the sauce as required.

RABBIT PASTRIES Use kitchen paper to pat the marinated fillets dry then cut them into ½ cm ($^1/_8$ in) thick slices. Place the sliced fillets in a bowl and combine with sufficient of the rabbit braising liquid to just coat. Lay out 12 pastry circles. Brush with the whisked egg white and sprinkle with chopped coriander. Place another pastry round on top of each and brush with whisked egg white again. Place slices of rabbit – the equivalent of half a fillet – on the bottom half of each double-layered pastry round and season with salt and pepper. Fold the doubled pastry over the rabbit slices to make turnovers. Store on a tray until ready to cook.

TO FINISH AND SERVE Reheat the stored rabbit meat in the sauce. Adjust the seasoning as necessary. Spread a film of oil on the base of a large frying pan and place over medium heat. When ready to serve the dish, fry the rabbit pastries for approximately 1 minute on each side or until golden brown and crisp. Spoon some rabbit braise onto each plate and top with two pastries. Garnish with parsley salad, harissa and a little yoghurt if desired.

VARIATION USING FILO PASTRY If you have difficulty sourcing the Tunisian pastry use filo as follows. Stack three sheets of filo on top of one another, sprinkling chopped coriander and brushing melted butter in between each layer. Cut 10 cm (4 in) diameter circles from the pastry. Top each circle with rabbit fillet slices as described above, brush the pastry edges with the whisked egg white and fold over to seal and create turnovers. Repeat with more filo until you have made 12 filled pastries. Place the pastries on a non-stick baking tray, brush the top of them with melted butter and bake in a preheated oven at 180°C (350°F) for 12–15 minutes until golden.

❖ Braised hare with shallots and mushrooms, roasted fillet ❖ and soft polenta

Serves 4

This recipe requires dusting the hare with a little flour and slow-cooking in the oven. I offer two different finishing treatments for the basic braise. The hare fillets are cooked separately – roasted rare while still attached to the carcass, rested, removed and sliced when ready to serve.

1 x 2 kg (4 lb 6 oz) hare, with heart, lungs and liver removed and discarded, front and back legs removed ready for use, saddle and fillets left intact and set aside

HARE BRAISE

½ cup plain (all-purpose) flour, seasoned with salt and freshly ground white pepper
vegetable oil for browning
small knob of butter
1 carrot, cut into 3 cm (1¼ in) dice
1 stick celery, cut into 3 cm (1¼ in) dice
1 leek, cut into 3 cm (1¼ in) dice
1 onion, cut into 3 cm (1¼ in) dice
1 tablespoon brandy (optional)
300 ml (10 fl oz) red wine
6 juniper berries
3 sprigs thyme
5 cloves garlic
1 bay leaf
1 litre (34 fl oz) chicken stock
1 litre (34 fl oz) beef stock
salt and freshly ground pepper

HARE BRAISE Preheat the oven to 150–160°C (300–320°F). Roll the hare legs in the seasoned flour. Heat a film of oil in a heavy pan, add the butter and sear the hare legs on all sides then remove them and set aside. Put all the vegetable dice in the pan, stir well and allow to colour. If using, pour in the brandy and cook down until it has almost evaporated. Remove the vegetables and reserve. Add the red wine to the pan, stir to deglaze any sediment then boil to reduce by two-thirds.

Spread the reserved browned vegetables in a baking pan, top with the browned hare legs and add the juniper berries, thyme, garlic and bay leaf. Pour over the reduced red wine. Combine the stocks and add to barely cover the contents of the baking pan. Cover tightly with foil or an airtight lid. Place the baking pan over direct heat and gently bring to a simmer. Transfer the baking tray to the preheated oven and allow the hare to braise gently for around 2 hours until the meat is meltingly tender and falling off the bone.

When the hare is cooked, take the baking pan from the oven and carefully remove the hare pieces and set them aside. While still warm, strip the meat from the bones, keeping the pieces as large as possible. Strain the liquid, pour it into a saucepan and boil to reduce it by one-third. Adjust the seasoning and replace the hare meat in sauce.

GARNISH FOR HARE BRAISE Combine the onions, sugar, vinegar and butter in a saucepan and add the 2 pinches of salt. Pour in enough water to come level with the onions. Cover and cook until the onions are soft and tender then uncover and boil to evaporate the liquid, stirring occasionally so the onions are glazed and evenly coloured. Set aside. Sauté the lardons in the duck fat or oil then remove them with a slotted spoon and set aside. Fry the button mushrooms in the fat remaining in the pan then set aside.

GARNISH FOR HARE BRAISE

150 g (5 oz) baby onions or shallots

½ teaspoon sugar

½ tablespoon red wine vinegar

10 g (½ oz) butter

2 pinches salt

60 g (2 oz) Kaiser fleisch, cut crosswise into lardons

½ tablespoon duck fat or vegetable oil

75 g (2½ oz) small button mushrooms

ROASTING THE SADDLE

oil for cooking

30 g (1 oz) butter

Soft Polenta or Fried Polenta (see page 281) for serving

ROASTING THE SADDLE Preheat the oven to 200°C (400°F). Heat oil in a pan over high heat, add the butter and put in the saddle, one fillet side facing downwards. Cook for 1 minute. Turn over and cook the other fillet side for 1 minute. Remove from the heat and place the saddle flat on the bones, fillets facing upwards, on a baking tray in the preheated oven and roast for 5 minutes. Remove from the oven and rest the saddle, fillets downwards, on a warm platter, tented with foil, for at least 6 minutes. When ready to serve, carve the fillets off the bones and slice thinly.

TO SERVE Reheat the reserved hare meat in the reduced red wine sauce over a gentle heat. Stir in the lardons, onions and mushrooms. Simmer until completely heated through. Serve with soft or fried polenta and garnish with the thin slices of oven-roasted fillet.

VARIATION An alternative and somewhat simpler dish using the braised hare is as follows. To the reduced hare braising liquid, add 4–6 peeled, seeded and chopped very ripe tomatoes (tinned ones are fine also) and a handful of pitted, sliced black olives. Simmer for a few minutes to allow the flavours to blend. Add the hare meat and heat through. Toss in a pan with some precooked pappardelle (see Basic Pasta Dough, page 290). Adjust the seasoning, pile into bowls and scatter chopped herbs over the top. You will be left with the hare fillets to use separately.

Hare cannelloni with spiced carrot cream
Serves 6

This is a more challenging recipe, which converts raw hare meat into a rich mousse to use as a filling for cannelloni. The pasta is imprinted with parsley leaves. The dish is labour-intensive but is always a hit in the restaurant. If you wish to omit the stage with the parsley, continue to roll out the dough to between the last and second-last setting.

1 x 2 kg (4 lb 6 oz) hare, fully boned and all sinew removed from meat
1 teaspoon salt
1 egg white
1 egg yolk
500 ml (17 fl oz) thickened cream (35% butterfat)
½ cup port, reduced to 1 tablespoon and cooled
1 teaspoon finely chopped fresh sage
1 teaspoon finely diced truffle (optional)
salt and freshly ground pepper
½ quantity Basic Pasta Dough (see page 290)
plain (all-purpose) flour for dusting
leaves from ½ bunch flat-leaf parsley
additional egg yolk for sealing
1 quantity Spiced Carrot Cream (see page 295)

GARNISH (OPTIONAL)
300 ml (10 fl oz) Elderberry Glaze (see page 40), reduced by half and with 40 g (1½ oz) butter swirled in just prior to serving

Place the hare meat in a well-chilled processor, add the salt and process to a fine purée. With the machine running continuously, add the egg white then the egg yolk, processing until well combined. Add 100 ml (3½ fl oz) of the cream and process until well combined. Pass the mousse through a tamis into a bowl over ice. Add the port reduction and sage, and the truffle if using. Gradually beat in more cream to achieve a light and delicate mousse. Season the mousse. To test the mixture, roll 1 tablespoon of mousse into a sausage shape in plastic wrap and tie the ends. Poach in simmering water until firm, then taste. The sausage should be well seasoned and smooth rather than crumbly or dry. If dry, add a little more cream and repeat the testing process until the desired texture is achieved. Put the mousse in a piping bag and chill.

Using a pasta machine, roll the dough through successive settings until the second last setting is reached. Place the rolled dough on a lightly floured surface and lay out the parsley leaves, flat, on top of half the dough. Fold the other half over the top and seal shut with a rolling pin. Roll twice through the pasta machine on setting 1½.

Cut the dough into even length rectangles, around 20 x 12 cm (8 x 4¾ in). Blanch the pasta in a very large pot of salted rapidly boiling water. Drain and refresh by rinsing with cold water then draining again well. Pat dry. Cut each pasta sheet in half. Pipe 3 cm (1¼ in) diameter logs of hare mousse across one of the narrow ends of each rectangle. Roll the pasta around the logs until there is a slight overlap. Use a little egg yolk to seal, and cut away excess pasta. Spray a sheet of plastic wrap with non-stick cooking spray, place the cannelloni on top, wrap tightly and tie off each end of the plastic wrap.

TO FINISH AND SERVE Poach the cannelloni in simmering water for 4 minutes. The filling should be springy to touch. Remove the plastic wrap and square off each end of the cannelloni with a sharp knife. Plate two to three hot cannelloni per person, with warm spiced carrot cream, and garnish with elderberry glaze if using.

KANGAROO

In Victoria, the overabundance of kangaroos sometimes causes considerable devastation to grazing land. Roos are culled but the subsequent processing is for pet food only. We rely on our supply of kangaroo meat for the table from suppliers in South Australia, where processing the meat for human consumption is allowed.

Roast kangaroo fillet with beet greens, glazed beetroot and sage fritters

Serves 6

Kangaroo is one of the few meats from the wild that can be enjoyed in Australia. Hanging or marinating can enhance its gaminess. We tend to serve it with many of the accompaniments that are traditionally served with game. Like most game meats it is best served rare.

18–20 baby beets, unpeeled, trimmed and washed

ELDERBERRY GLAZE
180 ml (6 fl oz) Elderberry Glaze (see page 40)
60 g (2 oz) butter
salt and freshly ground pepper

OR

RED WINE GLAZE
50 g (2 oz) sugar
55 ml (2 fl oz) red wine vinegar
55 ml (2 fl oz) shiraz
100 g (3½ oz) butter
salt and freshly ground pepper

6 x 190 g (6¾ oz) pieces kangaroo fillet, trimmed
oil for searing

SAGE FRITTERS AND BEET LEAVES
1 quantity Tempura Batter (see page 280)
3 dozen sage leaves
oil for frying
80 g (3 oz) butter
500 g (1 lb 2 oz) baby beet leaves, all tough stalks removed
salt and freshly ground pepper

BABY BEETS Either cook the beets in water (place them in a saucepan of water, bring to the boil, reduce heat to a simmer and cook gently for 15–20 minutes until tender) or steam them (place in a steamer and steam until tender). Remove the beets from the heat, drain if necessary and peel while still warm. Slice the beets in half. When ready to serve glaze the beets. If using elderberry glaze, heat the glaze in a pan over medium heat to reduce it to a slightly thicker consistency. Add the beetroot then toss to glaze and heat through. Remove from the heat, swirl in the butter and adjust the seasoning to taste. If using the red wine option, heat the sugar in a heavy-based pan until it begins to melt and caramelise. Add the vinegar to deglaze then reduce the liquid to a syrup. Add the shiraz and reduce to a syrup again. Add the beets and toss through to glaze and heat through. Remove from the heat, swirl in the butter and adjust the seasoning to taste.

KANGAROO FILLET Preheat the oven to 180°C (350°F). Season the trimmed pieces of kangaroo fillet. Spread a fine film of oil on the base of a pan and place over high heat. Sear the fillet pieces on all sides, for roughly 30 seconds in total, then roast on a flat tray in the oven for 5 minutes. Remove the fillet from the oven and rest, tented with foil, for 8 minutes.

SAGE FRITTERS AND BEET LEAVES Make the tempura batter. Dip the sage leaves into the batter and fry in hot oil until crisp. Drain on sheets of paper towel and season with salt. Meanwhile melt the butter over medium heat and sauté the beet leaves for about 3 minutes until just wilted then season.

TO SERVE Spread the sautéed beet leaves on six plates. Slice the kangaroo fillet and place on top of the beet leaves. Drizzle with elderberry or red wine glaze. Garnish with beets and scatter with sage leaf fritters.

Chapter Ten

FROM THE PADDOCKS

Nowadays we're confronted with many choices when purchasing beef. There's Wagyu with various grades of marbling, beef that's either grain- or grass-fed and also regional beef brands that reflect the specific flavours of regional pastures and herbages. The government's cooperative research centres have also identified that genes for temperament are related to genes for tenderness. So just the way an animal behaves may offer us clues to how good the meat will be.

It is all getting to be quite a business.

BEEF

The justifiable clamour for Wagyu is considerable. A breed originally from Japan but now also in Australia, Wagyu are generally reared for two to three years in comparison with other beef cattle that are often slaughtered at 18 months old. As a consequence, the considerably longer care and extra feed contribute to the very high cost of the Wagyu meat.

The very desirable distribution of fat through the meat, resulting in its superior juiciness and flavour, is referred to as marbling and its extent is scored on a scale of 1 to 12. That this fat tends to be mostly unsaturated as opposed to fat found on the outside of the muscles is an added bonus. But one of the biggest advantages of this well-marbled meat, apart from its superior flavour and tenderness, is that it can stand a little longer cooking without sacrificing juiciness.

One of the best influences on meat products in Australia has been the boning techniques of the Japanese. In practices refined over centuries, chefs in Japan have always pursued smaller portions of higher quality. Nowadays here also, the old ever-popular Aussie 700 g (1 lb 9 oz) lump of steak is mostly a thing of the past. In the case of rump, for example, it often was a mishmash of tenderness and textures in one slab. Nowadays we see it being separated into its muscle groups. Cooks now have some advance notice of how a cut will behave and what is the best way to prepare it.

But as a general guide the old basic principles apply across the board. Muscle (meat) that does little work – for example fillet – inevitably carries with it less flavour but requires very simple and often quick cooking. Pan, grill or barbecue it. Muscle that does a lot of work – cheek (all that chewing the cud), ox tail (fly swatting), shank (getting from the pasture to the waterhole) – is the most flavoursome and will develop a rich gelatinous sauce when cooked slowly at low temperatures.

Britain's contribution to our enjoyment of beef has got to be that famed roast extender – the Yorkshire pudding. Frankie, my Liverpudlian mother-in-law, made a mean 'pud' in the traditional way. Baked in the fat of the roast once the meat had been removed and was being carved, it was crunchy and delicious and puffed up with all the fat and juices. The following recipe is but a pale imitation, however it still does the job of offering something with which to mop up the delicious juices generated by the slow braising of the beef.

Braised beef cheek with Yorkshire pudding and horseradish cream

Serves 6

1 quantity Horseradish Cream (see page 289)

MARINADE

300 ml (10 fl oz) red wine

300 ml (10 fl oz) port

300 ml (10 fl oz) Madeira

2 bay leaves

6 sprigs thyme

1 tablespoon black peppercorns

1 carrot, peeled and chopped

2 stalks celery, chopped

2 onions, chopped

1 whole head of garlic, split

BEEF CHEEKS

3 x 400–450 g (14–16 oz) cleaned and trimmed beef cheeks

50 ml (2 fl oz) oil

plain flour (all-purpose) for dusting

water or chicken stock

YORKSHIRE PUDDING

2 eggs

125 g (4 oz) plain (all-purpose) flour

½ teaspoon salt

300 ml (10 fl oz) milk

1 tablespoon cold water

3 teaspoons oil

BEEF CHEEKS Combine all the marinade ingredients in a non-reactive container. Sit the beef cheeks in the marinade and place in the refrigerator for 12 hours. Remove the cheeks from the marinade and dry well. Heat the oil in a heavy-based ovenproof pan – ideally it should be large enough to fit the cheeks snugly, side by side, for braising. Dust the cheeks with flour and brown them on all sides, over high heat until crusty. Remove the cheeks from the pan and tip out any excess oil or fat.

Preheat the oven to 160°C (320°F). Replace the pan on high heat and strain in the marinade liquid, reserving the solids. Bring the liquid to the boil, reduce to a simmer, skim the top and reduce it by half. Add the browned beef cheeks and the vegetables from the marinade. Add sufficient stock or water to cover the beef. Cover the pan with a lid or greaseproof paper and tightly fitted foil. Bake in the preheated oven for 3½ hours or until the beef cheeks are completely tender. Remove the pan from the oven and allow the beef to rest in the liquid. Remove the beef cheeks, reserving the liquid, and when the cheeks have cooled, wrap them in damp greaseproof paper and refrigerate.

Strain the hot marinade and allow it to cool. Remove any fat that rises to the surface. Strain the liquid once again, through a fine sauce sieve, into a clean saucepan and reduce this liquid by one-third or more until it is thick and syrupy. Season this sauce.

YORKSHIRE PUDDING Preheat the oven to 190°C (375°F). Lightly beat the eggs in a bowl. Sift the flour and salt onto the beaten egg and stir it through. Pour in the milk gradually, whisking to produce a smooth batter. Beat in the cold water. Using a 6–8 piece non-stick muffin tray, pour ½ teaspoon of oil into each muffin mould. Place the tray in the preheated oven for about 5 minutes until the oil is hot. Distribute the batter among the moulds and return to the oven for 15 minutes. The puddings should be well risen, crisp and brown.

TO SERVE When ready, slice the beef cheeks and gently reheat the slices in the sauce. Serve with Yorkshire pudding and horseradish cream.

Beef carpaccio with crisp twice-cooked potatoes and sauce Gribiche

Serves 6–8

The original version of Carpaccio, named after the Renaissance Italian painter, made its debut at Harry's Bar in Venice. As a very young woman I perched there, transported by the unwavering attention of the wonderfully smooth waiters, while spending my precious dollars on outrageously expensive, but most elegantly presented carpaccio, chicken sandwiches and of course bellinis. In our version, fried crisp potatoes, moist beef, crunchy salad and a creamy sauce garnish make for a more-ish combination. Being basically a dish of thinly sliced raw beef requires the meat to be completely sinew-free and tender. Fillet is by far the easiest cut to use as it fulfils both prerequisites. The flavour, however, may not be as good as other cuts (but those might require more trimming and can be considerably less tender).

750 g (1 lb 10 oz) piece eye fillet, well trimmed
100 ml (3½ fl oz) extra virgin olive oil
8 medium-sized firm radishes, sliced and stored in iced water or 3 medium-sized artichokes, trimmed, sliced and fried (see Preparing Artichokes, page 293)
70 g (2⅓ oz) rocket (arugula) leaves
2 tablespoons Basic Vinaigrette (see page 284)

Crisp Twice-cooked Potatoes (see page 296)
150–180 ml (5–6 fl oz) Soft Egg Gribiche (see page 286)
fresh parmesan for serving (optional)

Chill the eye fillet in the freezer until firm and very cold but not frozen. Cut the fillet into ½ cm (¼ in) slices and divide these among six or eight 30 cm (12 in) squares of greaseproof or silicon paper that have been brushed with olive oil. The slices of beef should be pushed together but not overlapping and should roughly form a circle. Place a second square of paper on top of each portion of meat and using a flat-surfaced mallet gently pound the meat to flatten it to about a quarter of its thickness. Do not tear the meat. Smooth over lightly with a rolling pin and refrigerate the parchment packets of meat for at least 2 hours.

Remove the beef from the refrigerator, peel off the top layer of the paper and turn the carpaccio out onto individual plates. Drain and dry the radish slices, combine them (or the fried artichoke slivers if using) with the rocket and the vinaigrette and toss well. Brush the carpaccio on the plates with some extra-virgin olive oil. Sprinkle radish or artichoke slices and rocket leaves over the beef. Scatter the warm crusty potatoes over the surface. Place intermittent dollops of soft egg Gribiche all over the plate. Shave over fine slivers of parmesan, if using.

LAMB

I've had a chequered relationship with this stalwart of the Australian kitchen. When my mother roasted a leg of lamb for the family table she would choose the smallest she could find or otherwise do without. Most of the fat was removed and it was punctured all over with pockets into which slivers of garlic, anchovy or rosemary were placed. It would be rubbed with olive oil (obtainable only from chemists when I was very young) and roasted slowly for a long time until the meat was almost falling off the bone.

Meanwhile, at school barbecues, everyone was ripping into tough fatty chops and snags – cooked quickly over high heat – that tasted nothing like the lamb at home. A decade and a half later, I was being instructed by chefs to sear the blazes out of meats including lamb to ensure the retention of all the juices. Another decade on and culinary scientist Harold McGee put paid to that notion. Searing does no such thing. Apart from how it is cooked, the age of 'lamb' remains important for me. I somehow associate the fat of older sheep with the smell and flavour of lanolin. Interestingly, mutton – the meat from sheep over two years of age – is apparently currently having a resurgence with chefs in the United Kingdom. Frankly, I'm not rushing off to give it a go.

In Australia, the term 'lamb' is very loosely used to refer to an animal less than 12 months of age with no permanent teeth. Spring lamb – generally available towards the end of winter – is already four to five months old but continues to be referred to as spring lamb to up to 10 months of age. Spring lamb is often still suckling but because it is also grazing on pasture it is already developing a distinctive lamb flavour. Herbaceous flavours can already be detected especially with lambs grazing on clover or irrigated lucerne.

This early spring lamb is my favourite. We chase it eagerly and pair it with the first baby vegetables of spring. It can be difficult to find – with drought conditions and the proliferation of dry pasture grazing and hand-grain feeding, those early herby flavours are quite often lost. Milk-fed lamb – under eight weeks old (around 6 kg/13 lb 2 oz) – is another meat altogether. It is buttery and delicious but does not really taste of lamb.

Summer lamb – the animals are eight to ten months old – shows all the signs of long-term pasture. The flavour is robust and it is coarser in texture. When we do use it we treat it differently, marinating and adding spice and strongly flavoured accompaniments.

Generally, like most meat, lamb benefits in flavour and texture from a few days of hanging and ageing. If your lamb is tough or coarse ask your butcher how long he ages his meat.

Cheaper cuts of meat of all kinds – shoulder, shank, neck and cheek – have a special place in my heart. They were the stuff of my father's long-simmered stews. When I put these on to braise on a misty, rainy Daylesford day I hear the opera play once again and see his glass of wine by the stove. '*Pozhaluisto k ctoly* (Please to the table),' he would say.

❧ Winter lamb: braised neck with beans and sweetbreads ❧

Serves 6

In this recipe, the braised boned lamb neck is re-formed into a cylinder and chilled ready for slicing and reheating. Once in its cylindrical shape, we top it with garlic purée and breadcrumbs in an echo of the classic cassoulet before returning it to the oven. The effort is worthwhile if you wish to bother with the presentation. The braised lamb is also wonderful just served simply with polenta or mashed potatoes. In this dish of lamb in many guises, we include crisp fried sweetbreads and sometimes a garnish of our lamb and fennel sausage, together with a cassoulet-style braise of beans.

BRAISED LAMB NECK

2 lamb necks, each split lengthways
375 ml (12½ fl oz) red wine
750 ml (25 fl oz) port
1 carrot, chopped
1 stick celery, sliced
1 leek, sliced
1 onion, chopped
1 bay leaf
1 teaspoon peppercorns
2 cloves garlic
6 stalks thyme
seasoned plain (all-purpose) flour
oil for browning
2 litres (68 fl oz) chicken stock
50 ml (2 fl oz) Roasted Garlic Purée (see page 296)
100 g (3½ oz) breadcrumbs
dry breadcrumbs

BRAISED LAMB NECK Place the lamb necks in a bowl together with the red wine, port, carrot, celery, leek, onion, bay leaf, peppercorns, garlic and thyme, ensuring that the necks are completely covered with liquid. Leave the necks to marinate overnight then remove them from the liquid and pat dry. Pass the liquid through a sieve, reserving the solids. Reduce the liquid by three-quarters and set aside for later use.

Preheat the oven to 160°C (320°F). Dust the necks in seasoned flour. Spread a film of oil in a pan and colour the necks until golden and crusty all over. Place the necks and reserved solids from the marinade in a baking dish and add the chicken stock. Cover with aluminium foil and bake in the medium oven for approximately 3½–4 hours until the meat falls from the bone. Remove the necks from the liquid and allow them to cool slightly. Carefully remove the bones from the necks.

Strain the braising liquid through a sieve then return to a pot and reduce it until a good sauce consistency is achieved. Add 4 tablespoons of the reserved wine reduction. Lay 20 cm (8 in) of plastic wrap out on your work surface. Re-form the necks by placing each of the two halves on top of each other. Drizzle about 50 ml (2 fl oz) of reduced sauce over the necks. Roll the plastic wrap firmly around the necks to form a tight cylindrical shape and tie off the wrap at both ends. Refrigerate and leave to set.

Once the necks are set, remove the plastic wrap and slice each neck into three. Coat one end of each piece with a small amount of the roasted garlic purée then dip it into the breadcrumbs. Set aside until ready to complete the dish. »

~ recipe continued ~

CRUMBED LAMB SWEETBREADS
200–300 ml (7–10 fl oz) milk
1 bay leaf
2 cloves garlic, crushed
1 sprig thyme
500 g (1 lb 2 oz) lamb sweetbreads
1 cup plain (all-purpose) flour
2 eggs, beaten
Japanese (Panko) breadcrumbs or dry breadcrumbs

ACCOMPANIMENTS
Lamb and Fennel Sausages (optional; see page 247)
Cassoulet of Beans (see page 280)

CRUMBED LAMB SWEETBREADS Combine the milk, bay leaf, garlic, thyme and sweetbreads in a large heavy-based pot and bring to the boil. Turn down the heat to a simmer. After 5–10 minutes remove from the heat – the sweetbreads should be slightly firm. Drain and discard the milk and all ingredients other than the sweetbreads. Peel the sweetbreads and roughly chop. Lay out a sheet of plastic wrap and place 3 heaped tablespoons of the sweetbreads in the centre. Roll into an even cylinder approximately 2½ cm (1 in) in diameter. Tie off each end. Place in the freezer and leave until just semifrozen. Slice into 1½–2 cm (¾ in) thick disks then remove the plastic wrap. Dip the sweetbread discs in the flour, egg and breadcrumbs in succession. Set aside on kitchen paper to set the crumbs.

TO FINISH AND ASSEMBLE Preheat oven to 180°C (350°F). Bake the lamb neck 'cylinders' upright, with the garlic and crumbs on top, on a non-stick baking tray in the preheated oven for 15–20 minutes until the crumbs are coloured and the lamb is hot through the middle. Gently reheat the cassoulet of beans. Pan-fry the lamb sausages if using. Fry the sweetbreads in oil at 160°C (320°F) until golden brown.

TO SERVE Spoon a little of the bean cassoulet onto each plate. Place a lamb neck cylinder upright on top. If using, slice the sausage and place three to four slices on each plate. Garnish with crisp sweetbreads.

❖ Spring lamb with sauce Paloise and shepherd's croquette ❖

Serves 6

The delicate flavour of spring lamb is enhanced here with a touch of mint in the sauce and the sweet buttery classic combination of peas and lettuce. Ask your butcher to trim and bone the cutlets, as described. The cooking times in the recipe are for double cutlets with a trimmed weight of around 200 g (7 oz) each. The shepherd's croquette, composed of braised shank inside a mashed potato coating, is a playful variation of a shepherd's pie. Once again the separate components in what is a fairly complex restaurant dish can be individually useful.

SHEPHERD'S CROQUETTE

6 lamb shanks
plain (all-purpose) flour for dusting
oil for searing
1 carrot, chopped
6 shallots, peeled and halved
1 stick celery, chopped
3 cloves garlic, sliced
6 sprigs thyme
2 sprigs rosemary
6 peppercorns
1 bay leaf
2 litres (68 fl oz) chicken stock
2 egg yolks
6 potatoes, cooked and passed through a mouli or ricer while still warm
salt and freshly ground white pepper
1 additional egg yolk
plain (all-purpose) flour
beaten egg
Japanese (Panko) breadcrumbs or dry breadcrumbs

SHEPHERD'S CROQUETTE Dust the shanks lightly with flour then place in a deep pan and sear in hot oil to colour them on all sides. Remove the shanks and drain off any excess fat. Add the carrot, shallots and celery to the pan and sauté over high heat. When the vegetables have coloured, add the shanks, garlic, thyme, rosemary, peppercorns, bay leaf and stock. Bring to the boil, skim and reduce to a simmer. Cook on a low heat for about 2 hours or until the meat readily comes away from the bones. Remove the shanks and allow them to partially cool. Strain the remaining liquid and bring it to the boil. Skim, turn down to a simmer and cook to reduce the liquid by two-thirds. Strip the shank meat from the bones, removing and discarding any fat or sinew. Break the meat down or chop it into small pieces. Fold the reduced liquid through the meat, season then allow the meat to cool.

Place 6 heaped tablespoons of cooled moist shank mix on a sheet of plastic wrap. Use the wrap to roll a cylinder approximately 24 cm (9½ in) long and 2½ cm (1 in) in diameter. Roll to completely enclose then twist and tie the ends tightly. Place the roll in the refrigerator to set. When ready to make the croquettes, cut the lamb roll into 4 cm (1½ in) long pieces.

Beat the 2 egg yolks into the mashed potato by hand and season with salt and pepper. On pieces of plastic wrap, spread rectangles of potato mash about 5 x 15 cm (2 x 6 in) and about ½ cm (¼ in) thick. Place a cylinder of braised shank in the centre of each. Brush the shank with the additional egg yolk and wrap the mash around and up each end, using the plastic wrap to help roll a tight cylinder and to completely encase the lamb. Tie off each end and place in the freezer to firm the potato. Once firm, remove the plastic wrap and roll each croquette quickly in flour, egg and breadcrumbs. Repeat to double coat the croquettes then place them on a tray in the refrigerator to hold until ready to cook. »

❖ recipe continued ❖

LAMB CUTLETS

30 ml (1 fl oz) oil

6 x 200 g (7 oz) trimmed and boned double lamb cutlets (one bone removed and the other trimmed to 5 cm/2 in)

salt and freshly ground pepper

GARNISH AND ACCOMPANIMENTS

Braised Peas and Lettuce (see page 296)

Sauce Paloise (see page 288)

'Pesto' Emulsion (optional; see page 288)

LAMB CUTLETS Preheat the oven to 180°C (350°F). Heat the oil in a large pan over high heat. Season the cutlets on both sides with salt and pepper and place them in the pan, three at a time or whatever number fit comfortably without crowding. Brown the meat on all sides, cooking for a total of about 4 minutes. Remove and reserve while you repeat the process with the remaining cutlets. Finish the cooking in the preheated oven, for 2 minutes if you like your lamb medium–rare. Remove the cutlets from the oven, tent with foil and rest in a warm place for 5–6 minutes.

TO FINISH AND SERVE Bake the croquettes on a tray at 180°C (350°F) for 12 minutes until the exterior is golden brown. Test the middle with a metal skewer to ensure the meat is hot right through. Spoon the braised peas and lettuce onto each plate. Place a cutlet on each with a croquette alongside. Spoon a little Paloise sauce over each cutlet and the 'pesto' emulsion, if using, around the plate.

PORK

More than 40 per cent of all meat consumed around the globe is pork. Some years ago in an attempt to increase pork consumption in Australia, new breeding, housing and feeding techniques were introduced with the intent of causing a 60–65 per cent reduction in overall fat content.

As a result of a great deal of marketing and our pursuit of low-fat produce, pork increased in popularity. But that pork, widely available at the supermarket nowadays, is a pale imitation of the real thing.

Inherently a dry-ish texture when cooked, even in its naturally bred state, pork relies very much for its succulence and flavour on its fat content. Lean supermarket pork comes with recipes inevitably awash with sugary marinades and glazes that attempt to emulate that succulence and improve the dry texture. Replacing fat with excess sugars is a practice not to be condoned.

Lessons can be learned from the United States, which while boasting the greatest variety of low-fat products on its store shelves, also has a population with a considerable obesity problem. Sugar meanwhile invades virtually every product on our shelves from bread to mustard and is highly addictive. Take some time to read the labels.

Pork raised for the Lake House table is sourced from Judy Croagh at Western Plains Free Range Pork and, just down the road, Fiona Chambers who breeds Wessex Saddlebacks at one of Australia's few organic pork farms. Judy's pigs live a privileged existence in which their whole pasture and pens are regularly moved to freshly planted-out paddocks. Fiona's herd contains some of the last remaining Wessex Saddleback sows in the world. And here is an outstanding case for agricultural biodiversity and the preservation of rare breeds. The Wessex Saddleback pig is quite hairy with a distinctive thickish coating of black and white striped bristle (see photograph on page 248). This coat serves to protect the pigs from sunburn, allowing them to have extensive grazing time in the outdoors. At Fernleigh Farm, Fiona's paddocks of organic carrots are replanted after harvest with oats and other crops for the pigs to graze on. Standard common white pigs can spend only limited time outdoors because of the sun factor and are most often to be found in indoor pens. If indeed temperament truly is an indicator of flavour and texture, Wessex Saddlebacks already genetically predisposed to be calm and friendly, have the added advantage of a charmed existence. And I would have to say the quality of their meat supports the notion of temperament as an indicator of taste and texture.

Eating rare breed organic pork or pork raised in good conditions is a revelation. I would rather eat my pork with a bit of extra fat and walk an extra couple of kilometres any day.

Assiette of pork
Serves 8

A pork dish of this nature, displaying different cuts and cooking methods on the one plate, is rarely off our menus. The embellishments and accompaniments change with the seasons. Here the dish is served with a little creamed celeriac and cabbage in winter as an echo of the classic choucroute. We sometimes reduce the amount of belly and serve a small crisp crumbed Galette of Pork Trotter (see page 241), or garnish with strips of crisp pig's ear, introducing a third pork variation. In summer the dish may have an accompaniment of a sweet–sour sauce of morello cherries. The brining of the fillet affords more flavour to what is otherwise a fairly flavourless cut.

4 pork fillets, well trimmed
oil for searing

BRINE
2 bay leaves
1 dried chilli
6 dried juniper berries, crushed
7 coriander seeds, crushed
1 litre (34 fl oz) water
90 g (3¼ oz) sugar
45 g (1¾ oz) rock salt

PRESSED AND ROLLED PORK BELLY
1.5 kg (3 lb 5 oz) boneless pork belly, skin on
4 tablespoons rock salt
1 tablespoon fennel seeds, crushed
1 tablespoon coriander seeds, crushed
1 teaspoon cardamom pods, crushed
2 star anise, crushed
vegetable oil
2 cloves garlic, peeled and sliced
1 carrot, peeled and roughly chopped
2 sticks celery, roughly chopped ≫

BRINE Place the herbs and spices in a pan with a little of the water. Bring to a simmer, remove from the heat and leave to infuse. When cool add the remaining water, the sugar and salt and combine. Place the pork fillets in the brine, ensuring that the fillets are completely covered with liquid. Cover and refrigerate for 24 hours.

PRESSED AND ROLLED PORK BELLY Lightly trim the pork belly, removing any excess meat or fat until you have a flat rectangular piece of belly. Combine the salt and crushed spices and spread the mix over the belly, leave overnight then rinse off. Cut the piece of belly in half along the grain. Remove and discard the skin from one piece of belly. Roll this piece into a sausage across the grain of the meat and tie it in three places with string. Leave the other half with skin on, flat and trimmed.

Place a little oil in a pan over medium heat and cook the vegetables until they begin to colour. Remove the pan from the heat and put in the pieces of rolled and flat pork. Add the stock, or water if using, to cover the meat. Poach in water for about 3 hours or until each piece of pork can be pierced easily with a knife. The rolled belly will take longer to cook than the flat piece. Allow the pork to cool slightly in the liquid.

Cut the string on the rolled piece of pork, re-roll it tightly in plastic wrap to form a cylinder and tie off at each end. Roll in a piece of foil and place in iced water overnight to set. Place the flat piece of cooked pork on a lined tray, cover with plastic wrap, and weigh down with a board or another tray and a couple of cans. Refrigerate overnight.

When ready to serve, remove the foil and plastic wrap from the roll and slice the meat into rounds ready to be pan-fried. Slice the flat piece of pork into neat rectangles ready to be pan-fried also. ≫

~ recipe continued ~

1 onion, peeled and roughly chopped
1.5 litres (51 fl oz) stock or water, to cover
50 ml (2 fl oz) oil
salt and freshly ground pepper

ACCOMPANIMENTS
Choucroute-style Cabbage (see page 294)
Celeriac Purée (see page 295)

TO FINISH Preheat the oven to 200°C (400°F). Rinse the cured pork fillets under cold running water then dry and rub with olive oil. Sear the fillets on all sides in a hot pan. Place the fillets in the hot oven and continue to cook for a further 10 minutes. Remove the fillets from the oven and allow them to rest in a warm spot, tented with foil, for 5–10 minutes. Slice to serve. Heat the 50 ml of oil in a pan over high heat. Add the pork belly slices and cook both sides until crisp and coloured. Drain the slices on kitchen paper and season.

TO SERVE Mound the hot cabbage onto plates and top with fillet slices. Place the pan-fried pork belly pieces on the plate and spoon the celeriac purée alongside.

CHARCUTERIE

We have always produced a range of charcuterie, including terrines, pâtés and sausages.

These feature on our signature Lake House Changing Plate.

DUCK LIVER PARFAIT

Makes 1.2 litre (2 lb 10 oz) terrine

125 ml (4 fl oz) port
125 ml (4 fl oz) sherry
60 ml (2 fl oz) brandy
3 shallots, finely diced
1 clove garlic, finely chopped
3 sprigs thyme, finely chopped
400 g (14 oz) duck livers, picked over and cleaned
400 g (14 oz) butter, softened
14 g (½ oz) salt
5 whole eggs

Preheat the oven to 170°C (340°F). Combine the port, sherry, brandy, shallots, garlic and thyme in a saucepan, bring to the boil and reduce to 80 ml (3 fl oz). Leave the mixture to cool. Warm the livers in the butter by placing both in a stainless steel bowl, covering with plastic wrap and placing the bowl in a very warm place (approximately 40°C/110°F) for about 1 hour. Purée the reduction in a blender and add the warm livers and butter, and the salt. Once the mixture is smooth, add the eggs and pass through a very fine sieve. Pour immediately into an enamelled cast iron terrine mould, place in a bain-marie and bake in the preheated oven until just set. Allow the parfait to cool then refrigerate. Serve this parfait simply with warm toast or on Crostini (see page 281).

Chicken galantine with tarragon

Makes 2 x 450-500 g (1-1 lb 2 oz) galantines

1.2–1.3 kg (2 lb 10 oz–2 lb 10½ oz) chicken, boned and halved

TARRAGON CHICKEN MOUSSE

1 x 150 g (5 oz) chicken fillet
1 teaspoon salt
1 egg, separated
230 ml (8½ fl oz) thickened cream (35% butterfat)
2 tablespoons Tarragon Pesto (see page 289)
salt and freshly ground pepper

CHICKEN MOUSSE Roughly chop the chicken fillet and process in a chilled food processor with 1 teaspoon of salt until a paste forms. Add the egg white and process until combined. Add egg yolk and process until combined. Add 130 ml (4¼ fl oz) of the cream and process until combined. Remove the mixture from the processor and place it in a bowl over ice. Gradually beat in the remaining cream. For a superior lighter mousse, pass the mix through a tamis. Add the tarragon pesto and stir through to combine well. Tie a small ball or sausage of the mixture in plastic wrap and poach it in a saucepan of simmering water until firm. Unwrap and taste then adjust the seasoning accordingly.

ASSEMBLING GALANTINES Place one half of the fully boned bird, skin side down, on your work surface, with the leg meat furthest away from you. Lay a sheet of plastic wrap over the flesh and gently pound it flat with a rolling pin until the meat is about 1 cm (½ in) thick. Remove the plastic wrap and season the chicken with salt and pepper. Spread 3 heaped tablespoons of tarragon mousse over the flattened chicken, to a thickness of approximately 3 mm (⅛ in). Roll the chicken into a tight cylinder and wrap in plastic wrap, tying off at each end. Wrap in foil, twisting the ends closed. Repeat the process with the other half of the bird. Place the chicken galantines in a pot of cold water, fully covered. Place the pot on the stove and bring to a gentle simmer. Poach the chicken for 25–30 minutes until the core temperature of the galantines is 68°C (155°F). Remove the galantines from the pot and allow them to cool then refrigerate overnight. Remove the plastic wrap and foil and slice to serve.

❧ Ox tongue salad ❧
Makes 350 g (12 oz)

I once made the mistake of using a whole glazed tongue as one of the centrepieces of a banquet. I thought it looked rather spectacular. Not everyone agreed. Clearly tongue served whole can be confronting. Once cooked, sliced or diced it is more acceptable. In the following recipe you are likely to need half of the tongue. I suggest you slice the remainder thinly and try it on good rye bread with dill pickles. Thin pink slices of tongue arranged on a plate, topped with horseradish cream and a good peppery radish salad, also makes a nice change to usual antipasto-style starters.

COOKING THE TONGUE

1 x 700 g (1 lb 9 oz) pickled ox tongue
water for blanching
250 ml (8½ fl oz) white wine
100 ml (3½ fl oz) white wine vinegar
1 onion, chopped
1 carrot chopped
1 stick celery, chopped
1 bay leaf
1 sprig thyme
1 teaspoon black peppercorns
2 cloves garlic
2 litres (68 fl oz) water or chicken stock

FINISHING THE SALAD

30 g (1 oz) small salt-packed capers
65 g (2¼ oz) dill cucumber
150 ml (5 fl oz) Lake House Dressing (see page 284)
salt and freshly ground pepper

COOKING THE TONGUE Note that a 700 g (1 lb 9 oz) cooked tongue yields about 500 g (1 lb 2 oz) of clean trimmed meat. Unless you are organising a sizeable party you are unlikely to need that much as a salad. The salad here uses only around half of the cooked tongue, which can be stored for up to 3 days, as detailed below.

Place the tongue in a pot covered with cold water and heat until simmering. Remove from the heat and after a couple of minutes drain off the water. Leave the tongue in the pot and add all the remaining ingredients, using enough of the water or stock to cover the tongue. Bring to a simmer, skim the surface of the liquid and continue to cook very gently for at least 3 hours or until the skin offers no resistance to the tip of a knife. Remove from heat and leave the tongue to cool a little in the pot. Remove the tongue, peel off the skin, trim the gristle and place the tongue in a storage container. Strain the poaching liquid, bring it to the boil, skim and season. Pour the liquid over the poached tongue. When cool, store the tongue under its liquid in the refrigerator until ready to use.

FINISHING THE SALAD Take 200–250 g (7–9 oz) of the cooked, pickled ox tongue, slice it then cut it into julienne strips. Rinse and drain the capers. Slice and cut the dill cucumber into julienne strips. Combine the tongue, capers and cucumber in a bowl, add the dressing and season to taste. Serve the salad as part of an array of things or just in a bowl to pile onto crusty bread.

Galette of pork trotter with mustard crust

Makes 6–8 galettes

This is a variation on the crumbed whole pork trotters of French charcuterie.

3 pork trotters
1 medium-sized carrot, chopped
1 small onion, chopped
1 bay leaf
3 sprigs thyme
1 teaspoon olive oil
3 sticks celery, very finely diced
1 clove garlic, finely chopped
1 tablespoon parsley, chopped
2 tablespoons plain (all-purpose) flour
salt and freshly ground pepper
⅓ teaspoon mustard powder
2 eggs, whisked with 1 teaspoon Dijon mustard
Japanese (Panko) breadcrumbs or dry breadcrumbs
oil for frying

Place the trotters, carrot, onion and herbs in a pot and cover with water. Bring to the boil, skim and reduce to a simmer. Continue to cook for about 45 minutes until the skin is falling off the bone. Strain and reserve the stock. While warm, strip skin and meat off the bones and chop it finely. Heat the olive oil in a pan and add the celery and garlic and cook until softened but not coloured. Add the cooked aromatics to the trotter meat, add the parsley and season well. Press the mixture to about 1.5 cm (¾ in) in thickness, into metal rings 5 cm (2 in) in diameter. Refrigerate until set then press the galettes out of the moulds. Season the flour with salt, pepper and mustard. Lightly dust the moulded trotter meat with the seasoned flour then dip it into the into the whisked egg and coat with breadcrumbs. Refrigerate for at least a ½ hour to set. When ready to serve lightly fry in hot oil until golden brown on both sides.

Many of our guests request hampers for their excursions into the countryside. Crusty bread, home-made terrines and relishes provide splendid picnic fare.

Country terrine

Makes 1.5 kg (3 lb 5 oz) terrine

SPICE MIX

3½ teaspoons ground allspice

½ teaspoon ground nutmeg

½ teaspoon ground cloves

½ teaspoon ground cinnamon

2 bay leaves, crumbled

10 juniper berries

2 teaspoons peppercorns

500 g (1 lb 2 oz) lean pork mince

500 g (1 lb 2 oz) veal mince

250 g (9 oz) pork back fat

50 g (2 oz) pistachio nuts, shelled, blanched and rubbed in a towel to remove skins

zest and juice of 2 oranges

2 pinches salt

50 ml (2 fl oz) brandy

7 rashers middle bacon, rind removed

SPICE MIX Grind all the ingredients together with a mortar and pestle or spice grinder. Store in a screw-top jar and use for terrines or sausages (note that you will only need 1½ tablespoons of the spice mix for this terrine).

MAKING THE TERRINE Preheat the oven to 160°C (320°F). Process the mince and fat in small batches to combine well and create an even texture. Add 1½ tablespoons of the prepared spice mix and all the remaining ingredients, except the bacon, and mix well. Line the terrine dish with bacon and fill with mince mix. Fold the bacon over the top. Place the terrine in a bain-marie, cover with foil and cook in the oven for 45 minutes or until the interior of the terrine registers 70°C (140°F).

SAUSAGE-MAKING daunts most domestic cooks. Using a piping bag to fill casings requires a lot of strength and the best solution is to buy a funnel-like attachment for your mincer. In the recipes that follow there are some sausages that do not require casings.

For others that do, sausage casings can be purchased from most butchers. You will need roughly about 30 g (1 oz) of casings for every 1 kg (2 lb 3 oz) of sausage mix. There are bound to be some defective ones and occasional mishaps in your production line, so purchase more rather than less. Rinse the casings well and thread them over the spout of the tap to wash the insides. Drain and store in brine in the refrigerator until ready to use. Left-over casings will keep indefinitely stored this way.

At Lake House we make many different sausages. However, the recipe for our house-made Bullboars – specific to our region – is just as guarded as the many local family recipes that have been handed down from our original settlers here for generations. These settlers came from the Swiss-Italian canton of Ticino to try and make their fortune on the local goldfields. Many stayed on and established vineyards and olive groves. They relished spicy rustic sausages made of beef and pork, which made wonderful salamis once hung and dried. The Lake House version of Bullboars, which we now produce and distribute to various outlets, are similarly strong in flavour and are perfect grilled or barbecued. Making sausages is a nice way to spend a wintry afternoon with friends.

Chicken sausages
Serves 6

This is the most basic of recipes for this classic sausage, or Boudin Blanc. Alter the herbs or add other spice or embellishments such as sautéed bacon, mushrooms and onions as you wish.

500 g (1 lb 2 oz) skinless chicken breast, cut into small pieces and chilled
salt
1 whole egg
2 egg whites
400 ml (13 fl oz) chilled thickened cream (35% butterfat)
2 teaspoons chopped tarragon
freshly ground white pepper
¼ teaspoon freshly grated nutmeg

Pre-chill the processor bowl and blade. Place the chicken in the processor and, using a pulsing action, process to a paste. Add salt and the eggs and process until just combined. Add half the cream and process until just amalgamated. Scrape the contents of the processor into a large bowl and beat the remaining cream in with a spoon. Stir in the tarragon, pepper and nutmeg then refrigerate. Meanwhile test the mix for seasoning by poaching off a tablespoon of it in barely simmering water. Adjust seasoning with salt and pepper.

Using the method described in Smoked Trout Sausage (see page 156), use squares of foil, or plastic wrap, to roll the mixture into sausage shapes then refrigerate. Bring a wide pan of water to the boil, reduce it to a simmer and slip in the sausages. Poach them for around 10 minutes or until springy to the touch. Remove the sausages with tongs and drop them briefly into iced water to stop the cooking process. Drain the sausages, slip them from their 'skins' and store, covered, on a tray in the refrigerator until ready to serve. The sausages may be steamed, gently pan-fried, brushed with butter and heated in the over or sliced and slipped into hot soup. We use them in many dishes including Assiette of Chicken with Summer Herb Bouillon (see page 182) and with Chicken Wings with Sweet Corn Sauce (see page 185).

❖ Duck neck sausages ❖
Makes 6 sausages

If you would prefer a more Asian flavour to these sausages, add ginger, chopped coriander and a touch of chilli to the forcemeat. A couple of cooked sausage slices slipped into an Asian variant of the Duck Broth (see page 190) – infuse it with ginger and chopped coriander and add noodles and Asian mushrooms – and you are really talking.

400 g (14 oz) duck meat, cut into small pieces
500 g (1 lb 2 oz) fresh belly pork, skinned, boned and cut into small pieces
100 ml (3½ fl oz) port
100 ml (3½ fl oz) water
4 tablespoons fresh breadcrumbs
4 sprigs fresh thyme, leaves finely chopped
6 sprigs flat-leaf parsley, leaves finely chopped
pinch of ground allspice
pinch of ground cloves
pinch of ground coriander
salt and freshly ground pepper
6 duck neck skins, excess fat removed, well washed and dried

Pass all the meat through the coarse blade of a mincer or place it all in a processor and pulse to obtain coarsely ground meat. Do not overprocess the meat into a paste. Put the ground meat into a bowl and add the port, water, breadcrumbs, herbs, spices and seasoning. Combine the mix to disperse the ingredients evenly. Make a little patty of the mix, pan-fry it and taste for seasoning then adjust if necessary.

Preheat the oven to 190°C (375°F). Tie one end of each duck neck with string and stuff the necks fairly loosely as the skin will contract when it is roasted. Tie the other end of the necks with string and refrigerate until ready to cook. Heat a non-stick ovenproof pan large enough to hold all the sausages snugly. Brown the sausages in turn over medium-to-high heat then roast them in the oven for 10 minutes. Reduce the heat to 170°C (340°F) and continue to cook for another 10 minutes or until the juices from the sausages run clear when they are pricked with a skewer.

❧ Lamb and fennel sausages ❧

Makes about 15 thick or 24 thin sausages

Often used as an accompaniment to winter lamb dishes, these sausages are also wonderful with a little Soft Polenta (see page 281) and a tomato ragout. The quantity allows for thick sausages of around 80 g (3 oz) or thin sausages of around 50 g (2 oz).

1 bundle sausage casings
½ teaspoon juniper berries
1 tablespoon black peppercorns
3 tablespoons fennel seeds
1 clove
1 teaspoon coriander seeds
1 kg (2 lb 3 oz) lamb mince
60 g (2 oz) fresh breadcrumbs, soaked in 250 ml (8½ fl oz) water or stock
½ tablespoon chopped fresh thyme
1 tablespoon chopped rosemary
2 cloves garlic, chopped
30 ml (1 fl oz) red wine
30 ml (1 fl oz) port
30 ml (1 fl oz) Pernod
salt to taste

Toast then grind the juniper berries, peppercorns, fennel seeds, clove and coriander seeds. Place the ground spices with all the other ingredients, apart from the casings, in a bowl and mix together thoroughly. Season then make a small tester patty and pan-fry it. Taste and adjust the seasoning as required. Either spoon the mixture into a piping bag and pipe into the casings or pass it through the largest blade on your mincer and through the sausage attachment. Take care to work any air pockets out of the sausages, twisting them into 10 cm (4 in) lengths. The sausages may be gently pan-fried, grilled or oven-roasted.

Jellied ham hock sausages

Makes 6 x 20 cm (8 in) sausages just over 2 cm (8¾ in) in diameter

4 medium-sized salted ham hocks, soaked overnight
2 bay leaves
3 sprigs thyme
1 leek
1 carrot
6 sprigs flat-leaf parsley
2 onions, halved
½ whole head garlic, split in half

Place the hocks in a pot with the remaining ingredients. Totally cover with water, bring to the boil then simmer the hocks for about 4 hours or until the skin is completely soft and basically falling apart. Allow the hocks to partially cool in the stock then strain off the stock and reserve it. Discard the vegetables. Strip the skin from the hocks. Remove and discard any pockets of fat from the underside. Remove the meat from the bones, breaking it up into lobes and fibres (discard any sinew) and place in a bowl. Chop the skin up very, very finely and add to the meat. Using the skin creates a more interesting texture in the sausage but may be omitted if preferred. Heat 250 ml (8½ fl oz) of the reserved stock and reduce by two-thirds. Add this reduction to the meat and mix through thoroughly. (You can use 1 litre/34 fl oz of the remaining ham stock to cook lentils for a garnish or make Ham Hock and Lentil Soup, see page 251).

Place a kitchen towel on the bench and cover with three or four layers of plastic wrap. Divide the ham mix into six portions. Spoon one portion of the mixture in a mound along the long side of the plastic. Roll the plastic over to encase the ham and continue to roll into a long sausage shape, using the towel for assistance. Twist up one end of the plastic, forcing the meat to compact and expelling as much air as possible. Repeat with the other end. Repeat the process with the remaining portions of ham mix. Refrigerate the sausages until firm. To serve, unwrap the sausages and slice.

Spicy venison sausages

Makes about 20 sausages

We serve these spicy sausages with a warm salad of lentils tossed with Salsa Verde (see page 288) and with a demitasse of frothy Ham Hock and Lentil Soup (see page opposite) alongside.

750 g (1 lb 10 oz) pork belly, diced
700 g (1 lb 9 oz) venison, diced
110 g (3¾ oz) pork fat, diced
½ tablespoon ground coriander
½ tablespoon ground allspice
½ teaspoon ground cloves
1 tablespoon peppercorns, ground
1 teaspoon garam masala
1 teaspoon ground juniper berries
2 teaspoons chopped garlic
2 tablespoons salt
150 ml (5 fl oz) port
30 ml (1 fl oz) brandy
30 ml (1 fl oz) Madeira
35 g (1¼ oz) breadcrumbs
100 ml (3½ fl oz) water
additional 300 g (10½ oz) venison, cut into 1 cm (½ in) dice reserved to fold through mix

Put the pork belly, the larger quantity of venison and the pork fat through the mincer. Combine the mince well in a bowl, add all the ground spices, garlic, salt, port, brandy and Madeira and mix through thoroughly. In a separate bowl, soak the breadcrumbs in the water until the water is fully absorbed. Add the mince mixture then the additional diced venison. Place 100–120 g (3½–4 oz) mounds of mixture on double-layered squares of plastic wrap. Roll the mix into thick sausage shapes, twisting and tying both ends of the plastic, compacting the meat and ensuring that as much air is expelled as possible. Refrigerate the sausages.

Poach the plastic-wrapped sausages in a large pot of gently simmering water for about 15 minutes or until the sausages are completely set (they should still be raw in the middle). Allow the sausages to cool then refrigerate until ready to use.

Unwrap the sausages from the plastic and gently pan-fry, grill or oven-roast them until hot and cooked right through (about 10 minutes on gentle heat). Slice the sausages with a sharp knife and serve, if desired, on warm lentils tossed with salsa verde and with a demitasse of ham hock and lentil soup.

HAM HOCK AND LENTIL SOUP

The quantity here is for four substantial serves as a soup or eight or more demitasse cups as an *amuse bouche*, or accompaniment.

2 large shallots
2 tablespoons olive oil
2 large cloves garlic, peeled and squashed flat
125 g (4 oz) Puy lentils, washed and drained
850 ml (28¾ fl oz) ham hock stock (see Jellied
   Ham Hock Sausages, page 249)
salt and freshly ground pepper
150 ml (5 fl oz) pure cream (45% butterfat)

Peel and chop the shallots. Put them in a saucepan with a little olive oil and cook over a moderate heat until soft but not coloured. Add the garlic and cook for a minute or two. Add the lentils and hock stock, ensuring the lentils are covered at least twice over. Bring to the boil then turn down the heat so the liquid slowly simmers. Partly cover the pot and continue to cook gently until the lentils are very soft and disintegrating. Pour the liquid and lentils into a processor and blend until the soup is completely smooth. Return to the saucepan and taste and adjust the seasoning. Add the cream and return the liquid to the boil, allowing it to reduce a little if necessary to concentrate the flavour. Adjust the seasoning once again. Froth with a hand-held beater before serving.

Chapter Eleven

SWEETNESS AND FRUITFUL ANTICIPATION

Taking the trouble to round off a meal you have prepared with a flourish makes sense. If a three-course meal is to be some kind of journey then the appetiser or entrée is the teaser – just enough to make you wish there was more. The second course should help make sense of that wine you are drinking, offer a little more robustness in flavour and help almost sate the appetite.

But the last course should be all about delicious temptation. Just when you thought you had had enough, along comes something that is so wickedly playful it makes you smile and makes it impossible to say no. A touch of the whimsical – shiny, colourful, glistening and ... sweet.

Finishing off with just a main course is like getting the business of refuelling over and done with. It is more about feeding yourself than having a dining experience. You have eaten, you move on. Degustation menus, shared plates and 'small tastes' menus are no different. The role of the sweet course or plate is to make you want to yield when you were so absolutely sure you would not.

In the early years of my career I was often disappointed to find that many restaurants, and male chefs in particular, could not be bothered with this last bit of fanfare. So much so, that the job was often relegated to an inexperienced commis – usually a female. It was the job I fell into in many kitchens in the early days. Pastry chefs other than in bakeries and large hotels were not commonplace in Australian kitchens. This has remained the case.

At Lake House we celebrate desserts and use them to celebrate special occasions. Birthday and anniversary plates are embellished with best wishes scrolled in chocolate. Sculptured tuiles, the finest chocolate and toffee 'straws', towering peach melbas and deliciously wobbling jewel-like jellies, never fail to raise a smile. Just the sight of the array of miniature sweets on our Six Tastes Platter always has people reaching for their spoons. It is really just all about being kids in a lolly shop.

It is not an accident that fruit forms the basis for many desserts at Lake House. With keenly felt seasons and the produce of each, mostly available just down the road, we are rarely at a loss when it comes to the best ingredients. Anticipation provides the inspiration for each seasonal dessert change as we plan dishes incorporating quinces, figs, cherries, berries, peaches, blood oranges, pink grapefruit and rhubarb.

Apple soufflé with apple sorbet

Serves 4

With the bounty of Daylesford organics as well as the apple-growing centres of Bacchus Marsh and Harcourt nearby, you can track the change of apple varieties being picked locally by the flavours of our warm apple charlottes, apple soufflés and sorbets. Excellent ciders are also produced in the district, which we frequently use in our cooking as well as enjoying ice cold. If you are after something special to finish a dinner, bake these apple soufflés in little demitasse coffee cups with the sorbet alongside garnished with an apple crisp. Granny Smiths produce a sorbet with the lightest of green hues.

APPLE SOUFFLÉ

3 apples, peeled, cored and roughly chopped

2 tablespoons lemon juice

1 teaspoon caster (superfine) sugar

100 ml (3½ fl oz) milk

40 g (1½ oz) additional caster (superfine) sugar

1 tablespoon plain (all-purpose) flour, combined with 1–2 tablespoons milk to form a paste

15 g (½ oz) butter

2 egg yolks

2 tablespoons Calvados

4 egg whites

APPLE SORBET

6 apples (or more), unpeeled and roughly chopped

1 tablespoon lemon juice, or to taste

250 ml (8½ fl oz) Sugar Syrup (see page 293)

Apple Crisps (see page 291) for garnish

APPLE SOUFFLÉ Place the apples, lemon juice and the 1 teaspoon of caster sugar in a saucepan and cook, covered, over low heat for about 10–15 minutes or until the apples completely soften and break down. Stir with a wooden spoon until a purée forms. Remove from the heat but keep warm.

Place the milk and additional caster sugar in a small saucepan and bring to the boil. Reduce to low heat, add the flour–milk paste and cook, stirring with a wooden spoon, for 2–3 minutes or until the mixture thickens. Remove the saucepan from the heat then stir in the butter, egg yolks and liqueur. Stir in the warm apple purée. Using an electric beater, whisk the egg whites in a bowl until stiff peaks form then fold into the apple mixture.

Preheat the oven to 180°C (350°F). Spoon the mixture into 8 x 125 ml (4 fl oz) demitasse cups or 4 x 250 ml (8½ fl oz) soufflé dishes. Bake for 8 minutes for the demitasse cups and 12–16 minutes for the larger dishes, or until golden and puffed. Serve with apple sorbet and garnish with an apple crisp.

APPLE SORBET Process the apples and lemon juice in a food processor until completely pulped. Pass the pulp through a fine mesh strainer, catching the juices in a large bowl. You will need 500 ml (17 fl oz) of juice for the 250 ml (8½ fl oz) of sugar syrup. Add the apple juice to the sugar syrup, stirring to combine well. Cover and refrigerate for at least 1 hour then churn in an ice cream maker. Serve topped with an apple crisp alongside the soufflé. Alternatively, scoop into chilled martini glasses and drizzle with a little Calvados.

Through winter and early spring there are blood and Seville oranges, ruby grapefruit and lemons mostly from the north of our state. Meyer lemons, the only ones able to withstand our local frosts, need a fair bit of cosseting in their first years with canopies and Hessian bag overcoats for the mornings. When zesting lemons not obtained direct from a grower, scrub them well. Nowadays they are usually waxed. If you have a lemon tree, you'll have a glut from time to time. Take a bag when visiting friends. Lemons are among the most useful of kitchen ingredients.

~ Lemon charlotte with citrus salad ~
Makes 8 individual charlottes

This is a winter treat, warm and oozing beautiful hot lemon curd. You can embellish it with our very easy Lemon Ice Cream (see page 277). Several of the components of this dish are useful separately. The curd quantity (about 1.5 litres/51 fl oz) is sufficient to allow you to bottle half of it. Enjoy it on hot toast. If you visit us in winter you may be offered a little pot of curd with warm citrus madeleines. If the assembly of the charlotte is too fiddly for you, slice the sponge up into fingers and sandwich them with the curd and freshly whipped cream. Serving alongside a salad of mixed citrus will turn that teatime treat into a dessert.

LEMON CURD

6 large lemons

550 g (1 lb 3½ oz) caster (superfine) sugar

230 g (8¼ oz) diced butter, softened

6 eggs

LEMON CUSTARD

250 ml (8½ fl oz) milk

250 ml (8½ fl oz) thickened cream (35% butterfat)

3 eggs

125 g (4 oz) caster (superfine) sugar

20 ml (1 fl oz) lemon juice

CHARLOTTES

Genoese Sponge (see page 292) *or*
    1 packet sponge biscuits

SERVING SUGGESTIONS

Lemon Ice Cream (see Lemon Ice Cream
    'Sandwiches', page 277)

mixed citrus segments

Citrus Powder (see page 291) for dusting

LEMON CURD Remove the zest of three of the lemons. Extract the juice of all the lemons, measuring the liquid to ensure that you have 300 ml (10 fl oz). Place the zest, juice and other ingredients in a stainless steel bowl and whisk to combine. Place the bowl over a pot of warm water off the heat and whisk until the butter has melted, the sugar has dissolved and the eggs are thoroughly incorporated. Place the pot of water and the bowl over a gentle heat and bring the water to a simmer. Continue to cook, stirring frequently until the mixture begins to thicken. Stir continuously for about 20 minutes until it coats the back of the spoon. Pour the curd into warm sterilised jars, seal tightly and leave to cool. Store in the refrigerator.

LEMON CUSTARD Combine the milk and cream and bring to the boil. Remove from the heat. Whisk the eggs and sugar until creamy then pour on a little of the hot liquid and stir through. Add remaining liquid then lemon juice and stir to combine.

CHARLOTTES Line the sides and bases of the dariole moulds with trimmed sponge (or sponge biscuits if using) that has been well soaked in the lemon custard. The sponge, no more than 1½ cm (¾ in) thick, must fit tightly or even overlap slightly. Set aside any offcuts. Fill each lined mould with chilled curd and top with soaked sponge offcuts – this will be the base of the charlotte. Cover each mould with a piece of greased greaseproof paper and seal tightly with foil. Preheat the oven to 170°C (335°F). Place dariole moulds in a baking dish and pour in hot water to reach halfway up the sides of the moulds. Cover

the dish with foil. Carefully place in the oven and bake for 20 minutes. Remove and allow charlottes to cool slightly before turning out. Serve with ice cream, cream or a little salad of mixed citrus segments. Dust the plate with citrus powder.

VARIATION The charlotte can be adapted by filling it with sweetened puréed apple. Serve it with warm custard, scattered with a few toasted walnuts and perhaps a drizzle of honey.

Honey panna cotta with quince soup

Serves 6

We eagerly anticipate the arrival of quinces every year. Freshly picked and piled into large bowls around the house and the restaurant, they perfume the air. The quince soup in this recipe reminds me of my mother's beautiful late summer and autumn fruit compotes, which sat cooling in their cooking pots in the water-filled concrete laundry troughs. The use of 10 quinces in this recipe makes an intensely flavoured 'soup' and the remaining poached fruit can be used for breakfast or in a cake or tart.

HONEY PANNA COTTA

560 ml (19 fl oz) thickened cream (35% butterfat)
200 ml (7 fl oz) milk
150 g (5 oz) honey
90 g (3¼ oz) sugar
4½ leaves gelatine (gold), soaked in cold water

QUINCE SOUP

10 medium-sized quinces
pinch of salt
1 cup sugar
1 vanilla bean, split and scraped
juice of 1 lemon
4.4 litres (149 fl oz) water

GARNISH (OPTIONAL)

Tuile Biscuits (see page 293)

HONEY PANNA COTTA Bring the cream and milk to the boil with the honey and sugar. Drain the soaked gelatine leaves, add them to the milk mixture and stir until it comes back to a simmer. Allow the mixture to cool slightly, pour it into dariole moulds then leave for approximately 3 hours to set.

QUINCE SOUP Peel and core the quinces and place them in a bowl of acidulated water. Put the flesh, skin and cores in a pot with the sugar, vanilla bean, lemon juice and water. Bring to the boil and simmer until the liquid has reduced by one-quarter. Strain through a fine mesh sieve into a saucepan. Cut five of the quinces into quarters and roughly chop the rest. Add the quince quarters and chopped quince to the reduced strained liquid and bring to the boil. Reduce the heat and simmer until the flesh and liquid turns red in colour. Strain the liquid through a fine mesh sieve, reserving the quince flesh and taking care not to break the quince quarters. Chill the soup then adjust flavour with either sugar and/or lemon juice. Set aside the quince quarters. Process the remaining quince to a purée and adjust the flavour with sugar and/or lemon juice.

TO ASSEMBLE AND SERVE Using soup bowls to serve, place a dollop of purée in each one. Wrap a hot towel around the panna cotta moulds for a few seconds and gently unmould them onto the purée. Carefully pour soup around the panna cotta. Slice and fan one quince quarter per serve and use as a garnish in the soup or sit each on a tuile biscuit on top of the panna cotta. Any remaining sliced quince and quince purée are delicious as a breakfast fruit.

❧ Rhubarb, rhubarb, rhubarb ❧
Serves 8

During rambles with the dogs in spring, across paddocks and along forgotten rail tracks from the gold diggings, I'll often collect bunches of rhubarb from old plantings. If you've any space at all in your garden put in some rhubarb. It's a forgiving plant, even of the most neglectful of gardeners. Although the leaves are poisonous it's worth purchasing rhubarb intact rather than the plastic-wrapped stems often offered in supermarkets. Wilted leaves will indicate a lack of freshness.

RHUBARB SORBET
500 g (1 lb 2 oz) rhubarb, trimmed and cut to 1 cm (½ in) pieces
¾ cup caster (superfine) sugar
1 tablespoon liquid glucose

RHUBARB JELLY
1 kg (2 lb 3 oz) rhubarb, cooked (see method, page 84)
lemon juice to taste
gelatine leaves (gold)

RHUBARB CRUMBLE
150 g (5 oz) plain (all-purpose) flour
100 g (3½ oz) brown sugar
½ teaspoon ground cinnamon
80 g (3 oz) butter
4 rhubarb stalks, trimmed

GARNISH (OPTIONAL)
rhubarb crisp (see Pear Crisps, page 291)

RHUBARB SORBET Toss all the ingredients together in a bowl and leave it over a pot of warm water for 30 minutes. Pour all the ingredients into a saucepan and cook over low heat for 10–15 minutes or until tender. Purée in a blender and pass through a fine tamis. Cool, refrigerate then churn.

RHUBARB JELLY Strain the juice from the cooked rhubarb, reserving the flesh to use in the rhubarb crumble. Adjust the flavour of the strained syrup with lemon juice or Sugar Syrup (see page 293) if needed. For eight small jellies you will need about 800 ml (27 fl oz) of liquid. Measure out the liquid and heat gently. For each 120 ml (4 fl oz) of liquid soak 1 leaf of gelatine in a small bowl of cold water. When completely wet and pliable, drain and squeeze out the gelatine leaves. Add to the warm liquid and stir through until dissolved. Allow the liquid to cool then pour into moulds and refrigerate.

RHUBARB CRUMBLE Preheat the oven to 200°C (400°F). Combine the flour, sugar and cinnamon. Add the butter and rub in until crumbly. Sprinkle the crumble mix onto a baking tray, bake for 15 minutes or until golden then set aside. Reduce the oven temperature to 180°C (350°F). Line 8 ring moulds (about 4 cm/1½ in high and 3½ cm/ 1⅓ in diameter) with silicon paper and place them on a baking tray. Using a vegetable peeler, shave long ribbons of rhubarb from the stalks. Use these to line the inside of the moulds. Fill the moulds with the cooked rhubarb reserved from the jelly and top with crumble, packing it down gently. Bake crumbles for 8–10 minutes then remove from the oven.

TO SERVE Place each crumble on a plate and slip off the ring and silicon paper. Unmould the jellies onto the same plates and serve a quenelle of the sorbet alongside. Top with rhubarb crisp if using.

Apricot tarte tatin, amaretto parfait and praline
Serves 6

Cooked apricots go particularly well with almond-flavoured amaretto liqueur. Here miniature apricot tarte tatins are made from dried apricots. I prefer to cook with these because they provide an intensity of flavour generally lacking nowadays in the fresh fruit. As a consequence this is a fruit dessert that can still be produced in the dead of winter.

AMARETTO PARFAIT

300 ml (10 fl oz) thickened cream (35% butterfat)

½ vanilla bean

4 egg yolks

50 g (2 oz) caster (superfine) sugar

100 ml (3½ fl oz) thickened cream (35% butterfat), whipped to soft peaks

4 tablespoons amaretto

Praline (see page 292) for sprinkling

TARTE TATINS

500 g (1 lb 2 oz) dried apricots

300 g (10½ oz) sugar

500 ml (17 fl oz) water

8 discs puff pastry, cut slightly larger than tin diameter, and refrigerated

200 g (7 oz) sugar combined with 100 ml (3½ fl oz) water

50 g (2 oz) additional sugar for sprinkling

AMARETTO PARFAIT Bring the cream and vanilla bean to a simmer in a saucepan, remove from the heat and allow to infuse for ½ an hour. Whisk the yolks and sugar in a bowl, pour the warm cream onto the mix then return to the saucepan. Cook over a gentle heat, stirring until the mixture has thickened and coats the spoon. Cool then chill in the refrigerator. Fold in the whipped cream and amaretto, pour into moulds, leaving a little space at the top, and freeze. The quantity makes 6 pyramid moulds or can be poured into a loaf pan and served sliced.

TARTE TATINS Simmer the apricots with the sugar and water until soft but still holding their shape. Drain well. Sit on several layers of kitchen paper. Make a light toffee with the combined sugar and water as described in Praline (see page 292). As soon as the syrup colours, remove it from the heat and swirl the pan by the handle to even out the heat (the syrup will continue to cook and colour). Sit the pan in a bowl of cold water to stop the cooking process. Preheat the oven to 165°C (330°F). Place a teaspoon of the warm toffee in the base of each well-greased tart tin (we use 5 cm/2 in diameter tins). Place four whole poached apricots upright, firmly packed side by side, in each tin. Add a fifth apricot if necessary or some halved pieces of fruit around the sides. Cover each tin with a disc of greased paper. Place on a baking tray and cook for 10–15 minutes. The apricots will combine with the caramel to form a dense filling. Remove from the oven and allow to cool.

TO FINISH AND SERVE Purée any remaining apricots until smooth. Top the amaretto parfait moulds with the purée, sprinkle densely with praline then return to the freezer. Preheat the oven to 200°C (400°F). Once tarts have cooled, press down on the apricots to condense. Place a disc of chilled puff pastry over each tart, sprinkle with a little sugar and bake for 15–20 minutes or until golden. Carefully turn out each tart onto a plate – there will be some hot caramel and juices. Turn out a moulded parfait and garnish around with praline.

Sour cherry and almond pithivier with sour cream ice cream
Serves 8

Our Brandied Cherries (see page 38) and home-made Cherry Brandy (see page 39) already contain nuances of almond flavour from the use of cracked cherry pits in their cooking and production.

PITHIVIERS
600 g (1 lb 5 oz) good-quality puff pastry made with butter
plain (all-purpose) flour for dusting

FILLING
200 g (7 oz) blanched almonds
200 g (7 oz) caster (superfine) sugar
4 egg yolks
80 g (3 oz) butter
8 tablespoons kirsch or vodka
40 (about 300 g/10½ oz) pitted morello cherries, cooked (see Cherry Brandy, page 39), drained well and syrup reserved

1 beaten egg for glazing
2 teaspoons icing (confectioner's) sugar

Sour Cream Ice Cream (see page 292)

PITHIVIERS Cut off one-third of the pastry dough and roll it out to a sheet 2 mm (⅛ in) thick. Using a plain cutter, cut out eight circles, 6 cm (2½ in) in diameter. Dust with flour and store on a tray in the refrigerator. Roll out the remaining pastry, 3–4 mm (¼ in) thick, and cut out eight circles, 7 cm (2¾ in) in diameter. Store in the refrigerator.

FILLING Process the almonds and caster sugar until finely ground. Add the yolks, processing to incorporate. Repeat with the butter, adding the alcohol towards the end. The mixture should be smooth and creamy. Divide the almond cream in half then divide each half into eight roughly equal portions. Chill until cold and firm.

ASSEMBLY AND BAKING Place the eight smaller pastry circles on a baking sheet. Centre a portion of almond cream on each, three morello cherries on top and cover with another portion of almond cream. Place two cherries on top, pushing them into the cream a little. Moisten the border of the pastry with a little water. Centre a large pastry circle on top of each cream and cherry mound. Press down the edges of the pastry but ensure the mounded contents remain a centred small dome. With a small knife, mark lines radiating down from the centre of the pastry. Cut a small hole in the centre of the top. Mark around the edges of the dough with the knife, glaze each top with beaten egg and place in the refrigerator for at least ½ an hour or until ready to bake and serve.

Preheat the oven to 220°C (430°F) then bake the pithiviers for 8–10 minutes or until pastry is well risen and golden. Sprinkle the tops with icing sugar, raise the oven temperature to 240°C (465°F) and let the pithiviers caramelise. Remove from the oven and serve warm with the sour cream ice cream and cherry brandy.

❧ Duet for two divas ❧
Serves 6

This is a celebration of some very special dishes created long ago in honour of Dame Nellie Melba and Anna Pavlova. Our Peach Melba and Pavlova are by no means classics, but arriving as a duet on a large plate they always create a sense of fun. In our version of Peach Melba, the poached peach and vanilla ice cream sit on a mirror of raspberry jelly, concealing a layer of champagne sabayon underneath. These additional elements are inspired by a dessert done by friend, colleague and probably the finest pastry chef in Australia, Phillipa Sibley, for our Two Decades Dinner celebration.

CHAMPAGNE SABAYON
4 egg yolks
65 ml (2¼ fl oz) Sugar Syrup (see page 293)
2 leaves gelatine (gold)
50 ml (2 fl oz) thickened cream (35% butterfat)
juice of ½ lemon
90 ml (3¼ fl oz) champagne
100 ml (3½ fl oz) additional thickened cream (35% butterfat), whipped to soft peaks

RASPBERRY JELLY
500 g (1 lb 2 oz) fresh raspberries
100 g (3½ oz) sugar
zest of ½ lemon
2 leaves gelatine (gold)

THE PEACHES
300 g (10½ oz) sugar
500 ml (17 fl oz) water
zest of 1 lemon
1 vanilla bean
3 white peaches »

CHAMPAGNE SABAYON Whisk the yolks in an electric mixer. Heat the sugar syrup to 118°C (245°F) and pour it slowly onto the yolks with the mixer still running. Continue to whisk until cooled. Soak the gelatine leaves in cold water then drain and squeeze them dry. Heat the 50 ml (2 fl oz) of cream, add the softened gelatine and stir until completely dissolved. Cool the cream mix and fold it into the yolks with the lemon juice. Whisk in the champagne and the whipped cream. Divide the mixture between six small flat dishes (recipe makes 500 ml/17 fl oz) and refrigerate to set. We use 4 cm (1½ in) square dishes.

RASPBERRY JELLY Combine the ingredients, except the gelatine, in a metal bowl. Cover the bowl with plastic wrap and place over a pot of warm water. Stand in a warm spot for approximately 2 hours, allowing the juices to seep from the berries. Strain through a fine sieve, discarding the pulp. Measure out 250 ml (8½ fl oz) of juice. Heat half the juice. Soak the gelatine leaves in a bowl of cold water, drain and squeeze dry then add them to the heated juice and stir through to dissolve. Add to the remaining juice and cool to the point of setting. The recipe makes about 270 ml (9 fl oz) of jelly. Spoon a thin layer over the set sabayon in each of the 6 dishes. Refrigerate.

THE PEACHES In a small saucepan dissolve the sugar in the water over low heat. Add the zest and the vanilla bean, split and with its seeds scraped into the water. Bring to the boil over medium heat and remove from stove. Add the peaches to the saucepan, ensuring they are covered by syrup. Bring to a very gentle simmer and cook for 6–10 minutes. Lift out the peaches, allow them to cool slightly then remove the skins.

Vanilla Ice Cream (see page 292)
1 quantity Raspberry Sauce (see page 292)
6 Tuile Biscuits (optional; see page 293)

STRAWBERRY PAVLOVA
120 g (4 oz) egg whites
250 g (9 oz) caster (superfine) sugar
1 teaspoon vinegar
½ tablespoon cornflour (cornstarch)
½ teaspoon pure vanilla essence
200 ml (7 fl oz) thickened cream
   (35% butterfat), whipped
strawberries to decorate
icing (confectioner's) sugar for dusting

Store the peaches in the cooled syrup until ready to use – you can reuse the poaching liquid to poach more.

ASSEMBLING PEACH MELBA Remove the peaches from the syrup and drain and dry. Slice flat cheek halves from either side of the peach stone and place each half on the raspberry jelly surface of each of the 6 dishes. Place a quenelle of vanilla ice cream alongside. Spoon raspberry sauce over the peach and drizzle a strip over the ice cream. Garnish with a tuile if desired.

STRAWBERRY PAVLOVA Preheat the oven to 110°C (230°F). Whisk the egg whites to soft peaks. Whisk in the sugar, vinegar, cornflour and vanilla. Continue to whisk until the meringue forms stiff peaks. Spoon the meringue into a piping bag with a large plain nozzle. Line a baking tray with silicon paper. To make individual pavlovas, use a 4 cm diameter x 5cm deep (1½ x 2 in) well-greased mould as a guide and pipe the meringue into the mould on the tray. Lift off the mould, respray it and repeat the process until all the mixture is used up. Bake in the oven for 10 minutes then reduce the heat to 100°C (210°F) and bake for an additional 20 minutes. Pavlovas should not colour. They should be crisp on the outside and marshmallow soft in the centre.

ASSEMBLING PAVLOVA Drizzle a little raspberry sauce on a plate and place a meringue on top. Pipe whipped cream over the surface of the meringue and decorate with sliced strawberries. Dust with icing sugar.

TO SERVE THE DUET Place the assembled Peach Melba on a large plate with the completed pavlovas alongside.

❖ Individual tiramisu trifle ❖
Serves 8

This is one of the components of our changing La Dolce Vita plate, which celebrates the Italians' contribution to sweetness and desire.

MASCARPONE

3 egg yolks
100 g (3½ oz) sugar
250 g (9 oz) mascarpone
2 leaves gelatine (gold)
a little thickened cream (35% butterfat)
250 ml (8½ fl oz) thickened cream (35% butterfat), whipped

ESPRESSO JELLY

100 ml (3½ fl oz) coffee liqueur
1 litre (34 fl oz) strong brewed coffee
sugar to taste
9 leaves gelatine (gold)

Genoese Sponge (see page 292) or purchased sponge fingers

MASCARPONE Cream the eggs and sugar until pale and fluffy. Fold the mascarpone through the egg mix. Soak the gelatine leaves in water, heat the small quantity of cream then squeeze out the gelatine leaves and add them to the warm cream. Stir until the gelatine is completely dissolved then add to the mascarpone mixture. Stir to amalgamate evenly then fold the whipped cream into the mixture.

ESPRESSO JELLY Add the liqueur to the coffee. Sweeten the coffee to taste. Soak the gelatine leaves in cold water until completely soft. Squeeze out the leaves, add to the warm coffee and stir until the gelatine has completely dissolved. Allow the jelly to cool and when completely cold check for sweetness once again.

TO ASSEMBLE AND SERVE TIRAMISU You will need 8 martini glasses. Have the mascarpone mixture and coffee jelly cool and close to the point of setting. Pour out a little coffee mixture into a small bowl and soak some pieces of sponge, or sponge fingers, in it. Place a little soaked sponge in the base of each glass. Press down with a teaspoon to create an even surface. Spread a layer of mascarpone over the sponge and place the glasses in the refrigerator. Once set pour in a layer of coffee jelly and return to the refrigerator to set. Continue the process with another layer of mascarpone and finish with a layer of jelly. Place in the refrigerator until ready. Serve one assembled trifle per person. At Lake House, as part of our La Dolce Vita plate, the trifle may be served with crostolli, biscotti, espresso granita and other indulgences.

SWEET TASTES

The following are some of the many things we serve as small tastes for those of our guests who visibly waver with indecision when offered our list of complete desserts. 'Perhaps just a morsel … ?'

❧ STRAWBERRY FRITTERS ❧
WITH RASPBERRY SAUCE
Makes 30 fritters

Fabulous served in a little pile alongside a Kir Royale. Just try saying no.

80 g (3 oz) plain (all-purpose) flour
pinch of salt
1 whole egg
8 teaspoons beer
4 egg whites
30 strawberries
100 ml (3½ fl oz) Grand Marnier
oil for deep-frying
1 quantity Raspberry Sauce (see page 292)
caster (superfine) sugar for sprinkling

Combine the flour and salt with the whole egg and beer, stirring to produce a smooth batter. Allow it to rest for at least 2 hours. Stiffly beat the egg whites and fold into the batter. Stem the strawberries and marinate in the Grand Marnier for 20 minutes. Heat some oil to 150°C (300°F). Drain the strawberries and, using a skewer, dip each strawberry in batter and deep-fry until golden. Drain briefly on kitchen paper. Brush raspberry sauce across the plates and pile a few fritters on each. Serve additional sauce alongside.

❧ CHOCOLATE FONDANT SACHER ❧
Serves 8

Really just your classic gooey baked fondant that oozes hot chocolate when you cut into it. Inspired by the wonderful Viennese Sacher torte, in this version I add an insert of soft apricots and a warm apricot glaze coating.

60 g (2 oz) butter
115 g (3¾ oz) chocolate, with at least 70% cocoa solids
1 teaspoon flour
1 whole egg
1 egg yolk
30 g (1 oz) sugar
60 g (2 oz) dried apricots, cooked in water until soft
100 ml (3½ fl oz) smooth apricot jam,
　　heated with 1 tablespoon rum and passed
　　through a fine sieve to form a glaze

Preheat the oven to 170°C (340°F). Melt the butter and chocolate together in a bowl over a pot of warm water. Stir in the flour. Whisk the eggs and sugar together until creamy, add to the chocolate mix and stir through to combine. Chop the apricots into small pieces and divide into 8 portions, squeezing the pieces together to form 8 small balls. Spoon sufficient chocolate mixture to half fill 8 half-cup metal dariole moulds. Drop an apricot ball onto the mix and spoon more chocolate mixture on top to cover. Fill the moulds seven-eighths full. Bake the fondants in the preheated oven for 7 minutes. Turn the fondants out of the moulds onto a serving plate, brush with warm apricot glaze and serve immediately.

Lemon ice cream 'sandwiches'

Makes 8 x 4 cm (1 ½ in) sandwiches

I'm forever playing with variations on little ice cream sandwiches. It's something to do with one of the treats of my youth. A 'Kreem b tween' – a slice of creamy vanilla ice cream sandwiched between two wafers – was something worth saving up for. Rather than bite into the 'sandwich', which would demolish it far too quickly, one would daintily lick at the outside edges to prolong the treat. Our dessert repertoire includes many variations on this theme: honey wafers with lavender ice cream, chocolate crisps with rum and raisin ice cream, and this one, which sandwiches lemon ice cream between a pair of nutty meringues. The ice cream is a particularly simple one, made using an uncooked base.

LEMON ICE CREAM

600 ml (20 fl oz) cream
1 vanilla bean
zest of 1 lemon
6 egg yolks
200 g (7 oz) caster (superfine) sugar
75 ml (3 fl oz) strained fresh lemon juice
1 tablespoon Limoncello liqueur

ALMOND MERINGUES

200 g (7 oz) ground almonds
120 g (4 oz) sugar
120 g (4 oz) icing (confectioner's) sugar
8 egg whites

ICE CREAM Place the cream, vanilla bean and zest in a pan and bring to a simmer over gentle heat. Turn off the heat, allow to infuse then strain. Cream the yolks and sugar, pour the warm cream onto the mix and whisk well. Stir through the lemon juice and limoncello then chill and churn.

MERINGUES Preheat the oven to 135°C (270°F). Line baking trays with silicon paper and use a cutter to draw 16 circles, each 4 cm (1½ in) in diameter. Combine the ground almonds, sugar and icing sugar. Beat the egg whites until stiff. Carefully fold the almond mixture into the egg whites, scrape the mixture into a piping bag and pipe flat spiral rounds onto the drawn circles. Place the trays in the oven to bake for up to 1 hour or until the discs are firm. They will crisp up as they cool.

TO ASSEMBLE Sandwich the ice cream between two layers of meringue.

Chapter Twelve

BASICS AND EMBELLISHMENTS

This chapter contains most of the basic building blocks for producing the recipes in this book. There are also embellishments that are found in the larders of professional kitchens, which can serve to transform a very simple dish into something a little more special.

BATTER

TEMPURA BATTER

Makes 2 cups

2 eggs
2 cups rice flour
¼ teaspoon salt
2 cups chilled soda water

In a bowl use a whisk to combine the eggs, rice flour, salt and enough soda water to make a wet batter — do not be concerned if it is slightly lumpy. You can refrigerate the batter for up to 1 hour before use but it is best made just before using.

BEANS, PULSES AND GRAINS

COOKING BARLEY

1 tablespoon butter
1 cup pearl barley
2 cups chicken stock
½ teaspoon salt

Melt the butter in a saucepan over medium heat. When hot, add the barley and cook, stirring, for about 5 minutes or until the grains are lightly toasted. Pour in the stock, add the salt and simmer partially covered for around 30 minutes or until the barley is the texture you like. Add a little water if necessary. The barley should be reasonably chewy. Uncover and boil off any excess liquid.

CASSOULET OF BEANS

1½ cups cannelloni beans, soaked in water overnight
1 small leek, white part only
1 small carrot, cut in half
1 small onion, cut in half
20 g (¾ oz) butter
1 tablespoon olive oil
1 teaspoon finely chopped garlic
2 rashers middle bacon, finely chopped
1 tablespoon finely chopped carrot
1 tablespoon finely chopped onion
3–4 tablespoons chicken or beef stock
2 sprigs fresh rosemary, very finely chopped
1 Roma tomato from a can (as you are most likely cooking this in winter!), seeded and diced
salt and freshly ground pepper

Rinse the soaked beans, drain then place in a saucepan with enough water to cover them. Add the leek and carrot and onion halves and bring to the boil. Reduce to a simmer and cook for approximately 1 hour or until tender. Drain and reserve. Heat the butter and oil in a saucepan over medium heat. Add the garlic, bacon and chopped carrot and onion and stir for 2–3 minutes until the carrot and onion are cooked. Add the reserved cooked bean mix, stock and rosemary. Cover and cook for a further 2 minutes. Add the diced tomato and heat through. Season to taste and keep warm until ready to serve.

BUCKWHEAT

500 ml (17 fl oz) water or stock
30 g (1 oz) butter
1 cup buckwheat
salt

Bring the water or stock to a simmer. Melt the butter in a saucepan over medium heat, add the buckwheat and stir for 3–4 minutes. Pour the simmering liquid into the buckwheat and add salt. Reduce the heat. Cover and simmer for 15–20 minutes or until the liquid is absorbed. The buckwheat is cooked at this stage.

If you are using buckwheat as an accompaniment and you want a fluffy dry pilaf texture, cook the buckwheat as above to this point in an ovenproof casserole. Then stir through another 30 g (1 oz) butter and 1 cup of stock and place, uncovered, in a preheated oven at 170°C (340°F) for a further 15–20 minutes. Give the buckwheat a stir and a turn halfway through the cooking time. The finished buckwheat will be quite dry and have a toasted aroma.

FRIED CHICKPEA CHIPS

Makes 24 finger-sized chips

This is one of the many things Matt enjoyed during his time at Daniel's in NYC.

900 ml (30 fl oz) milk
2 tablespoons olive oil
1 tablespoon butter
salt and freshly ground pepper
2¼ cups chickpea flour
fine polenta for dredging
oil for frying

Put the milk, olive oil and butter in a saucepan. Season and bring to the boil. Reduce to a simmer and gradually whisk in the chickpea flour, stirring constantly. Continue to cook until very thick. Pour into a non-stick baking pan and leave to cool. Turn out the chickpea 'slab' onto your work surface and cut it into the desired shapes. Dredge with polenta and shallow-fry at 160°C (320°F) until crisp on the outside.

SOFT POLENTA

Gradual addition of the polenta, steady constant heat, a heavy-based saucepan and regular stirring to prevent sticking and scorching are the required elements of success when cooking polenta. If I wish to hold the polenta for some time before serving, I use a little more water. Once cooked, the polenta will swell and soften while being held.

salt
800–1000 ml (27–34 fl oz) water
200 g (7 oz) polenta
50 g (2 oz) butter
1 tablespoon chopped flat-leaf parsley (optional)
1 teaspoon chopped fresh sage (optional)
1 tablespoon freshly grated parmesan or 2 heaped tablespoons of mascarpone (optional)

Add salt to the water and bring to the boil. Gradually add the polenta, stirring constantly with a wooden spoon. Reduce the heat and cook, uncovered, for about 45 minutes, stirring as needed. The polenta is ready when it comes away from the side of the pan. Add the butter – and the herbs and parmesan or mascarpone if using. Cover with wet or greased greaseproof paper to avoid the top from hardening. The best way to hold the polenta is in a double boiler over simmering water. Tightly covered, it will hold for at least ½ an hour without any loss of its deliciously soft creamy texture.

FRIED OR BAKED POLENTA

Spread hot soft polenta (see above) to a depth of about 2 cm (¾ in) in a well-greased or non-stick tray and leave it to cool and set. Cut the polenta into 5 cm (2 in) diamonds or use a cutter of your desired shape or size. Either fry the pieces in oil at 160°C (320°F) until crisp on the outside or brush with melted butter or olive oil and bake in a preheated oven at 140°C (275°F) for about half an hour. The polenta will be crisp on the outside and soft in the middle.

WILD RICE

Makes 2-3 cups of cooked rice

Wild rice is not really rice at all but is related to oats. I enjoy its nutty texture, a quality further enhanced if the rice is sautéed in a little butter after its initial cooking.

1 cup wild rice
6 cups water
60 g (2 oz) butter
salt and freshly ground pepper
chopped fresh herb for flavour (optional)

Place the rice in a fine colander, wash with plenty of running water then drain. Bring the 6 cups of water to the boil with some salt. Add the rice and cook for 15–20 minutes or until the rice is tender and the grains have opened up. Drain out the liquid. Heat the butter in a large pan and, when foaming, add the cooked rice. Cook over medium heat, stirring and turning the rice to ensure it is evenly coated in the butter. You will smell the delicious nutty aroma of the rice. Season to taste. Add chopped fresh thyme, chives or other herb that enhances your dish.

BREAD

Every day we produce our own bread, bread rolls, flat breads, brioche and specialty fruit and nut breads for cheese. There is inevitably much left at the end of the day. Many cultures use bread to extend dishes, such as the Italian panzanella and Middle Eastern fattoush. The following suggestions for dealing with leftovers also provide useful items to have in your store cupboard. At Lake House, when all of these uses are exhausted, there are always very hungry ducks, water hens, swans and goslings on the lake at the bottom of our garden.

BREAD RINGS

1 square loaf day-old bread, thinly sliced lengthways
olive oil, infused with garlic

Slice the long bread slices into strips about 4–5 cm (2 in) wide. Brush the strips with oil and wrap them around egg rings or other metal circles of the required diameter. Place the rings tightly against each other on a baking tray to hold the bread in place and bake in the oven at 125°C (255°F) until crisp. Remove the bread rings from the oven, allow them to cool then slide out the metal rings. Store in an airtight container until ready to use.

CROUTONS AND CROSTINI

Croutons are added to salads such as a classic Caesar, but are also delicious with many other ingredients, such as spinach, blue cheese and walnuts. Crostini can act as a base for hors d'oeuvres and as an accompaniment to cheese, but also go well with vegetable purées, pâtés and rillettes. Try crostini with a fresh broad bean purée in the height of spring with some shaved pecorino and a drizzle of peppery olive oil.

- stale bread, cut into 1–2 cm (½–¾ in) cubes (for croutons)
- two-day-old dinner rolls or baguette, cut into ½ cm (¼ in) slices (for crostini)
- olive oil or butter

Drizzle or brush the bread with olive oil to barely coat it. Place the bread in a single layer on a baking tray and bake at 170°C (340°F) until golden. For the best result, turn the slices/cubes over halfway through the cooking time. Alternatively, the bread can be gently fried in melted foaming butter over medium heat for about 5 minutes. Stir the slices/cubes around to ensure they are well coated in the butter. Drain on kitchen paper.

'Soldiers', used as a garnish with savoury custards such as the Smoked Trout Custards (see page 159) or as a base for hors d'oeuvres, are made by cutting day-old bread, crusts removed, into finger-width lengths before frying. Cool and store all these fried breads in an airtight jar.

FRIED BREADCRUMB TOPPINGS

Any bread that has been sprinkled with oil and baked or fried in butter (as above) produces wonderful, moist but crunchy breadcrumbs when rolled with a rolling pin or processed. Well seasoned, we use these as a topping for our cassoulets. Combined with herbs, zest and even nuts they make wonderful embellishments for many dishes.

CRUNCHY GREMOLATA

Process fried bread to coarse crumbs and combine with equal quantities of finely chopped parsley, lemon zest and puréed garlic. Season well and you have gremolata with a crunch, which is lovely over lamb.

WALNUT CRUMBLE

- 50 g (2 oz) fried bread
- 3 tablespoons toasted finely chopped walnuts
- zest of ½ orange, finely chopped
- 5 mint leaves, finely sliced
- 1 clove garlic, finely chopped

Process the fried bread into coarse crumbs and add the remaining ingredients. Seasoned well this is a wonderful embellishment for duck, especially with the addition of a little Duck Crackling (see page 191).

BUTTER

CLARIFIED BUTTER

For making a quantity of 500 g:
(1 lb 2 oz) or more:

Without its milk solids butter provides a flavoursome but less risky medium in which to sauté or fry.

Cut the butter up into cubes. Place the butter cubes in a saucepan over the lowest possible heat and allow them to melt — the saucepan can also be placed over a pilot light. (Alternatively, the cubes can be placed in a double boiler and can take up to 4 hours to melt.) Without disturbing the butter, skim and discard any white foam on the surface. Gently ladle out all the clear golden butter into a container with an airtight lid. Discard all the milk solids that will have fallen to the bottom of the saucepan. Keep the clarified butter in the refrigerator for up to a week.

For making a quantity of less than 500 g:

Melt the butter in a small saucepan over a low heat. Increase the heat and boil for about 10–15 minutes until the milk solids begin to colour. Cool slightly and pour through a coffee filter or muslin-lined sieve. Discard the milk solids.

CHEESE

FROMAGE FRAIS

We are fortunate in having regular deliveries of this really fresh cheese. It is delicious with Slow-baked Figs (see page 97), ripe strawberries or simply seasoned and mixed with chopped herbs and piled on Crostini (see page 281). Occasionally we have had to make a quick version of our own.

- 1 litre (34 fl oz) milk, warmed to no higher than 37°C (95°F)
- 3 tablets junket, dissolved in 3 tablespoons cold water
- salt and freshly ground pepper
- selected spices or freshly chopped herbs (optional)

Place the milk in a stainless steel bowl and heat slowly in a warm place. Combine the dissolved junket liquid with the milk then cover and leave in a warm place to set firm. Once set, put the mixture into a coffee filter or muslin-lined sieve and leave it to drain overnight. Turn the cheese into a bowl and add seasoning, spice or fresh herbs as desired.

MARINATED GOAT'S CHEESE

Makes 12 small medallions

250 g (9 oz) fresh goat's cheese
160 ml (5½ fl oz) mild-flavoured olive oil
2 shallots, thinly sliced
3 sprigs thyme
1 clove garlic, thinly sliced
½ teaspoon black peppercorns

Put the cheese in a bowl and knead to soften. Place the softened cheese on a 30 cm (12 in) double layer of plastic wrap. Elongate the mound of cheese along the plastic, using the wrap to roll the cheese into a log approximately 22 cm (8¾ in) long. Wrap the plastic tightly, tying the ends, and refrigerate the cheese for at least 2 hours or until firm. Cut the cheese into 12 discs then remove the plastic from each disc. Place the discs in a glass dish and add the remaining ingredients. For the best results, refrigerate the marinating cheese for 3 days then bring it back to room temperature before using.

PARMESAN CRISPS

Makes 10–12 crisps

150–200 g (5–7 oz) freshly grated parmesan

Sprinkle the parmesan evenly across a non-stick baking tray and bake at 160°C (320°F) for 10 minutes or until the parmesan is golden brown. The parmesan will melt together to form a sheet. Turn this out onto a chopping board and cut it into 'crisps' of the required size and shape while it is still warm. Store the crisps in an airtight container for up to a week.

PARMESAN FOAM

200 ml (7 fl oz) thickened cream
  (35% butterfat)
100 ml (3½ fl oz) milk
4 sprigs thyme
100 g (3½ oz) parmesan, chopped
3 cloves garlic
salt and freshly ground pepper
2 drops truffle oil (optional)

Combine the cream and milk and bring to the boil. Remove from the heat, add the thyme, parmesan and garlic and allow them to infuse for 15 minutes. Return the liquid to a simmer then remove from the heat. Discard the thyme sprigs and purée the liquid in a blender and pass through a tamis. Season well and add the truffle oil if using. Just before serving, blitz the liquid with a hand-held beater.

CRÊPES

PLAIN CRÊPES

Makes at least 12 crêpes

These are one of the most versatile items in our kitchen repertoire and provide an interesting way to package things other than using pasta or pastry.

260 g (9½ oz) plain (all-purpose) flour
salt and freshly ground white pepper
2 eggs
550 ml (19 fl oz) milk
50 ml (2 fl oz) olive oil

Place the flour, salt and pepper in a bowl. Make a deep well in the middle of the flour and break the eggs into it. Add 400 ml (13 fl oz) of the milk, and the olive oil. Using a whisk, stir the wet ingredients to combine well. Continue to stir, gradually drawing in the flour from around the edges. Continue until all the flour is incorporated. Gradually add the remaining milk, stirring to form a smooth batter. Pass the batter through a fine sieve and store in a jug in the refrigerator for 1 hour before using. To cook the crêpes, spread a film of oil on the base of a 20 cm (8 in) pan. Place the pan over medium heat then pour in enough batter to coat the base in a thin layer. Cook until set on top. Turn the crêpe over using a spatula and cook until it is coloured. Slide the crêpe out of the pan and continue the process until all the batter is used. The first crêpe is inevitably a disaster. If the batter seems too thick (flour can vary) to spread quickly over the base of the pan, you may need to add a little more milk to the mixture, stirring it through well. Transfer the cooked crêpes to a plate and stack one on top of the other as they are cooked.

DRESSINGS, OILS AND SAUCES

We use canola, grapeseed, peanut or blended vegetable oils when cooking with considerable heat or when a neutral-flavoured oil is required. Cold-pressed hazelnut and walnut oils, combined with one of the neutral oils, add a delicious quality to salads, especially where toasted nuts are one of the ingredients. We have several excellent suppliers of extra-virgin olive oil in the region. Those that are a little peppery or even a touch bitter may sometimes be offered at the table to add an extra layer of flavour as, for example, on a beef carpaccio or a sweet pepper compote. Olive oil is also used in dressings, usually combined with a little neutral-flavoured oil. Moroccan Argan oil is a rather expensive newcomer to our place and I am enjoying playing with its nutty flavour. Rice oil is also a new arrival and one of the new breeds of 'healthier' oils. Good red and white wine vinegars are staple ingredients. My personal favourites include sherry vinegar and, more especially, one made from the sultana-tasting Pedro Ximinez grape. This and cabernet vinegar are often used for dressings combined with meat juices in 'split' vinaigrettes, as our modern palates move further away from highly reduced sauces. Wine vinegars are also used to deglaze pans. I find champagne vinegar useful when a more delicate touch is required and rice vinegar offers a very mild and considerably less acidic flavour. Cider vinegar is produced in nearby Harcourt, along with a range of other apple products, and is a lovely addition when apples and pears are in a salad or when apples are cooked with cabbage. It also adds an extra layer of flavour when a touch is added to apple or pear sorbets. We keep and use a little barrel-aged balsamic vinegar. It is not as frequently used as the others. We had a decade-long abuse of this ingredient in Australia, when often-cheap olive oils and balsamic vinegars, largely comprised of caramel, were offered in a myriad of cafés for dunking bread. A little of the best balsamic judiciously used, on the other hand, goes a very long way.

Acidity can be added to a dressing in a variety of ways: citrus juice and rind, verjuice, a splash of wine and even pomegranate molasses can prove good additions. Generally dressings have a ratio of 3–4 parts oil to 1 part acid. To cut acidity, add finely chopped shallots. The addition of mustard (we use Dijon) helps emulsify a dressing and acts to balance the oil and the acid. The stronger the flavour of the salad leaves, the more robust your dressing can be. With bitter leaves such as witlof, cream can also be added to smooth out the flavour. Hard- or soft-boiled eggs add body, as does crumbled cheese.

BASIC VINAIGRETTE

Makes 300 ml (10 fl oz)

120 ml (4 fl oz) extra-virgin olive oil
120 ml (4 fl oz) grapeseed or other neutral-flavoured oil
60 ml (2 fl oz) red wine vinegar
salt and freshly ground pepper

If desired you can combine all the ingredients and emulsify with a hand-held blender for immediate use or combine them with a whisk and store in a bottle in the refrigerator. Shake well before using.

LAKE HOUSE DRESSING

Makes 200 ml (7 fl oz)

This is our house dressing, an emulsified vinaigrette we serve over a selection of salad leaves. With the addition of chopped dill it also makes a beautiful sauce to serve with poached trout or salmon. Alternatively, leave the fish plain and use the dill dressing on an accompaniment of poached or sautéed cucumber batons. We also sometimes toss the dressing over and around some steamed baby potatoes.

2 teaspoons Dijon mustard
2 shallots, finely diced
30–40 ml (1–1½ fl oz) red wine vinegar
40 ml (1½ fl oz) extra-virgin olive oil
80 ml (3 fl oz) grapeseed oil
salt and freshly ground pepper

Put the mustard, shallots and vinegar in a bowl and blend with a hand-held blender. Slowly drizzle in the oils to emulsify. Season to taste.

HAZELNUT DRESSING

Makes 220 ml (8 fl oz)

This dressing is useful with robust flavoured leaves such as witlof.

2 tablespoons white wine vinegar
½ teaspoon Dijon mustard
a splash of Frangelico (optional)
120 ml (4 fl oz) extra-virgin olive oil
1 teaspoon hazelnut oil
60 ml (2 fl oz) thickened cream (35% butterfat)
salt and freshly ground pepper

Combine the vinegar and mustard, and add the Frangelico if using. Whisk while adding olive oil in a thin drizzle then whisk in the hazelnut oil. Place in the refrigerator to chill. Just before serving whisk in the cream and season to taste.

BLACK BEAN DRESSING

Makes about 450 ml (15 fl oz)

75 ml (3 fl oz) vegetable oil
2 medium-sized shallots, finely chopped
1 piece ginger (about 30 g/1 oz), finely chopped
1 clove garlic, finely chopped
80 g (2½ oz) salted black beans, rinsed for a minute in a colander, then drained
100 ml (3½ fl oz) salt-reduced soy sauce
2 tablespoons mirin

225 ml (8 fl oz) olive oil
salt and freshly ground pepper

Pour about 1 tablespoon of the vegetable oil into a small pan over medium heat and add the shallots, ginger and garlic. Sweat gently for a few moments to release the aroma and to soften without colouring. Add the drained beans, soy sauce and mirin. Stir through and remove from the heat. Scrape the pan contents into a bowl and add the remaining oils in a slow drizzle, whisking to amalgamate. Taste and adjust seasoning. The dressing is best served immediately while it is still a little warm or at room temperature, and is delicious stirred through buckwheat noodles.

SPICED DRESSING

Makes 225 ml (8 fl oz)

45 ml (1¾ fl oz) lemon juice
1 clove garlic, peeled and crushed
1 teaspoon Dijon mustard
½ teaspoon curry powder
½ teaspoon ground cumin
½ teaspoon ground ginger
pinch of cayenne pepper
80 ml (3 fl oz) vegetable oil
80 ml (3 fl oz) olive oil
salt and freshly ground pepper

Combine the lemon juice, garlic, mustard and spices in a blender or in a bowl using a hand-held blender. With the machine running, gradually add the oils until the dressing emulsifies. Season with salt and pepper to taste and add extra lemon juice or oil as necessary.

HERB OILS

bunch of chosen herb
neutral-flavoured oil

Wash and pick over your chosen bunch of herbs. Bring a large pot of water to the boil. Add the herbs and blanch for 15 seconds or a little longer for robust herbs such as rosemary. Drain and refresh the herbs in iced water then drain again and dry. When dry, place the herbs in a blender with sufficient neutral-flavoured oil to cover them. Blend until smooth but do not allow the herbs to heat up in the process. Pour into a muslin-lined sieve over a bowl and allow the flavoured oil to drain through. Store the oil in a bottle out of the light for up to 1 week.

MAYONNAISE

Makes 400 ml (13 fl oz)

Here is the method for making mayonnaise by hand. The processor method is described in the next recipe. Choose whichever method is convenient for you, bearing in mind that small quantities tend to puddle around below the processor blade while larger quantities are quite difficult to handle by hand. All sauces of this kind must be well covered and stored in the refrigerator.

2 egg yolks
2 pinches salt
360 ml (11½ fl oz) mild-flavoured olive oil
freshly squeezed lemon juice

Place the yolks in a bowl. Use a damp cloth under the bowl to anchor it to your work surface. Whisk the yolks, add the salt and whisk again. Whisk in a little trickle of oil. When thoroughly amalgamated, whisk in a little more oil. Gradually increase the flow of the oil until nearly all of it is added. You will find that the sauce is very thick. Add a squeeze of lemon and whisk again. When almost all the oil has been added, taste and add more lemon, salt or oil as required. A little warm water added to the sauce while processing is useful if at any point the mixture becomes too thick.

AÏOLI

Makes about 400 ml (13 fl oz)

Traditionally aïoli is garlic and salt pounded together using a mortar and pestle and then emulsified with olive oil. The result is a thick, glossy but not very stable sauce. The emulsification takes anywhere from 20–30 minutes of pounding with the pestle and requires considerable patience. Unlike an egg-based sauce, if the emulsion breaks there is no saving it. I suggest you leave the practice to a real slow food afternoon when you are unlikely to stress when things go wrong. The following processor method uses eggs and produces a creamier, more mayonnaise-like sauce.

2 large cloves garlic, peeled and chopped
½ teaspoon salt
2 eggs yolks
25 ml (1 fl oz) white wine vinegar
350 ml (11½ fl oz) oil
25 ml (1 fl oz) lukewarm water
additional oil if required

Combine the garlic and salt and using the face of a knife rub them until they are well minced. In a food processor combine the minced garlic mix, egg yolks and vinegar. With the machine running, drizzle in the oil – commencing slowly – in a steady stream. Continue until all the oil is used up and the mixture is quite thick. Adjust seasoning to taste. The mixture can absorb more oil and this may be necessary if you find the strength of the garlic too overpowering for the end use of the aïoli. In this case, with the motor running, add a little tepid water. The sauce will thin down and lighten. Continue to drizzle in additional oil as required.

Variations
- For saffron aïoli, infuse the vinegar with ½ teaspoon of saffron pistils.
- For tarragon aïoli, use tarragon vinegar if you have some. But whether you are using it or not, add 4 tablespoons of finely chopped fresh tarragon to the completed aïoli and stir through to disperse evenly.

CAESAR DRESSING

Makes 500 ml (17 fl oz)

2 eggs
75 g (2½ oz) freshly grated parmesan
1–2 anchovy fillets, washed and dried
1 clove garlic, peeled
30 ml (1 fl oz) red wine vinegar
30 ml (1 fl oz) lemon juice
1 teaspoon Dijon mustard
350 ml (11½ fl oz) mild-flavoured olive oil
2 tablespoons lukewarm water
freshly ground white pepper

Combine all the ingredients, except the oil, water and pepper, in a food processor and blend until the mix is as smooth as possible. Continue to process while adding the oil in a steady stream until the mix becomes quite thick. Add a couple of tablespoons or more of lukewarm water and pulse to re-emulsify. Continue to add oil until you have close to 500 ml (17 fl oz) of thick Caesar dressing. Seasoning may be adjusted with freshly ground pepper and additional lemon juice.

SOFT EGG GRIBICHE

Makes 500 ml (17 fl oz)

This is not the classic vinaigrette with hard egg chopped into it but rather a creamy sauce.

1 soft-boiled egg (see cooking method, page 290)
salt
1 tablespoon Dijon mustard
1 large shallot, finely diced
1 tablespoon tarragon vinegar or sherry vinegar
400 ml (13 fl oz) mild olive oil
1 teaspoon finely chopped tarragon
1 teaspoon finely chopped dill
1 teaspoon finely chopped flat-leaf parsley
1 tablespoon capers

Peel the egg and put it into a bowl with the salt, mustard and shallot. Break up the egg with a whisk and stir the ingredients together. Add the vinegar and combine. Place a damp tea towel on your work surface to stabilise the bowl. Begin adding oil in a drizzle, continually whisking. When you have added three-quarters of the oil, stop and taste the sauce, which should be thick and shiny. Season with salt if required. If the balance of acid is right to your taste do not add any more oil without adding additional vinegar. To finish, stir through the herbs and capers.

COCONUT DRESSING

Makes 600 ml (20½ fl oz)

1 stalk of lemongrass, sliced
1 knob ginger, peeled and diced
1 spanish onion, peeled and sliced
2 bird's-eye chillies, seeded and diced
vegetable oil
600 ml (20 fl oz) coconut milk

In a pan, sweat the lemongrass, ginger, onion and chilli in a little oil over medium heat until the onion is soft. Add the coconut milk and simmer for 15 minutes then remove from the heat and allow the mixture to cool. Purée and pass through a fine sieve, discarding the residue. This dressing can be made in advance, covered and refrigerated.

AROMATIC CARROT EMULSION

Makes 125 ml (4 fl oz)

4 cups fresh carrot juice
6 whole star anise
¼ cup peanut oil
salt and freshly ground pepper

Put the carrot juice and star anise in a stainless steel saucepan. Over a low flame reduce the liquid to a quarter of a cup, whisking constantly. Strain out the star anise and transfer the concentrated juice to a blender. While blending on high speed, slowly add the peanut oil to emulsify. Season with salt and pepper to taste. The sauce can be reheated and re-emulsified with a hand-held blender.

MUSHROOM EMULSION

Makes about 400 ml (13 fl oz)

Vegetable oil for sautéing
500g (1 lb) button mushrooms or a combination of mushrooms, stalks and trimmings
50 g (2 oz) butter
1 shallot, finely chopped
1 clove garlic, finely chopped
2 sprigs thyme
100 ml (3½ fl oz) milk
salt and freshly ground pepper
100 g (3½ oz) butter, diced and chilled

Heat the oil in a pan and when hot sauté the mushrooms until golden then remove them and drain well. Melt the butter and sauté the shallots, garlic and thyme, cooking until translucent but not coloured. Add the sautéed mushrooms, cover with water and simmer gently for 30 minutes. Strain the stock into a clean saucepan, return to the heat and reduce by two-thirds. Add the milk, bring to the boil then reduce to a gentle simmer. Season and hold. When ready to serve, gradually add the chilled butter, blending with a hand-held blender. Preferably do not reheat and certainly do not boil. Give the sauce another blitz with the blender just on serving.

ORANGE GASTRIQUE

Makes about 250 ml (8½ fl oz)

The texture and depth of gastriques normally rely on the addition of a greatly reduced jus to finish them off. As you are unlikely to have these on hand the plum sauce makes an expedient substitute in this orange gastrique for use with duck.

65 g (2¼ oz) caster (superfine) sugar
100 ml (3½ fl oz) red wine vinegar
400 ml (13 fl oz) orange juice, strained through a fine sauce sieve
1 piece of star anise
60 ml (2 fl oz) plum sauce

Using a heavy-based pan, spread the sugar over the base and warm over a moderate heat until the sugar melts and begins to colour. Lift and swirl the pan by its handle to even the cooking of the sugar. Do not allow it to burn. Once the sugar is an even caramel, carefully add the vinegar. Swirl the pan to melt the caramel in the liquid then reduce by a half. Add the orange juice, star anise and plum sauce and reduce to around 250 ml (8½ fl oz). Adjust the seasoning.

SAUCE BEURRE BLANC

Makes about 500 ml (17 fl oz)

6 tablespoons white wine vinegar
6 tablespoons dry white wine
4 shallots, very finely chopped
a splash of cream
500 g (1 lb 2 oz) butter, very cold and cut into small pieces
salt and freshly ground white pepper

In a small saucepan (not aluminium), boil the vinegar, wine and shallots until the liquid has reduced down to about 2 tablespoons. Add the splash of cream. Remove from the heat and whisk in the butter gradually in small pieces to make a smooth creamy sauce. If you find the mixture is getting a little too cool to absorb more butter, you may need to return your pan to a very low heat for a few seconds while still continuing to whisk. Work in this way, sometimes over low heat and sometimes off the heat, so the butter softens and thickens the sauce without separating. Season to taste and serve as soon as possible. This white butter sauce can be kept warm for a little time in a vacuum flask.

VARIATION Once all the butter has been incorporated, add a fine chiffonade of sorrel. This is delicious with fish.

SAUCE JACQUELINE

Makes about 1 litre (34 fl oz)

500 ml (17 fl oz) vegetable stock
50 ml (2 fl oz) Pernod
100 ml (3½ fl oz) orange juice
1 piece star anise
½ tablespoon very finely chopped ginger
500 g (1 lb 2 oz) carrot, chopped
1 medium-sized onion, chopped
160 g (5½ oz) butter, diced and chilled
salt and freshly ground white pepper

Pour the stock into a medium-sized saucepan. Add the Pernod, orange juice, star anise and ginger. Heat to boiling point then simmer for a few minutes. Remove from the heat and allow to infuse. Add the chopped carrot and onion to the saucepan, bring to a simmer once again and continue to cook until the vegetables are very soft. Remove from the heat. Pick out and discard the star anise. Blend the remaining mixture with a hand-held blender until completely smooth. Pass through a fine sieve and return to the saucepan. To finish, whisk the cold butter into the warm liquid, a small piece at a time. Season. Blitz with a hand-held blender before serving.

SAUCE PALOISE

Makes about 250 ml (8½ fl oz)

This sauce is basically a mint-flavoured hollandaise, made here using a much less time-consuming processor method.

3 tablespoons dry white wine
3 tablespoons white wine vinegar
1 heaped tablespoon finely chopped shallots
2 sprigs fresh mint
3 egg yolks
salt and freshly ground white pepper
175 g (6 oz) butter
3–4 tablespoons chopped fresh mint

Put the white wine, wine vinegar, chopped shallots and sprigs of mint in a saucepan and boil vigorously until the quantity is reduced to about 2 tablespoons. Strain the liquid, pressing down on the mint to squeeze out the last drops of flavour. Allow the mint reduction to cool then pour it into a food processor and add the egg yolks and a little salt and pepper. Pulse to mix together.

Melt the butter and remove from the heat once hot. Turn on the processor and slowly trickle in the hot butter, cautiously at first. Continue until only the milky white sediment from the butter remains (discard this). Place the chopped mint in a sieve and shower with boiling water to release the flavours. Drain well and stir into sauce. Taste and adjust seasoning if required.

CURRY SAUCE

Makes 250 ml (8 fl oz)

vegetable oil
2 onions, sliced
1 tablespoon tomato paste
1½ tablespoons curry powder
50 ml (2 fl oz) white wine
350 ml (11½ fl oz) coconut milk

Barely coat the base of a small stainless steel pot with oil. Add sliced onions and sauté over medium heat until translucent. Add tomato paste and curry powder and cook for 1 minute. Deglaze the pan with the white wine then simmer the mix until the wine has evaporated. Add the coconut milk. Simmer until the liquid has reduced by one-third. Purée in a blender and season with salt and pepper. This sauce can be made in advance and reheated.

SALSA VERDE

Makes about 350 ml (11½ fl oz)

2 bunches flat-leaf parsley, washed and dried
3 fillets anchovies (optional)
2 tablespoons salt-packed capers, rinsed and drained
½ clove garlic
50 ml (2 fl oz) lemon juice
100 ml (3½ fl oz) extra-virgin olive oil
salt and freshly ground pepper

Place the parsley in a blender and process on a low setting. Add the anchovies, capers, garlic, and lemon juice and process until ingredients are well combined. Slowly drizzle in the oil until the sauce is thick and smooth. Season and if not using immediately store in the refrigerator in a jar with a tight-fitting lid.

BASIL PESTO

Unlike the classic version, this recipe produces a smooth pesto required for the emulsion sauce that follows. Otherwise use a mortar and pestle and do not blanch the basil leaves.

250 g (9 oz) basil leaves
125 ml (4 fl oz) extra-virgin olive oil
1 clove garlic
1 tablespoon toasted pine nuts
1 tablespoon freshly grated parmesan

Bring a pot of water to the boil. Add basil leaves and blanch for 30 seconds. Drain and refresh in iced water. Drain again and squeeze or spin dry. Place all the ingredients in a blender and process until smooth. Do not allow ingredients to heat up in the process. Scrape into a container with an airtight lid. Place a piece of plastic wrap directly onto the surface of the pesto before covering. Store in the refrigerator.

'PESTO' EMULSION

125 ml (4 fl oz) very smooth Basil Pesto (see above)
125 ml (4 fl oz) chicken or vegetable stock
30 g (1 oz) butter
salt and freshly ground white pepper

Heat the pesto in a saucepan with the stock. If desired, pass the pesto liquid through a fine sieve and return to the saucepan. Beat in the butter with a hand-held blender and season.

TARRAGON PESTO

This is really a mixed herb pesto with tarragon being one of the components. A small quantity is used in the Chicken Galantine recipe (see page 239) and once again a processor is used as a smooth result is required. A tiny quantity is difficult to make in a processor and not worth the effort – if you are going to make it at all I suggest you make the whole amount. The remainder will have many uses. Spread some on bread in a delicious chicken sandwich, top your breakfast poached egg with it, or stir it through pasta, risotto or an omelette mix.

1 tablespoon snipped tarragon
1 cup fresh chopped parsley, washed and spun dry
1 clove garlic
2 tablespoons toasted pine nuts
12 large basil leaves
100 ml (3½ fl oz) olive oil
2 tablespoon grated parmesan
juice of ½ lemon
salt and freshly ground pepper

Purée all the ingredients, except the lemon juice and seasoning, in a blender until smooth. Add the lemon juice and season to taste.

CUCUMBER RAITA

Makes about 400 ml (13 fl oz)

500 ml (17 fl oz) sheep's milk yoghurt
1 teaspoon salt
1 teaspoon cumin seeds
1 medium-sized Lebanese cucumber, peeled, seeded and finely diced
6 mint leaves, very finely sliced

Combine the yoghurt and salt and leave overnight in a colander lined with a double layer of muslin or in a coffee filter paper. On the following day place the cumin seed in a non-stick pan over gentle heat until browned and aromatic then crush it lightly. Combine the crushed cumin with the drained yoghurt. Add the diced cucumber and mint slices and stir to combine. Store in a sealed container in the refrigerator.

HORSERADISH CREAM

Makes 250 ml (8½ fl oz)

Freshly grated horseradish is a considerably different product to the bottled variety, which lacks any real pungency. Horseradish is generally available through winter. It is best to make up small amounts as it quickly loses its pungency. Grate what you need and freeze the rest wrapped in foil. It can be retrieved and returned to the freezer as needed without ill effect.

2½ cm (1 in) piece fresh horseradish
1 cup sour cream or crème fraîche
pinch of salt

Grate the horseradish on a fine grater and combine it with the sour cream or crème fraîche. Add the salt and taste – you may prefer to make your mix stronger or weaker.

HARISSA

Makes 250 ml (8½ fl oz)

This is a relatively user-friendly harissa. Adjust the quantity of chilli if you prefer more heat.

3 red capsicums (bell peppers)
½ teaspoon caraway seeds, toasted and ground
½ teaspoon freshly crushed garlic
½ teaspoon chopped chilli
a little lemon juice
olive oil
salt and freshly ground pepper

Roast the capsicums in the oven at 160°C (320°F) for 30 minutes or until they have collapsed and are soft. Take the capsicums out of the oven and place them in plastic bag for 10 minutes. Remove the capsicums from the bag and core, peel and seed. Put the capsicum flesh, spices and garlic in a blender and process. Taste and adjust the flavour with olive oil, additional chilli, lemon juice, salt and pepper. Harissa should have a smooth dip-like consistency. Store in the refrigerator.

TAPENADE

This recipe makes a small quantity sufficient as a garnish for six serves. You may wish to make considerably more. It keeps well in the refrigerator in a screw-top jar with a thin film of oil drizzled over its surface. If you are making a considerably larger quantity, the pounding might become tedious. It is better to make smaller batches – say double or triple this quantity rather than having to resort to a food processor, which turns it all into a slurry-like paste with little of the distinguishing features of the original ingredients.

4 tablespoons pitted, finely chopped kalamata olives
1 tablespoon freshly grated parmesan
1 tablespoon salt-packed baby capers, rinsed and drained

1 clove garlic, finely chopped
1 tablespoon finely chopped flat-leaf parsley
zest of 1 lemon, finely chopped
2 anchovy fillets, finely chopped (optional)
1 tablespoon olive oil, or more as needed

Place the chopped olives in the mortar and begin incorporating the other ingredients using a pounding and crushing action with the pestle. Include the anchovies if using. Every now and then add a little of the olive oil. Once all the ingredients are well combined, place the mix in a bowl and stir in any remaining olive oil. The tapenade should be firm enough to hold its shape when spooned out.

EGGS

The most magic of ingredients, eggs can thicken, emulsify, trap air and much more. They also provide the simplest of nourishing meals. A soft-boiled egg with good toasted bread is hard to beat as a fast food. Added to dressings and salads it provides interest and flavour.

POACHED EGGS

1.5 litres (51 fl oz) water
1 teaspoon white vinegar
4 eggs

Bring the water to the boil then reduce to a simmer. Add the white vinegar, swirl the simmering water with a spoon and carefully slip the eggs into it. Poach the eggs for about 2½ minutes — the whites should be set and the yolks still runny. This quantity of water will be sufficient for up to four eggs at a time. Remove the poached eggs from the pot with a slotted spoon and place on kitchen paper to drain completely. If the leisurely breakfast à deux has turned into a party and you wish to poach more eggs, skim the poaching water first with a small strainer or a slotted spoon.

CRISP CRUMBED POACHED EGGS

soft poached eggs (1 per person), as cooked above
seasoned plain (all-purpose) flour
1 beaten egg
Japanese (Panko) breadcrumbs or dry breadcrumbs
oil for frying

Trim any excess bits of white from around the poached eggs with a sharp pair of scissors. Roll the eggs in flour, then in the beaten egg and finally in the breadcrumbs. Allow the crumbing to set by resting the eggs in the refrigerator for 10–20 minutes. Heat some oil to 160°C (320°F) and fry the eggs for 1–2 minutes, ensuring the yolk is warm, but remains runny. Remove the eggs with a slotted spoon and drain on kitchen paper.

SOFT EGGS FOR SALADS AND DRESSINGS

Bring a pot of water to a simmer and lower in your eggs with a slotted spoon. Take the pot off the stove and turn the eggs a few times to centre the yolks. Cover the pot and let the eggs sit for 6 minutes. Take the eggs out and put them in iced water. After 5 minutes, drain off the water and carefully peel the eggs.

HARD-BOILED EGGS

This offers you a method to reduce the chance of yolk discolouration through overcooking when a recipe calls for hard-boiled eggs.

Put the eggs in a pot and cover them with cold water. Bring to a rolling boil. If you are eventually going to cut the hard-boiled eggs in half, roll them around with a spoon as the water heats up, to centre the yolks. Reduce the heat to low, cover the pot and cook the eggs for 30 seconds. Remove the pot from the heat and let the eggs stand in the hot water (still covered) for 15 minutes. Drain and run the eggs under cold running water for 5 minutes.

PASTA

BASIC PASTA DOUGH

Makes 1 kg (2 lb 3 oz)

4 eggs
7 egg yolks
600 g (1 lb 5 oz) plain (all-purpose) flour
1½ tablespoons olive oil
1 teaspoon salt

Combine all the ingredients in a processor. When combined, place the dough on your work surface and knead well several times. Before using, allow the pasta to rest for at least 2 hours at room temperature, covered with plastic wrap.

SALT

We generally use sea salt in our cooking. Mass-produced 'table salt' is full of anti-caking agents and because of the way it is produced has little additional flavour-enhancing minerals. If we are using a large amount of salt for curing purposes we will often use rock salt. This is mined salt and can have additional mineral components depending on where it comes from. Sel gris – French sea salt made from the natural evaporation of sea water is milder and has a lower sodium content. For general table use we have Murray River salt flakes in the restaurant, although specific dishes may have varyingly flavoured salts served as an accompaniment. The pink colour of the Murray River salt reflects the minerals within the ancient inland sea from which it is harvested. Fleur de sel is the finest sea salt available. Hand-harvested, its collection is dependent on specific weather conditions. It is unrefined, slightly damp and has a depth of flavour that goes beyond salt. I have recently had some purists tell me that French sea salt harvested from the top of waves is superior to that from the seabed or marshes. No doubt the ticket price will reflect their obsessiveness. If you are confused about what you should spend on something that ought to be a basic cooking ingredient, think about how long a particular cooking process is and what the finished result is like. Short-term cooking with seasoning added just before or at the table may be perceptibly altered by which salt you choose to use. The texture of large flakes on a finished dish can be an additional enhancement. But adding expensive Fleur de sel to water used for cooking vegetables, pasta and grains makes little sense.

STOCKS

Virtually every cookbook offers good guidelines for making chicken, veal, fish and vegetable stocks. I have chosen not to include stock-making here but rather to offer many of the larder preparations, which you might find useful to put a little bit of a 'wow' factor into what you cook.

SWEETS

CITRUS POWDER

Thinly peel the zest of an orange or lemon with a vegetable peeler (ensure there is no pith). Lay the zest in a single layer on a baking tray and dry in a low oven at 100°C (210°F) for about 1 hour. The zest must be completely dry. Remove the zest from the oven and allow it to cool. Grind the dried zest in a spice mill until it is a smooth powder. Use for flavour and garnishing. Mix with a little sea salt to produce an intriguing seasoning for poultry and fish.

CANDIED ORANGE RIND

We use this garnish in both savoury and dessert dishes ...

2–3 large oranges
200 ml (7 fl oz) Sugar Syrup (see page 293)

Bring a small saucepan of water to the boil. Remove the rind from the oranges very thinly using a sharp vegetable peeler. Try and obtain long strips and ensure that you are removing it without any white pith. Cut the rind into fine julienne strips. Add the rind to the boiling water and continue to cook for a minute or two. Drain the rind then rinse it in cold water. Drain again and pat dry. Bring the sugar syrup to the boil in a small saucepan. Add the rind and simmer for 8–10 minutes. Remove from heat and allow to cool. The rind may be stored in the syrup if desired and drained when required as a garnish. Alternatively, drain the rind and arrange it on an oven tray lined with silicon paper. Place the tray into a switched-off gas oven overnight, or a very low oven for about an hour, to dry out.

PEAR CRISPS

This recipe and the following for Apple Crisps offer alternative methods for making crisps. The first method is better if you have the time as the crisps are less likely to colour. Either method will work with thinly shaved rhubarb. Orange slices take longer to dry and are better if allowed to sit for 15 minutes in hot sugar syrup before being slow-baked.

1 or 2 pears
250 ml (10 fl oz) Sugar Syrup (see page 293)

Preheat the oven to 100°C (210°F). Cut the pears into very fine slices using a mandoline or a sharp knife. Dip each piece into the syrup and place in a single layer on silicon paper or a non-stick baking tray. Bake for about 2 hours until crisp but not coloured. To check if they are done, peel a pear slice off the baking sheet, allow it to cool for a moment then try to break it. It should break crisply otherwise return the tray to the oven and cook a little longer. When done, peel crisps off the baking sheet and allow them to cool on your work surface. Use the crisps immediately or they will keep in an airtight container for a few days.

APPLE CRISPS

1 Granny Smith, unpeeled and cut into
   wafer-thin slices
100 ml (3½ fl oz) Sugar Syrup (see page 293)

Preheat the oven to 160°C (320°F). Dip the apple slices into the syrup. Lay them on a silicon-paper-lined oven tray and place in the preheated oven for 2 minutes. Remove the tray from the oven. Turn off the oven and leave the door ajar to allow the oven to cool. When the oven temperature has reduced to a maximum of 60°C (140°F), return the tray to the turned-off oven and leave until the apple slices are crisp (about 1 hour).

GENOESE SPONGE

This sponge is ideal for trifles and lining charlottes.

4 eggs
125 g (4 oz) sugar
125 g (4 oz) plain (all-purpose) flour, sifted
50 g (2 oz) butter, melted

Preheat the oven to 180°C (350°F). Whisk the eggs and sugar together in a stainless steel bowl. Place the bowl over a pot of simmering water and continue to whisk (you are trying to incorporate as much air as possible) until the mixture falls off the whisk in a ribbon. Remove the bowl from heat. Using a plastic spatula, gently fold the flour and melted butter, alternately, through the egg mixture without deflating it too much. Pour into two non-stick, shallow, Swiss roll-style baking pans and bake in the oven for 8 minutes. Allow the sponge to cool. It can be made in advance, cut into slices and stored in an airtight container.

VANILLA ICE CREAM

Makes about 1.5 litres (34 fl oz)

600 ml (20 fl oz) milk
200 g (7 oz) sugar
1 vanilla bean
6 yolks
500 ml (17 fl oz) cream (35% fat)

Add half the sugar and the vanilla bean split in half lengthwise, to the milk in a saucepan. Bring to the boil. Remove from the heat, cover and allow to infuse for 20 minutes. Beat the yolks with the remaining sugar until pale and thick. Return the milk to the boil. Pour hot milk in a slow stream onto the egg yolks and sugar, whisking to combine. Return the mixture to the saucepan and place over a low heat.

Stir the custard constantly, continuing to cook very gently until the mixture coats the back of a spoon and a line drawn across it with your finger holds it shape. Remove immediately from the heat and place the base of the saucepan into a bowl of cold water to stop the cooking process. Continue to stir the custard occasionally as it is cooling. Pour into a bowl or jug, cover and refrigerate. When ready to churn, scrape both halves of the vanilla bean into the cooled custard. Discard the bean. Add the chilled cream to the custard and stir to combine and distribute the small black vanilla specks. Pour the mixture into an ice cream machine and churn.

SOUR CREAM ICE CREAM

Makes about 1.6 litres (54 fl oz)

500 ml (17 fl oz) milk
4 egg yolks
250 g (9 oz) vanilla sugar
750 g (1 lb 10 oz) sour cream

Heat the milk to boiling point then remove from the heat. Cream the yolks and sugar until pale and creamy. Pour on a little of the hot milk, whisking thoroughly. Add this mixture back to the hot milk, stirring well. Return to a gentle heat and cook very carefully until thickened. Remove from the heat, cool, fold in the sour cream, refrigerate then churn.

PRALINE

300 g (10½ oz) sugar
½ cup water
100 g (3½ oz) blanched almonds

In a heavy-based saucepan over very gentle heat mix the sugar and water then bring to a simmer. Remove the pan from the heat and swirl it by its handle to be sure the sugar has dissolved completely and the liquid is clear. Return to the heat and boil for a few minutes over medium heat until the bubbles are thick. Continue to cook until the syrup begins to colour. Give the pan a swirl by its handle to even out the heat. Continue boiling until the syrup is a light caramel brown. Remove from the heat and add the nuts, turning them vigorously with a metal spoon. While still hot, turn out the mixture onto an oiled shallow tray, allowing the mixture to spread. Leave it to cool and set hard. Break into pieces and process into crumbs in a processor. Store in an airtight container until ready to use.

RASPBERRY SAUCE

Serves six as a dessert garnish

450 g (1 lb) fresh raspberries
150 g (5 oz) caster sugar
Sugar Syrup (see next recipe) and lemon juice to taste

Place the raspberries in a bowl and cover with the sugar. Stand for an hour to allow the berries to drop their juices. Blend to a purée and pass through a fine sieve. Taste and adjust flavour with sugar syrup or lemon juice as required. Store in the refrigerator until ready to use.

SUGAR SYRUP

Makes 500 ml (17 fl oz)

The sugar syrup generally referred to in the recipes in this book is produced as follows.

1 cup sugar
1 cup water

Put the sugar and water in a pan. Bring to the boil, stirring to dissolve the sugar. Simmer for 5 minutes. Remove from the heat, cool and store.

FLAVOURED SUGARS

Here are three variations.

ROSE SCENTED Use highly scented pink or red rose petals from plants that have not been sprayed. Do not wash. Lightly bruising the petals helps the scent permeate the sugar. Using 3 cups of icing (confectioner's) sugar or caster (superfine) sugar and a generous handful of rose petals, place alternate layers of sugar and petals in a jar. Cover the sugar with a tight-fitting lid and leave it in a warm place for at least 3–4 hours or until the sugar has taken on the scent of the roses.

LAVENDER Said to be good for everything from headaches to indigestion, this herb also has many culinary uses. Generously layer fresh lavender flowers with sugar in an airtight jar. Leaving it in a warm place will speed up the process but unlike the rose sugar the lavender can take up to a couple of weeks to produce a nicely scented sugar.

VANILLA (see page 293) Use two large vanilla beans to 1.5 kg (3 lb 5 oz) of sugar. Crush or pound the beans lightly and intersperse with sugar in a jar with a tight-fitting lid. The sugar will take around a week to reach its best flavour. If using vanilla beans to infuse milk or cream, wash the beans after use. Dry thoroughly and when completely dry store as a matter of course in a sugar jar before re-using.

TUILE BISCUITS

Makes 24 large and up to 40 small biscuits

125 g (4 oz) caster (superfine) sugar
125 g (4 oz) butter
125 ml (about 3) egg whites
125 g (4 oz) plain (all-purpose) flour

Preheat the oven to 180°C (350°F). In a food processor, beat the sugar and butter until the mixture is smooth and just changing to a lighter colour. Add the egg whites and beat well. Add the flour and pulse some more until the mixture is well combined. Do not overprocess. Spread or stencil the mixture onto well-greased trays or silicon sheets. Bake in the oven until firm and lightly coloured. Remove from the oven and, while still warm, roll around a rolling pin or glass if you wish to produce a curved crisp. When cool, the tuiles may be stored in an airtight container for up to a week.

VEGETABLES

PREPARING ARTICHOKES

Choose artichokes that feel heavy and are still tightly closed. Remove the dark green outer leaves of the vegetable, up to the softer pale leaves. Snap off the stem. Trim off the tip of the head then rotate the artichokes as you trim around the base of the leaves. As you finish trimming drop the artichokes into a bowl of salted acidulated water to stop them from discolouring.

To poach artichokes, allow enough water to cover them. Whisking a tablespoon of plain flour into the cooking water will help preserve the pallor of the artichokes. Add coriander seed, a sprig of thyme, a bay leaf and salt. Use a saucer to keep the artichokes submerged if necessary. Simmer for around 10 minutes or until tender. Remove the artichokes from the heat and allow them to cool in their poaching liquid.

Artichokes are also delicious trimmed as described above and thinly shaved raw for salads. Thinly sliced and grilled or fried until the edges crisp, they are a special treat dunked in aïoli or just seasoned and tossed through pasta with a little shaved parmesan.

PREPARING ASPARAGUS

Choose asparagus with firm stalks and tight heads. Thick stalks have considerably more flavour. It is best not to let asparagus hang about too long but if you have inadvertently bought too much, trim off the ends and stand the stalks upright in the refrigerator in a container with a couple of centimetres of water in the bottom.

To cook asparagus, snap off the woody end of each spear. If using thick asparagus, we prepare it for a secondary cooking of some kind. Peel away the toughest skin. Cook for about a minute in a large pot of boiling salted water in batches small enough to ensure a continuous boil. Remove and plunge in iced water until cool. Drain on kitchen paper. Reserve for further cooking. If serving immediately, cook about 4–6 minutes until tender. Check with a small sharp knife to see if they are done. If using skinny asparagus, break off the woody ends. Little or no peeling should be required. Generally with this sort of asparagus we just rapidly cook it to order.

BEETROOT RELISH

Makes about 850 g (1lb 13½ oz)

500 g (1 lb 2 oz) beetroot (beets)
250 g (9 oz) onions
vegetable oil
5 g (¼ oz) brown mustard seeds
5 g (¼ oz) grated horseradish
200 g (7 oz) sugar
200 ml (7 fl oz) red wine vinegar

Peel and grate the beetroot (use gloves) and onions on a coarse grater. Steam the grated beetroot lightly until it is cooked but still has texture. Sauté the grated onion in a little vegetable oil until soft – do not allow to colour. Add the mustard seeds and horseradish and stir to combine well. Heat the sugar in a heavy-based pan until it dissolves into a pale caramel. Remove from the heat and carefully add the vinegar. Replace on medium heat and stir until caramel is dissolved. Cook until thick and syrupy. Combine the beetroot with the onion mixture, pour the caramel syrup on top and stir through. Spoon into warm sterilised jars and seal or you can store the relish in a sealed container in the refrigerator for a week.

PREPARING BROAD BEANS

One of the oldest known cultivated food plants and one of the most prolific, these earthy beans are truly delicious. To pod the beans, pinch off the stem and pull away the string along the seam. Pry the shell open and remove the beans. Many cultures utilise broad beans in this state – with the casing intact. Some even use young broad beans with the outer pod. However, the beans within the beans are another thing altogether.

Blanch the broad beans in their casings for 30 seconds then cool in iced water. Using a small knife or your fingernail, cut off a sliver of the bean casing and slip out the bright green broad bean inside.

HOME-MADE SAUERKRAUT

Once you have bothered to make your own sauerkraut you are unlikely to go for the purchased variety. Crocks of this stuff usually sat outside the back door of our Daylesford dacha. It takes about 10 days for the cabbage to cure properly.

1½ kg (3 lb 5 oz) cabbage, cored and thinly shredded
4 tablespoons salt
4 tablespoons sugar
12 juniper berries, crushed

Place a quarter of the shredded cabbage in a bowl. Combine the salt, sugar and berries. Sprinkle a quarter of the salting mix over the cabbage in the bowl. Top with another quarter of the cabbage and repeat the process until all the ingredients are used up. Using the heel of your hand or a mallet press down on the cabbage, bruising and breaking it down until it begins to drop liquid. Place the bowl contents in a pottery crock or plastic tub, compacting and packing it down. Cover with a couple of pieces of damp muslin or cheesecloth. Weigh down the cabbage with a plate and a heavy can or two. Leave the cabbage to cure at room temperature in a dark cool area for 10 days. Wash or change the cloth every 3 days. After 10 days put the cured cabbage into a clean covered container in the refrigerator. Sauerkraut will keep for at least two months. To use, drain the sauerkraut and sauté in oil or duck fat over medium heat with a little onion for about ½ an hour. Alternatively, combine it with fresh cabbage and cook choucroute-style (see following recipe).

CHOUCROUTE-STYLE CABBAGE

Serves 6 as an accompaniment

This is a good accompaniment with pork or a meaty fish.

vegetable oil or duck fat
1 large onion, finely sliced
4 cloves garlic, crushed
60 g (2 oz) smoked bacon cut into lardons
1 tablespoon toasted caraway seeds
2 cups thinly shredded white cabbage
1 cup drained Home-made Sauerkraut (see left)
1 bay leaf
½ cup riesling
1–1½ cups vegetable stock or water
salt and freshly ground white pepper

Place a pan spread with a film of oil or melted duck fat over medium heat and sweat the onion, garlic, bacon and caraway seeds for about 10 minutes. Add the fresh cabbage and sweat for a further 5–6 minutes. Add the sauerkraut, bay leaf, wine and stock or water. Bring to a simmer, cover and cook for 10 minutes. Uncover and cook for at least a further 20 minutes until all the liquid is absorbed. The cabbage should be cooked but still retain some texture and crunch. Season with salt and white pepper.

SPICED CARROT CREAM

Serves 6

This is good with poultry, pork and spiced tuna or under seared scallops.

½ teaspoon cumin seeds
⅓ teaspoon coriander seeds
1 cinnamon stick
750 g (1 lb 10 oz) carrots, peeled and chopped
500 ml (17 fl oz) carrot juice
70 ml (2 ⅓ fl oz) thickened cream (35% butterfat)
100 g (3½ oz) butter
salt and freshly ground white pepper

Tie the spices in a piece of muslin and place in a saucepan with the carrots and carrot juice. Bring to a simmer and cook for about 30 minutes or until the carrots are tender. Remove from the heat, discard the spices and process the carrots and juice in a blender until a fine purée is achieved. Pass through a fine sieve. If using immediately, beat in the cream and butter and season with salt and pepper. Otherwise allow the mixture to cool and when ready to use, reheat, then beat in the cream, butter and seasoning.

CELERIAC PURÉE

Serves 4-6 as an accompaniment

100 g (3½ oz) butter
1 clove garlic
400 g (14 oz) celeriac, peeled and diced
3 sprigs thyme
100 ml (3½ fl oz) water or chicken stock
125 ml (4 oz) thickened cream (35% butterfat)
salt and freshly ground pepper

Melt the butter in a pan and sauté the garlic, celeriac and thyme over medium heat. Add the stock or water. Bring to the boil and reduce by half. Add the cream and simmer for 20 minutes. Purée in the blender and adjust seasoning.

COOKING CHESTNUTS

Preheat the oven to 175°C (340°F). Cut a cross in the rounded side of the nuts. Place them on a baking tray and roast for around 7–8 minutes until they have browned and the skins begin to burst. Alternatively they can be boiled to soften the skin. Whatever method, ensure the outer skin is pierced before cooking. When coolish, peel the nuts and also discard the inner skins. Do not cool completely as chestnuts are easiest skinned when still quite hot. When deciding the alternatives, burned fingers are inevitably my choice rather than what can be a very protracted process if the chestnuts are too cool.

SMOKY EGGPLANT PURÉE

Makes about 300 ml (10 fl oz)

2 medium-sized eggplants (aubergines)
50 ml (2 fl oz) lemon juice
salt and freshly ground pepper
1 teaspoon chopped fresh thyme
1 clove garlic
2 tablespoons olive oil
1 tablespoon tahina paste

Top and tail the eggplants and cut one in half. Bake the two halves on an oiled tray, skin side up, in a moderate oven (170°C/340°F) for 30 minutes. Remove the halves from the oven and allow them to cool in a bowl covered with plastic wrap. Take the other eggplant and scorch it over a direct medium gas flame to blacken the outside, turning with tongs to ensure even cooking. Place in a bowl and cover with plastic wrap. Once the eggplants are cool, remove the skin and place the flesh in a blender and blend until smooth. Add the remaining ingredients and season to taste. Pass the purée through a medium tamis and store it, covered, in the refrigerator until needed. Preferably bring the purée to room temperature before using.

EGGPLANT RELISH

Serves 10 as an accompaniment

This recipe will serve at least ten as an accompaniment but will keep in a covered container in the refrigerator and is a useful addition to your larder. It works well as a relish or warm vegetable. Try it with left-over roast lamb in a sandwich or as a condiment served with most meats.

5 medium-sized eggplants (aubergines), peeled, diced and salted
200 ml (7 fl oz) vegetable oil
7 cloves garlic, peeled and finely chopped
1 x 5 cm (2 in) piece ginger, peeled and grated
1½ red chillies, seeded and chopped
2½ teaspoons ground coriander
2½ teaspoons turmeric
2½ teaspoons ground cumin
150 g (5 oz) brown sugar

375 ml (11¾ fl oz) white wine vinegar
salt and freshly ground pepper

Allow the salted eggplant dice to drain in a colander for 30 minutes then rinse it and squeeze to remove excess water. Heat a large pan with some of the oil and sauté the eggplant in batches until tender. Put all the eggplant into a very large shallow pot and place over medium heat. Add the garlic, ginger and chopped chilli and continue to cook. Add the dry spices and sugar and sauté for another minute. Add the vinegar and stir to scrape up any sediment. Turn down the heat and simmer for 5 minutes. Do not allow all the liquid to evaporate. The mix should still be moist. Season the relish. It will keep covered in the refrigerator for at least two weeks. Reheat gently if desired.

ROASTED GARLIC PURÉE

Split whole heads of garlic across the middle and wrap each half tightly in greased foil. Bake at 100°C (210°F) for 30–45 minutes or until the flesh is very soft. Remove the garlic from the oven and cool a little. Push the pulp out of the open cloves and discard the skin. Blend the pulp with ½ teaspoon of extra-virgin olive oil for each clove of garlic. Push the purée through a tamis or fine sieve. Store in an airtight container in the refrigerator.

BRAISED PEAS AND LETTUCE

Serves 6 as an accompaniment

Fresh peas in the pod generally yield just over half their weight in podded peas.

1 small iceberg lettuce
120 ml (4 fl oz) water
20 g (¾ oz) butter

pinch of salt
pinch of freshly ground pepper
pinch of sugar
200 g (7 oz) podded or frozen baby peas
50 g (2 oz) sautéed fine bacon strips or lardons (optional)

Discard the outer large leaves of the lettuce, remove the core and separate the leaves. Wash the leaves well, drain then shred them into ½ cm (¼ in) slices. Combine the water, butter, salt, pepper and sugar in a saucepan. Add the shredded leaves and cover and cook for 30 seconds. Add the peas, and bacon if using, and cook for 2–3 minutes or until the peas are cooked and the lettuce no longer tastes raw, but retains some crunch. The vegetables should be bathed in a syrupy liquid. If this is too watery, you have the option of draining the lettuce and peas, reducing the liquid until it becomes syrupy then returning the peas and lettuce to the pan. Taste and adjust seasoning if required.

CRISP TWICE-COOKED POTATOES

Serves 6

These potatoes are delicious cooked at the last minute and scattered through a warm salad. They are a good way to use left-over boiled potato. If using with shreds of confit duck in a salad, use a little duck fat to cook them, rather than oil.

1 kg (2 lb 3 oz) non-waxy potatoes
oil or duck fat for cooking
salt and freshly ground pepper

Simmer the potatoes gently in their skins until tender. Allow them to cool then peel and cut into 2–2½ cm (¾–1 in) dice. Heat the oil or duck fat in a heavy-based frying pan, preferably large enough to accommodate all the potato dice snugly in a single layer. Have the oil or duck fat to a depth of 2 cm (¾ in) and when it is hot, add the potato dice and allow it to cook, sizzle and colour thoroughly. Resist the impulse to fiddle before attempting to turn and colour the other side. When you do, the side already coloured should be crusty and crunchy. Repeat the cooking process on the second side then remove the potatoes from the pan with a slotted lifter.

Depending on the potato variety used, there may be delicious small crunchy well-coloured bits of broken-off potato as well as the dice. Drain the lot on several layers of kitchen paper and season well.

SLOW-ROASTED TOMATOES

Slow roasting tomatoes is a way of removing some water and concentrating the tomato flavour. This is the basic recipe. The addition of various spices is worth experimenting with.

12 Roma tomatoes
2 shallots, finely sliced
3 cloves garlic, sliced
pinch of sugar
5 tablespoons extra-virgin olive oil
salt and freshly ground pepper

Halve the tomatoes and place them in a bowl with the shallots, garlic, sugar, oil, salt and pepper. Toss to ensure the tomatoes have been evenly coated. Place the tomatoes, cut side up, on a baking tray and scatter the shallots and garlic mix from the bowl over them. Roast in the oven at 140°C (375°F) for about 1½ hours or until completely tender. Remove from the oven and cool. The roasted tomatoes may be stored in the refrigerator under oil, with fresh herbs. However, always serve at room temperature.

VARIATIONS Before roasting, you can add various spices when tossing the tomatoes in the oil. For example, ½ teaspoon ground coriander, and a pinch each of ground cinnamon and cloves, together with an extra pinch of sugar, creates a pleasantly aromatic and slightly sweeter roast tomato, which is quite delicious with a young creamy goat's cheese. The addition of stronger spices can also yield interesting results.

CARAMELISED WITLOF

Serves 4 as a side vegetable or 8 as a garnish

This is excellent with duck or pork.

100 g (3½ oz) butter
2 medium-sized witlof, cut into quarters
100 g (3½ oz) additional butter
3 tablespoons sugar
2 tablespoons sherry or red wine vinegar
juice and zest of 2 oranges

Melt 100 g (3½ oz) butter over medium heat and pan-fry the witlof, turning the quarters over until they are coloured on all sides. Add the second amount of butter and, when it has foamed, sprinkle over the sugar and cook to caramelise. Add the vinegar and reduce to a caramel. Add the orange juice and zest. Reduce until the liquid has thickened. Turn the witlof over to glaze the other side.

Continue to cook over a low heat until the witlof is cooked through. Remove the witlof from the liquid and reserve until ready to use.

PARSLEY, PINE NUT AND CURRANT SALAD

Serves 6 as a garnish

40 g (1½ oz) currants
50 g (2 oz) pine nuts, lightly toasted
½ cup flat-leaf parsley leaves
1 teaspoon finely diced preserved lemon (optional)
½ cup mild-tasting olive oil
2 tablespoons lemon juice
salt and freshly ground pepper

Soak the currants in boiling water for 5 minutes. Drain, then combine with the pine nuts and parsley leaves in a bowl. Add preserved lemon if using. Whisk oil and lemon juice together, add seasoning then drizzle over salad ingredients. Toss to ensure salad is well coated.

Chapter Thirteen

DECADES OF CHANGE

We commenced building Lake House in 1980 at a time when regional Australia was not a considered choice for anyone with an inclination towards fine food and wine. We were warned that it was a most unwise business decision and that we were doomed to fail.

However, Australia's culinary landscape was soon to undergo great change. It was a heady time for Australian chefs as we sought our own unique identity. In a way Lake House was on the fringe of that, pursuing from the outset a sense of our location and the seasons in what we offered. These of course are now ubiquitous and ever popular notions and Australia is rich with great regional culinary destinations. Vineyards with cellar doors abound, provedores are springing up everywhere and 'local' and 'regional' are the words on everyone's lips.

None of this was the case in the 1970s. Generally, if one was after a special night out, one went to a European restaurant with a French menu where antiques and other embellishments served to create a cultivated air. Inevitably replete with grandiose velvet curtaining and balloon-backed chairs these dining rooms still shone largely with the presence of society's glitterati.

While in Australia we still persisted with attempting to re-create traditional European cuisine and the rarefied atmosphere to accompany it, in France it was already being dumped at the rate of knots by Fernand Point and his protégés Bocuse, Chapel and the Troisgros brothers. The entire focus of French haute cuisine was moving from overworked food to regional-produce-driven dishes where provenance of ingredients mattered. All of a sudden what was considered to be okay to cook in 'serious' restaurants had changed.

In 1980 the first *Age Good Food Guide*, edited by Claude Forell, was published in Melbourne. There was already a little of the best of Oz in the restaurant scene. Wealthy travelling Australians of the likes of the indomitable Staleys set about re-creating the best of the food and atmosphere of Europe but in a strikingly Australian way. Fanny's in Melbourne was an experience worth saving up for. Meanwhile, not far away, Herman Schneider was producing probably the best food in Australia in the less opulent surroundings of Two Faces.

The food of Europe was being embraced but the attitude was left behind. Gay and Tony Bilson's Berowra Waters opened just out of Sydney in 1977. The style of service, the setting and its eventual Glen Murcutt renovation, could not have been more Australian. Generally though, it was still about French food. In fact Charles Barrier's 'Brioche de Moelle au Beurre Rouge', an opening appetiser, lasted until the restaurant's closure in 1995.

In the United States, meanwhile, a movement to create a new personal culinary identity had begun with the opening of Alice Water's Chez Panisse. Californian place names began to trumpet the provenance of ingredients. In 1976 a Californian regional dinner was held and a whole new culinary aesthetic was launched.

Culinary activity was also developing a distinctly local voice in Australia. Stephanie Alexander, an extraordinary cook, took the contemporary culinary message of France, translated it into something suitable for the Australian sensibility, and paired it with wonderful self-sourced produce from all over Australia. For the first time Australian purveyors and provedores were written up in food articles and glossy magazines.

Stephanie Alexander's commitment to the style and sophistication of the dining experience was enhanced by the friendly and highly knowledgeable professionalism of her floor team eventually led by Dure Dara. The experience was one of a very special occasion but where a thick French accent was no longer an expected component. The fine dining establishment had a new and very Australian face.

Another decade on, and the excesses of the high-riding, high-spending mid-1980s saw a boom in upmarket dining, which brazenly brandished 'Modern Australian cuisine' as its new culinary idiom. Sumptuous kitchens rolling out superior food provided fertile training grounds for young chefs. Great front-of-house service and wine knowledge were lauded by a population of restaurant patrons beginning to truly appreciate and understand the craft and the profession. Australia was in the throes of creating a restaurant culture with a sustainable future.

Mediterranean cuisine was embraced with a vengeance. Interestingly, while a menu utilising French culinary terms now seemed exceedingly pretentious, the Italians continued to get away with their *Purea di patate* and *Pesce del giorno*, for mash and fish of the day. Their legions of good-looking and smartly attentive waiters often refused to speak anything but Italian. 'Ciao, bella', Campari and blood orange, parmesan and rocket, plenty of excellent olive oil on everything ... and of course we swooned.

Then the Brit pack arrived and turned us on our heads. Lambie, Strode, Szabo, Wilson, Cambray and Cooke pumped out their versions of the classics and upped the ante in what was a dynamic, thriving industry environment. Blood pudding appeared on menus, pork and seafood and oxtail and fish contributed a new style, surf 'n' turf. Bois Boudran, Antiboise and Gribiche were sauces we came to love. Elsewhere East was busily meeting West. The Australian Sommelier's Association burgeoned with young would-be sommeliers. Wine lists became serious.

THE DEMISE OF TABLECLOTHS AND SAUCES

Already building in the background, however, was a succession of events none of which can be said to have individually altered the dynamic of the food industry in Australia. However, cumulatively their effect has been considerable.

The recession of the late 1980s brought the nation and much of the industry to a grinding halt. At Lake House we held on as we watched property after property being taken over by banks. The introduction of the fringe benefits tax some time before had added to the gloom as the previously hugely lucrative business-lunch trade was wiped out overnight.

In Victoria the loosening of requirements for liquor licences had been much needed and welcome at the time. Many had taken advantage of the easing of regulations. Almost two decades later, Victoria now has the highest per capita number of liquor licences in Australia.

Into an already highly competitive atmosphere came the advent of ethnic cuisines, often driven by migrants who saw the opportunity to run small establishments while seeing their younger generation through school and university. These were able to offer particularly low-cost dining through the employment of family members and cuisines based generally on less-expensive ingredients. Rarely meant to be long-term enterprises and although delivering delicious bargain-priced food, they were not about training or the passing on of any craft.

By now, continuing low interest rates had created an over-mortgaged population of two career households with little or no time to cook. There was a need for inexpensive restaurants that served reasonable home-style food. The Australian public dined out more frequently but paid less. Special occasion dining became less of a priority. The arrival of the GST into this economic climate meant that most restaurateurs absorbed some or even all of the costs. Not confident that consumers would be prepared to pay an extra 10 per cent and concerned that many other establishments would not raise prices, they were further hampered by their inability to express the tax as the additional government charge that it is. To this day Australia remains one of the few countries where the tax remains hidden within purchase price.

Profitability in the industry plummeted. Restaurateurs cut corners. Elements such as training, not immediately relevant to the bottom line, became less of a priority. It was barely noticed. In times of global catastrophe and unrest, discussing one's wine choice with a trained sommelier and watching the ritual of its decanting sat a bit uneasily on our shoulders. Somehow an unclothed table, a relaxed laissez-faire waiter with sleeves rolled up who apologetically laughed off the fact that the dish served bore little resemblance to its misspelled description on the menu, made us feel less guilty when we were spending money on our own pleasure. The bill at the end, however, was now frequently not much less. The demise of tablecloths and sauces, the advent of shared tables, cuisines and food philosophies utilising cheaper cuts of meat, all considerably effective tools for reducing business costs, were being touted as new dining trends rather than a reaction to the economic climate. In fact, establishments of this type were regularly feted by the media. Many received high ratings and accolades.

The industry took very careful and calculated note. Why bother with much else? Three or four years on, food publications were lamenting the lack of excitement and the sameness of Melbourne establishments. All of a sudden when we did want to have a special night out, there was really no longer that much to choose from. But the real hidden costs of prolonged lack of viability in the industry have been the lack of training and lowering of working conditions. The restaurant industry is now fraught with skill shortages, low take-up of the profession and catastrophically high attrition rates. Many of our best operators have chosen to opt out of the industry altogether or run operations that do not even begin to test their talents. The wholesale uptake of cuisines based on the 'grill and garnish' school of cooking has led to the demise of depth in culinary knowledge among many of our young practitioners.

RESTAURANTS TODAY

The economic viability of restaurant operations taking a downturn is mostly a worldwide phenomenon. Perhaps only the US business model, with generally low-paid front-of-house professionals reliant on a public used to tipping a minimum of 17 per cent, remains highly profitable. In France, meanwhile, the 35-hour week, the five-week vacation and towering labour costs are altering the ability of restaurateurs to deliver at every level. Small bistros are cutting corners in order to ensure that the patron and his wife can manage all the cooking and cleaning on their own without the need for another employee. Franchised operations with greater purchasing power, and often with food produced offsite, are flourishing. Michelin-starred chefs are handing back their stars and opting out of the Michelin system. Better to give awards back than have them stripped, as through necessity corners are cut and operations are simplified.

The viability of the industry and where we stand in the international culinary arena of the future will be determined by what we as diners consider important and what we are prepared to pay for. If quality, consistency and creativity are important to us then generously staffed kitchens and floors are required as well as time for briefing and training sessions. Is it important for us as a wine producing nation to have restaurants with great cellars and sommeliers to match?

Then there is the dilemma of the contemporary restaurateur – to cloth, not to cloth or perhaps even to double cloth? Personally I find the crispness of starched white linen in a restaurant sexy. The fact that you are guaranteed an immaculate setting for your food and are not resting your hands on a surface that has been hastily wiped by a re-usable cloth also bears some consideration. It is not a question of formality either. The best meals I have had in rural European relais and cafés, indoors in farmhouses and outdoors under the spreading branches of fruit trees, have inevitably begun with the spreading of a freshly laundered cloth, by a proud host. Make no mistake, however, unless driven by consumer demand, nowadays clothing is a big expense willingly foregone by any cost-cutting restaurateur.

And we have not even touched on the quality of the settings. Do we care if it is imported fine china or will the sturdy Australian range do? Will we pay more for that plate of food if the chairs are gorgeous as well as comfortable? Are we happy with the discarding of all rituals and many of the accoutrements from the theatre of dining? Do we mind that many of our cooks no longer know how to make a bisque or a refined jus, or that elements of the craft are being lost?

For my money, I like food that is a bit challenging, which I would not bother to produce at home. I like it served on crisp linen by a waiter in a clean white shirt or jacket who is knowledgeable, accommodating and discreet and for whom the job is a profession. Why restaurants remain a place where we are prepared to suffer less than professional service remains a great mystery. I am delighted if there is an option of three or four wines from an intelligently put together list, which might go with the dishes I have selected. I enjoy listening to well thought out recommendations. 'The shiraz is popular' does not really pass muster. I like the restaurant fitted out so that I do not emerge hoarse from trying to converse with my partner. I like the place to have been around for long enough to acquire a patina and to have systems in place that afford consistency. At the very least, I would like it to still be there and to deliver the same result in a few months' time. I love the generosity of fresh flowers, which together with other similar touches, speak to me of an understanding of hospitality and a lack of obsession with the bottom line. I am also able to appreciate how much all of that is likely to cost.

The demise of top-end dining has often been remarked on over the past few years and nowhere more than in Melbourne where establishments of that calibre can now be counted on one hand. Melbourne has always done egalitarian well. Nowadays it is almost all it does. The implications have been profound. It was Alain Ducasse who noted that haute cuisine is like haute couture. You may perhaps never get to experience it, but it is what sets the standards for the industry to aspire to. It is a benchmark for young front-of-house teams and young chefs. In a city of pleasant casual bistros, yet more gastro pubs and wood-fired-pizza establishments, who sets the benchmarks? For destinations with gastronomic aspirations, it is the mix across the full spectrum that matters.

Melbourne, however, has always been a 'food' city and the tide is turning, driven by diners who are tired of the sameness of food establishments and who are prepared to pay. No doubt top-end dining as it returns will be a substantially different product. Having observed the cycles of the industry over the years I have no doubt there is glamour looming on the horizon. Bring it on!

A WORK IN PROGRESS

At our house on the lake, the journey continues. The challenges of remaining true to one's tenets no matter what the climate can be tricky. All our guests from near and far continue to reinforce what we do and what we aspire to. I enjoy their feedback, which often suggests a proprietary interest in the place. The exhilaration of working with young, passionate people continues to keep me motivated.

Evenings with more than a hundred in the restaurant, a wedding in full flight in our function room and a team that has not dropped the ball once despite a demanding night, continue to leave me energised and with the sort of high that I can imagine sports teams experience. That sort of effort, when the whole thing swings into action like some well-oiled machine, is one of the most addictive things about our industry. It is a performance of sorts. And when that curtain goes up you really want to be with a great cast.

Around me is also the sweet country air, the impossibly starry skies, the magnificent views and the far horizons. After service I'm sometimes known to indulge in a drink on the terraces overlooking the lake. I look about and can never quite believe what's become of this forsaken paddock that my mother wept over. After more than two decades, there probably should have been more cookbooks on my agenda, but the place continues to occupy much of my waking and often even my sleeping life. As others have taken over many of the physical tasks – even the day-to-day running of the kitchen – there has always been more to become involved with. I have had the privilege of watching a small country town and surrounding region resurrect its sense of self and become an attractive proposition for its community, visitors and new residents alike. Tourism, when carefully managed, is proving to be the saviour of many rural areas and has the potential to promote other associated industries. For some years now I have also concerned myself with wider industry issues, serving on state and national industry committees and boards. I find it difficult to say no. It is an exciting industry. Lake House continues to be a work in progress. The team has its sights set even further afield. There is more to come.

INDEX

A

Aïoli 285
   Saffron aïoli 286
   Tarragon aïoli 286
almonds
   Almond meringues 277
   Praline 292
   Sour cherry and almond pithivier with sour cream ice cream 269
Amaretto parfait 266
apples
   Apple crisps 291
   Apple soufflé with apple sorbet 255
   Napoleon torte 120
Apricot tarte tatin, amaretto parfait and praline 266
Aromatic carrot emulsion 286
artichokes
   preparing 293
   Spring salad with asparagus velouté and parmesan foam 135
asparagus
   Asparagus and morels in mustard cream 153
   Asparagus velouté 135
   preparing 293
   Spring salad with asparagus velouté and parmesan foam 135
Assiette of chicken with summer herb bouillon 182
Assiette of pork 235

B

Baked polenta 281
balsamic vinegar 284
bananas, Caramelised 82
barley
   Butter-poached pheasant breast with barley and mushrooms 199
   cooking 280
Basic pasta dough 290
Basic vinaigrette 284
Basil pesto 288
batter, Tempura 280

beans, Cassoulet of 280
beef
   Beef carpaccio with crisp twice-cooked potatoes and sauce Gribiche 222
   Blinchiki with chestnut soup 114
   Braised beef cheek with Yorkshire pudding and horseradish cream 221
beetroot
   Beetroot carpaccio with fetta and walnuts 133
   Beetroot relish 294
   Borscht terrine 119
   Roast kangaroo fillet with beet greens, glazed beetroot and sage fritters 217
   Russian salad 111
berries
   Blueberry jam 89
   Elderflower cordial 93
   Elderberry glaze 40
   Raspberry jelly 270
   Raspberry sauce 292
   Strawberry fritters with raspberry sauce 276
   Strawberry pavlova 271
biscuits
   Biscotti 99
   Coconut macaroons 98
   Tuile biscuits 293
Black bean dressing 284
Blinchiki with chestnut soup 114
Blue cheese crostini 132
Blueberry jam 89
Borscht terrine 119
Braises
   Braise of fresh eel with tomatoes and olives 148
   Braised beef cheek with Yorkshire pudding and horseradish cream 221
   Braised hare with shallots and mushrooms, roasted fillet and soft polenta 212
   Braised peas and lettuce 296
   Rabbit braise 208
   Winter lamb: braised neck with beans and sweetbreads 225
Brandied cherries 38
bread
   Blue cheese crostini 132

Bread rings 281
Crostini 281
Croutons 281
Crunchy gremolata 282
French toast 82
Fried breadcrumb toppings 282
Walnut crumble 282
brine 235
broad beans
   Broad bean falafel 137
   preparing 294
   Spring salad with asparagus velouté and parmesan foam 135
broths
   Duck broth 190
   Summer herb bouillon 183
   see *also* soups
buckwheat
   cooking 280
   Buckwheat vinaigrette 167
butter, Clarified 282
Butter-poached pheasant breast with barley and mushrooms 199

C

cabbage
   Cabbage roll of boned quail with pork farce and roasting juices 203
   Chicken cabbage rolls 182
   Choucroute-style cabbage 294
   Home-made sauerkraut 294
   Caesar dressing 286
cakes
   Chocolate fondant sacher 276
   Friandes 94
   Genoese sponge 292
   Madeleines 94
   Napoleon torte 120
   Sienna cake 98
   Summer rose cupcakes 95
Candied orange rind 291
Caramelised bananas 82
Caramelised witlof 297
carpaccio

Beef carpaccio with crisp twice-cooked
  potatoes and sauce Gribiche 222
Beetroot carpaccio with fetta and walnuts 133
carrots
  Aromatic carrot emulsion 286
  Spiced carrot cream 295
Cassoulet of beans 280
Cauliflower panna cotta with oyster fritters 169
Celeriac purée 295
Ceviche of Murray cod and steamed yabbies in
  coconut dressing 152
Champagne sabayon 270
cheese
  Beetroot carpaccio with fetta and walnuts 133
  Blue cheese crostini 132
  Fromage frais 282
  Mascarpone 272
  Marinated goats cheese 283
  Parmesan crisps 283
  Parmesan foam 283
  Poached eggs in cheese soufflés 85
  Ripe tomato salad, fried green tomatoes
    and buffalini 138
  with fruit and nuts 97
cherries
  Brandied cherries 38
  Cherry brandy 39
  Cherry syrup 39
  Sour cherry and almond pithivier with sour
    cream ice cream 269
  Sour cherry jam 89
chestnuts
  Blinchiki with chestnut soup 114
  cooking 295
  Chestnut soup 117
chicken
  Assiette of chicken with summer herb
    bouillon 182
  Chicken cabbage rolls 182
  Chicken galantine with tarragon 239
  Chicken sausage and chicken wings with
    sweet corn sauce 185
  Chicken sausages 245
  Confit chicken wings 185
  Roast herbed chicken 182

  Tarragon chicken mousse 239
chickpeas
  Fried chickpea chips 280
Chocolate fondant sacher 276
Choucroute-style cabbage 294
cider vinegar 284
citrus
  Citrus madeleines 94
  Citrus powder 291
  Lemon charlotte with citrus salad 258
Clarified butter 282
coconut
  Coconut dressing 286
  Coconut macaroons 98
confit
  Confit chicken wings 185
  Confit of tuna in a salad niçoise with salsa
    verde 168
  Duck confit 189
  process 188
  Roasted confit duck in coriander crêpe 192
Cooked rhubarb 84
Coulibiac 113
Country terrine 243
creams
  Horseradish cream 289
  Mascarpone 272
  Mustard cream 153
  Spiced carrot cream 295
  Wasabi crème fraîche 167
crêpes
  Blinchiki with chestnut soup 114
  Plain crêpes 283
  Roasted confit duck in coriander crêpe 192
Crisp crumbed poached eggs 290
Crisp twice-cooked potatoes 296
crisps
  Apple crisps 291
  Parmesan crisps 283
  Pear crisps 291
Crostini 281
Croutons 281
crumble
  Rhubarb crumble 262
  Walnut crumble 282

Crunchy gremolata 282
crystallised rose petals 95
Cucumber raita 289
curd, Lemon 258
Cured salmon 173
Curry sauce 288
custard
  Lemon custard 258
  Smoked trout custards 159
  Zucchini custard 141

D

dressings
  Basic vinaigrette 284
  Black bean dressing 284
  Buckwheat vinaigrette 167
  Caesar dressing 286
  Coconut dressing 286
  Hazelnut dressing 284
  Lake House dressing 284
  Spiced dressing 285
  Yabby dressing 152
  see also mayonnaise; sauces
duck
  Duck broth 190
  Duck confit 189
  Duck glaze 196
  Duck liver parfait 238
  Duck neck sausages 246
  Duck and potato galettes 195
  Duck skin cracklings 191
  Glazed roast duck breast with duck and
    potato galette 195
  Roasted confit duck in coriander crêpe 192
Duet for two divas 270

E

eel
  Braise of fresh eel with tomatoes and olives 148
  Jellied eel and smoked trout 111
  Smoked eel rillettes 149
  Smoked trout sausage and smoked eel with
    potato pancakes 156

eggplant
    Eggplant relish 296
    Smoky eggplant purée 295
eggs
    Crisp crumbed poached eggs 290
    Hard-boiled eggs 290
    Poached eggs 290
    Poached eggs in cheese soufflés 85
    Soft egg Gribiche 286
    Soft eggs for salads and dressings 290
    Stuffed eggs with horseradish 111
Elderberry glaze 40
Elderflower cordial 93
Escabèche of freshwater trout with
    remoulade-style salad 155
Espresso jelly 272

F

felafel, Broad bean 137
figs
    with cheese 97
    Pickled figs 40
    Slow-baked figs 97
fish
    Ceviche of Murray cod and steamed yabbies
        in coconut 152
    Confit of tuna in a salad niçoise with
        salsa verde 168
    Coulibiac 113
    Cured salmon 173
    Escabèche of freshwater trout with
        remoulade-style salad 155
    Gravadlax with flavours of Caesar and crisp
        crumbed poached egg 173
    Jellied eel and smoked trout 111
    Murray cod in a potato jacket with asparagus
        and morels 153
    Peppered and herbed seared tuna with
        cucumber and buckwheat 167
    Snapper and oysters with cucumber, sorrel
        and champagne 177
    Smoked trout custards 159
    Smoked trout sausage and smoked eel with
        potato pancakes 156
    Spiced blue eye with eggplant relish, sweet
        curried mussels and chickpea chips 174
Fish spice 174
Flavoured sugars 289
French toast 82
Friandes 94
Fried breadcrumb toppings 282
Fried chickpea chips 280
Fried green tomatoes 138
Fried polenta 281
fritters
    Oyster fritters 169
    Sage fritters 217
    Strawberry fritters with raspberry sauce 276
Fromage frais 282
fruit salad
    Winter salad of poached dried fruits 83

G

galantine with tarragon, Chicken 239
galettes
    Duck and potato galettes 195
    Galette of pork trotter with mustard crust 241
garlic
    Roasted garlic purée 296
Genoese sponge 292
glazes
    Duck glaze 196
    Elderberry glaze 40
    Glazed roast duck breast with duck and
        potato galette 195
    Red wine glaze 217
Gravadlax with flavours of Caesar and crisp
    crumbed poached egg 173
gremolata, Crunchy 282
ham hocks
    Ham hock and lentil soup 251
    Jellied ham hock sausages 249

H

Hard-boiled eggs 290
hare
    Braised hare with shallots and mushrooms,
        roasted fillet and soft polenta 212
    Hare cannelloni with spiced carrot cream 214
Harissa 289
hazelnuts
    Hazelnut dressing 284
    Witlof salad with hazelnuts and blue cheese
        crostini 132
herbs
    Herb oils 285
    Salsa verde 288
    Summer herb bouillon 183
    Summer herb tortellini 141
Home-made sauerkraut 294
Honey panna cotta with quince soup 261
Horseradish cream 289

I

ice cream
    Lemon ice cream 277
    Sour cream ice cream 292
    Vanilla ice cream 292
Icing 95
Individual tiramisu trifle 272

J

jams
    Blueberry jam 89
    Sour cherry jam 89
Jellied eel and smoked trout 111
Jellied ham hock sausages 249
jellies
    Espresso jelly 272
    Medlar jelly 88
    Quince and Seville orange jelly 88
    Raspberry jelly 270
    Rhubarb jelly 262
setting point 88

K

kangaroo fillet with beet greens, glazed beetroot
    and sage fritters, Roast 217
Khvorost 123

L

Lake House dressing 284
lamb
   Crumbed lamb sweetbreads 226
   Lamb cutlets 230
   Lamb and fennel sausages 247
   Spring lamb with sauce Paloise and shepherd's croquette 229
   Winter lamb: braised neck with beans and sweetbreads 225
Lavender sugar 293
Lemon charlotte with citrus salad 258
Lemon curd 258
Lemon custard 258
Lemon ice cream 'sandwiches' 277
lentil soup, Ham hock and 251
lettuce, Braised peas and 296

M

Madeleines 94
   Citrus madeleines 94
Marinated goat's cheese 283
Mascarpone 272
Mayonnaise 285
   see also Aïoli
Medlar jelly 88
meringue
   Lemon ice cream 'sandwiches' 277
   Coconut macaroons 98
   Strawberry pavlova 271
mousse, Tarragon chicken 239
Murray cod
   Ceviche of Murray cod and steamed yabbies in coconut 152
   Murray cod in a potato jacket with asparagus and morels 153
mushrooms
   Asparagus and morels in mustard cream 153
   Blinchiki with chestnut soup 114
   Butter-poached pheasant breast with barley and mushrooms 199
   Coulibiac 113
   Mushroom emulsion 287
   Mushrooms and sausage 186
   Ragout of wild mushrooms 136
Mustard cream 153

N

Napoleon torte 120
Noodle cakes 200
nuts
   Biscotti 99
   cheese with fruit and nuts 97
   Sienna cake 98
   Witlof salad with hazelnuts and blue cheese crostini 132
   see also almonds; walnuts

O

offal
   Braised beef cheek with Yorkshire pudding and horseradish cream 221
   Crumbed lamb sweetbreads 226
   Galette of pork trotter with mustard crust 241
   Ox tongue salad 240
oils 283
   Herb oils 285
   olive oil 283
   rice oil 284
olives
   Braise of fresh eel with tomatoes and olives 148
   Tapenade 289
oranges
   Candied orange rind 291
   Orange gastrique 287
   Quince and Seville orange jelly 88
Ox tongue salad 240
oysters
   Oyster fritters 169
   Snapper and oysters with cucumber, sorrel and champagne 177

P

pancakes, Potato 158
panna cotta
   Cauliflower panna cotta with oyster fritters 169
   Honey panna cotta with quince soup 261
parfait
   Amaretto parfait 266
   Duck liver parfait 238
Parmesan crisps 283
Parmesan foam 283
Parsley, pine nut and currant salad 297
pasta
   Basic pasta dough 290
   Hare cannelloni with spiced carrot cream 214
   Summer herb tortellini 141
pastries, savoury
   Coulibiac 113
   Rabbit pastries 211
pastries, sweet
   Apricot tarte tatin, amaretto parfait and praline 266
   Khvorost 123
   Napoleon torte 120
   Sour cherry and almond pithivier with sour cream ice cream 269
Pastry cream 120
pavlova, Strawberry 271
Peach Melba 270
Pear crisps 291
peas
   Braised peas and lettuce 296
   Pea ravioli 162
Penny's porridge 82
Peppered and herbed seared tuna with cucumber and buckwheat 167
pesto
   Basil pesto 288
   'Pesto' emulsion 288
   Tarragon pesto 289
pheasant
   Butter-poached pheasant breast with barley and mushrooms 199
Pickled figs 40
Plain crêpes 283

Poached eggs 290
   Crisp crumbed poached eggs 290
   Poached eggs in cheese soufflés 85
polenta
   Fried or baked polenta 281
   Soft polenta 281
pork
   Assiette of pork 235
   Pressed and rolled pork belly 235
porridge, Penny's 82
potatoes
   Crisp twice-cooked potatoes 296
   Duck and potato galettes 195
   Murray cod in a potato jacket with asparagus and morels 153
   Potato pancakes 158
   Russian salad 111
Praline 292
preserves see jams; jellies
Pressed and rolled pork belly 235

Q

quail
   Cabbage roll of boned quail with pork farce and roasting juices 203
   Quail marinade 200
   Quail salad 201
   Spiced quail with noodle cake and Asian salad 200
quince
   Quince and Seville orange jelly 88
   Quince soup 261

R

rabbit
   Rabbit braise 208
   Rabbit pastries 211
   Rabbit rillettes 207
   Spiced rabbit with Tunisian pastry and harissa 208
Ragout of wild mushrooms 136
raita, Cucumber 289

Raspberry jelly 270
Raspberry sauce 292
Red wine glaze 217
relishes
   Beetroot relish 294
   Eggplant relish 296
Remoulade-style salad 155
rhubarb
   Cooked rhubarb 84
   Rhubarb crumble 262
   Rhubarb jelly 262
   Rhubarb sorbet 262
rice, Wild 281
rice oil 284
rice vinegar 284
Ripe tomato salad, fried green tomatoes and buffalini 138
Roast herbed chicken 182
Roast kangaroo fillet with beet greens, glazed beetroot and sage fritters 217
Roasted confit duck in coriander crêpe 192
Roasted garlic purée 296
rose petals, Crystallised 95
Rose-scented sugar 293
Russian salad 111

S

sabayon, Champagne 270
Saffron aïoli 286
Sage fritters and beet leaves 217
salads
   Beetroot carpaccio with fetta and walnuts 133
   Ox tongue salad 240
   Parsley, pine nut and currant salad 297
   Quail salad 201
   Remoulade-style salad 155
   Ripe tomato salad, fried green tomatoes and buffalini 138
   Russian salad 111
   Salad niçoise 168
   Soft eggs for salads and dressings 290
   Spiced quail with noodle cake and Asian salad 200

Spiced roasted tomatoes with fresh soya beans and broad bean falafel 137
Spring salad with asparagus velouté and parmesan foam 135
Witlof salad with hazelnuts and blue cheese crostini 132
Salsa verde 288
salt 291
sauces
   Aromatic carrot emulsion 286
   Curry sauce 288
   Mushroom emulsion 287
   Orange gastrique 287
   'Pesto' emulsion 288
   Raspberry sauce 292
   Sauce beurre blanc 287
   Sauce Jacqueline 287
   Sauce Paloise 288
   Soft egg Gribiche 286
   Sweet corn sauce 185
   White wine sauce 162
sauerkraut, Home-made 294
sausages
   Chicken sausages 245
   Duck neck sausages 246
   Jellied ham hock sausages 249
   Lamb and fennel sausages 247
   Mushrooms and sausage 186
   Smoked trout sausage 156
   Spicy venison sausages 250
Sautéed yabbies with pea ravioli and pea tendril salad 162
seafood
   Oyster fritters 169
   Snapper and oysters with cucumber, sorrel and champagne 177
   Sweet curried mussels 174
Shepherd's croquette 229
Sienna cake 98
Slow-baked figs 97
Slow-roasted tomatoes 296
Smoked eel rillettes 149
smoked trout
   Jellied eel and smoked trout 111

Smoked trout custards 159
Smoked trout sausage and smoked eel with potato pancakes 156
Smoky eggplant purée 295
Snapper and oysters with cucumber, sorrel and champagne 177
Soft egg Gribiche 286
Soft eggs for salads and dressings 290
Soft polenta 281
sorbet
  Apple sorbet 255
  Rhubarb sorbet 262
soufflés
  Apple soufflé with apple sorbet 255
  Poached eggs in cheese soufflés 85
soups
  Chestnut soup 117
  Ham hock and lentil soup 251
  Quince soup 261
  see also broth
Sour cherry and almond pithivier with sour cream ice cream 269
Sour cherry jam 89
Sour cream ice cream 292
soya beans and broad bean falafel, Spiced roasted tomatoes with 137
Spiced blue eye with eggplant relish, sweet curried mussels and chickpea chips 174
Spiced carrot cream 295
Spiced dressing 285
Spiced honey walnuts 97
Spiced quail with noodle cake and Asian salad 200
Spiced rabbit with Tunisian pastry and harissa 208
Spiced roasted tomatoes with fresh soya beans and broad bean falafel 137
Spicy venison sausages 250
sponge
  Genoese sponge 292
Spring lamb with sauce Paloise and shepherd's croquette 229
Spring salad with asparagus velouté and parmesan foam 135
stock 291
Strawberry fritters with raspberry sauce 276
Strawberry pavlova 271
Stuffed eggs with horseradish 111
sugar
  Lavender sugar 293
  Rose-scented sugar 293
  Sugar syrup 293
  Vanilla sugar 293
Summer herb bouillon 183
Summer herb tortellini 141
Summer rose cupcakes 95
Sweet corn sauce 185
syrups
  Cherry syrup 39
  Sugar syrup 293

T

Tapenade 289
Tarragon aïoli 286
Tarragon chicken mousse 239
Tarragon pesto 289
Tempura batter 280
terrines
  Borscht terrine 119
  Country terrine 243
  Duck liver parfait 238
tiramisu trifle, Individual 272
tomatoes
  Braise of fresh eel with tomatoes and olives 148
  Fried green tomatoes 138
  Ripe tomato salad, fried green tomatoes and buffalini 138
  Slow-roasted tomatoes 296
  Spiced roasted tomatoes with fresh soya beans and broad bean falafel 137
  Tomato stew 148
trifle, Individual tirimisu 272
Tuile biscuits 293

V

Vanilla ice cream 292
Vanilla sugar 293

venison sausages, Spicy 250
vinaigrette
  Basic vinaigrette 284
  Buckwheat vinaigrette 167
vinegars 284

W

walnuts
  Beetroot carpaccio with fetta and walnuts 133
  Spiced honey walnuts 97
  Walnut crumble 282
Wasabi crème fraîche 167
White wine sauce 162
wild rice
  Blinchiki with chestnut soup 114
  cooking 281
  Coulibiac 113
wine vinegar 284
Winter lamb: braised neck with beans and sweetbreads 225
Winter salad of poached dried fruits 83
witlof
  Caramelised witlof 297
  Witlof salad with hazelnuts and blue cheese crostini 132

Y

yabbies
  Ceviche of Murray cod and steamed yabbies in coconut 152
  cooking 161
  Sautéed yabbies with pea ravioli and pea tendril salad 162
  Yabby dressing 152
Yorkshire pudding 221

Z

zucchini
  Spring salad with asparagus velouté and parmesan foam 135
  Zucchini custard, summer herb tortellini and sauce Jacqueline 141

Published in 2006 by
Hardie Grant Books
85 High Street
Prahran, Victoria 3181, Australia
www.hardiegrant.com.au

All rights reserved. No part of this publication may be reproduced, stored in a retrieval system or transmitted in any form by any means, electronic, mechanical, photocopying, recording or otherwise, without the prior written permission of the publishers and copyright holders.

The moral right of the author has been asserted.

Copyright text © Alla Wolf-Tasker 2006
Copyright photography © Simon Griffiths, Ashley Mackevicius, Earl Carter and Dean Cambray 2006
Paintings © Allan Wolf-Tasker

National Library of Australia Cataloguing-in-Publication data:

Wolf-Tasker, Alla.
Lake House : a culinary journey in country Australia.
Includes index.
ISBN 9781740663830.
ISBN 1 74066 383 7.

1. Lake House (Restaurant : Daylesford, Vic.) - History.
2. Cookery. 3. Restaurants - Victoria - Daylesford - History.
I. Title.

641.5099453

Design and typesetting by Gayna Murphy, Greendot Design
Principal photography by Simon Griffiths
Additional photography by Ashley Mackevicius, Earl Carter and Dean Cambray
Printed and bound in China by SNP Leefung

10 9 8 7 6 5 4 3 2 1

ACKNOWLDEGEMENTS

Many thanks to Sandy, Julie, Mary, Fran and all the folk at Hardie Grant Books for their patient and knowledgeable encouragement; Gayna Murphy for her sense of style; Helen Duffy for bringing order; Simon Griffiths for his formidable skills and always making it a good time; and Ashley Mackevicius, Earl Carter and Dean Cambray for their very special contribution.

In the continuing journey that is Lake House, nothing would be possible without the support and loyalty of Allan, Larissa and the extended family of the Lake House team. I thank you with all my heart.

Thanks also to Lois and David who shared some of our earliest experiences of France, Maria and John who were happy to spend New Year's Eve in the unfinished building of our dreams, Tom and Libby for their frequent and generous supply of a warm place in which to write, Dee and Greg for providing essential stress-free respite with hours of canasta over the years, Annie for compiling our memories and offering unconditional friendship, Gerry for sending the Queen and making us laugh on so many occasions, and our 'Tyro' friends for offering diversions and good times. Rita Erlich and Claude Forell, much thanks for writing about the regions at a time when they were considered anything but sexy.

To my many fellow chefs and industry colleagues, thanks for the continued support and the generosity of your tables.

To our Lake House clients and friends, thanks for continuing to be part of the place and for allowing us to create some very special memories. I look forward to many more good times ahead.